FROM CHAOS
TO CLARITY

FROM CHAOS TO CLARITY

HOW DATA VISUALISATION CAN SAVE THE WORLD

JAMES EAGLE

WILEY

This edition first published 2025
© 2025 John Wiley & Sons, Ltd.

All rights reserved, including rights for text and data mining and training of artificial intelligence technologies or similar technologies. No part of this publication may be reproduced, stored in a retrieval system or transmitted, in any form or by any means, electronic, mechanical, photocopying, recording or otherwise, except as permitted by law. Advice on how to obtain permission to reuse material from this title is available at http://www.wiley.com/go/permissions.

The right of 2025 John Wiley & Sons, Ltd, identified as the editorial material in this work has been asserted in accordance with law.

Registered Office(s)
John Wiley & Sons, Inc., 111 River Street, Hoboken, NJ 07030, USA
John Wiley & Sons Ltd, New Era House, 8 Oldlands Way, Bognor Regis, West Sussex, PO22 9NQ
John Wiley & Sons Singapore Pte. Ltd, 134 Jurong Gateway Road, #04-307H, Singapore 600134

For details of our global editorial offices, customer services and more information about Wiley products visit us at www.wiley.com.

Wiley also publishes its books in a variety of electronic formats and by print on demand. Some content that appears in standard print versions of this book may not be available in other formats.

Trademarks: Wiley and the Wiley logo are trademarks or registered trademarks of John Wiley & Sons, Inc., and/or its affiliates in the United States and other countries and may not be used without written permission. All other trademarks are the property of their respective owners. John Wiley & Sons, Inc., is not associated with any product or vendor mentioned in this book.

Limit of Liability/Disclaimer of Warranty

While the publisher and authors have used their best efforts in preparing this work, they make no representations or warranties with respect to the accuracy or completeness of the contents of this work and specifically disclaim all warranties, including without limitation any implied warranties of merchantability or fitness for a particular purpose. No warranty may be created or extended by sales representatives, written sales materials or promotional statements for this work. This work is sold with the understanding that the publisher is not engaged in rendering professional services. The advice and strategies contained herein may not be suitable for your situation. You should consult with a specialist where appropriate. The fact that an organisation, website or product is referred to in this work as a citation and/or potential source of further information does not mean that the publisher and authors endorse the information or services the organisation, website or product may provide or recommendations it may make. Further, readers should be aware that websites listed in this work may have changed or disappeared between when this work was written and when it is read. Neither the publisher nor authors shall be liable for any loss of profit or any other commercial damages, including but not limited to special, incidental, consequential or other damages.

Library of Congress Cataloging-in-Publication Data is Available:

ISBN 9781394292981 (Cloth)
ISBN 9781394293001 (ePub)
ISBN 9781394292998 (ePDF)

Cover Design: Jon Boylan
Cover Image: © Konstantin/stock.adobe.com

Set in 12.5/15pts Bembo Std by Straive, Chennai, India.

Mr Hugh Hargreaves (15.03.1947–16.02.2024)

There are people who leave a lasting mark on your life, and my English teacher was one of them. Without him, I might have wandered through life missing opportunities or doubting myself. Sometimes it only takes one person to believe in you and point you in the right direction.

Contents

Preface		**xi**
Introduction		**1**
Chapter 1	**Data Visualisation Is Written in Our DNA**	**7**
	The Dawn of Maps and Abstract Thought	9
	The Roots of Visual Communication	11
	Human Minds Are Pattern-Seeking Machines	12
	William Playfair and the Birth of Modern Charts	19
	Navigating the Era of Information Overload	20
	Why Visual Literacy Is the New Survival Skill	21
Chapter 2	**Technology Makes Us Fragile**	**25**
	Systems, Networks and Hidden Fragility	27
	The New Global Scale of Exploitation	28
	Floods of Data, Deficits of Wisdom	30
	Simulations, Pandemics and the Cost of Inaction	34
	The Transformative Power of Data Visualisation	35

Chapter 3 Fighting Data Pollution — 43
Lies Are the First Symptom of Data Pollution — 44
The Deadly Impact of Data Pollution — 47
Desensitisation and the Invisibility of Data Pollution — 49
Data Visualisation as a Tool to Combat Misinformation — 51
Cognitive Pitfalls and the Spread of Half-Truths — 53
Information Overload and Social Inequality — 55
Information Overload and Social Inequality — 56
The Moral Responsibility of Data Visualisation — 60

Chapter 4 AI and Data Visualisation Become Allies — 63
A New Technology Gold Rush — 64
The Cognitive Cost of Technological Reliance — 66
Fighting Misinformation with AI — 68
Defending Against Extremism and Manipulated Visualisations — 71
AI as a Sparring Partner and Impartial Critic — 75
Liberating and Democratising Data — 76
Mosaic Theory and the Risks of Weaponising Data — 77
Privacy, Intellectual Property and Open Data — 79

Chapter 5 Data Is Inherently Bias — 83
The Great Financial Crisis — 84
Subprime Mortgages: A Lesson in Hubris — 85
When Data Visualisation Fails Humanity — 86
The Flawed Assumptions Behind MBS — 87
Biased Data at the Heart of the Crisis — 91
Inflation and Evolving Economic Forces — 96
GDP and the Shifting Nature of Data — 98
Why Accepting Data Bias Matters — 99

Chapter 6 Economics Is a Dismal Science — 103
The Enduring Legacy of Malthus's Mistake — 104
The Lewis Model and the Promise of Industrialisation — 106
An Invented Lecture and the Power of False Stories — 109

Contents

Chapter 7	**Risk Should Be Seen Not Heard About**	**125**
	The Universal Allure of the Normal Curve	126
	A Self-Imposed Fog: When Scientists Shunned Visuals	128
	The Monte Carlo Moment: Random Numbers as Graffiti	133
Chapter 8	**The Dark Side of the Dial Tone**	**147**
	The Vulnerabilities in a Trust-Based System	151
Chapter 9	**Visualising the Climate War**	**165**
	Cutting Through Climate Data Overload	166
	When Animation Speaks Louder than Words	169
	The Future Is Interactive	170
	Shining a Light on Climate Injustice	176
	Burning Embers and the Paris Agreement	178
	A New Generation of Climate Activists	182
	Uniting Science, Society and Justice	183
Chapter 10	**Poverty and Wealth**	**187**
Chapter 11	**Data Deception in Politics**	**207**
	Cambridge Analytica's Origins and Influence	209
	The Dark Side of Politics	209
	Facebook Data Turn from Asset into Liability	211
	Re-evaluating Facebook's Transparency	213
	Election Misinformation and Data Manipulation	214
	Online Manipulation and the Arms Race Against Fake Accounts	217
	How Data Visualisation Can Help	218
	Data Visualisation and Freedom of Speech	220
	A Future Balanced on Data	223
Chapter 12	**Visualising Healthcare for a Better Tomorrow**	**227**
	Electronic Health Records and Patient Monitoring	229
	Medical Imaging and Diagnostics	231
	Disease Surveillance and Epidemiology	232

CONTENTS

A Shocking Murder and the High
  Cost of Healthcare   235
Public Health and Population-Level Interventions   238
Clinical Research and Drug Development   240
Healthcare Resource Management   242
Cognitive Biases in Medicine and the Role
  of Visualisation   243
Reshaping the Narrative of Healthcare   244
Towards a Healthier, Data-Driven Future   245

Chapter 13 Educating Through Data Visualisation   249
Education Is Crucial in a Data-Saturated World   252
Specialisation Can Actually Make Us Fragile   256
Data Visualisation Taps into the Power of
  Visual Thinking   257
Bring the World into the Classroom   259
Overcoming Misinformation Through
  Visual Literacy   260
How Technology Can Be Used for
  Data-Driven Learning   262
Barriers and Ethical Dilemmas   264
Data Visualisation as a Catalyst for Global Awareness   264

Chapter 14 Seeing Our Way to Survival   269
The Epoch of Data   270
Revisiting the Warning Signs   271
Data Visualisation as Human Storytelling   272
Ethical Frameworks and Education   274
The Imperative of Continuous Learning   275
A Call to Arms for Change   275
A Return to Ethan   277
Final Reflections   279

References   **283**
About the Author   **291**
Index   **293**

Preface

We constantly fret about carbon emissions polluting our atmosphere, yet a far more toxic threat lurks unseen: the flood of data overwhelming our lives. Misused, it fractures trust, distorts reality and undermines our ability to understand the risks we face. Our evolutionary wiring, honed over millennia for survival in simpler environments, struggles to keep pace with a world drowning in information.

This book explores how data visualisation could help save us from this modern crisis. We have forged a world so complex that our innate instincts can no longer interpret it effectively, creating dangerous blind spots where real threats go unseen or misunderstood. Yet paradoxically, data visualisation cuts through chaos to find clarity, harnessing data itself to fight this data overload. It could, therefore, become potentially our most powerful ally in safeguarding humanity's future.

Introduction

That evening, Dr Lena Sorensa watched her life's work discredited by a viral social media post. For years, disinformation campaigns had fractured society and eroded trust in the country's once-lauded academic institutions. Even highly respected news broadcasters no longer had a voice that the public listened to.

The true threat to humanity was not carbon emissions pumped into the atmosphere, but an invisible and more deadly pollutant: data.

Apologies for being so dramatic, but this is urgent. Consider this as a glimpse into the near future. Dr Lena Sorensen's character represents what many academics fear what might come true and a lot of that is linked to the fog of data.

Data could kill us off before climate change does. It is an even bigger threat than the risk of nuclear war. It could sweep away our human existence even without a mass extinction event. We haven't got there yet, but we are close to it.

Imagine, for instance, if we let artificial intelligence (AI) deprive us of our ability to think for ourselves. Or imagine our cognitive ability declining so much because our brains are choked by data that we can no longer think properly. Our own human biases in this data-rich world (the cause) could actually lead us to climate catastrophe or nuclear war (the effect) because we didn't understand what was in front of us — data.

To understand the magnitude of this problem, let's begin with some — dare I say — data. Every day, we create 463 exabytes of data (World Economic Forum 2019). On its own, this number is meaningless because the vast majority of normal human beings do not know what an exabyte is. This number is so large that it's not tangible in our human minds, which desensitises us to its size.

So please accept my humblest apologies. That was rather lazy of me to quote such a ridiculously big number. Let's put this into perspective: if every grain of sand on Earth represents a byte of data, then 463 exabytes represent more than 61,000 times every grain of sand on this planet (Science Atlas 2022). At first glance, this abundance of data might seem like a blessing. After all, knowledge is power and the more data we have at our fingertips, the better equipped we should be to tackle the world's most pressing problems. However, the reality is far more complex and dangerous for us.

For starters, most of the time we have no idea how much data we are creating. From social media posts and online transactions to sensor readings and surveillance footage, the sheer volume of data we produce today without realising is phenomenal. If we don't know we are creating data, then we cannot really harness it.

Worse still, the data we have created could be actively weaponised against us by those who seek to exploit us or sow confusion and discord to their advantage. State actors, terrorist groups and other malicious entities could use, for instance, the cover of data to spread disinformation, manipulate public opinions and undermine the very foundations of our democratic institutions.

We are already seeing this happen today with the rise of populist movements and the erosion of trust in experts and fact-checked traditional media. Much of what we described in Dr Lena Sorensen's story is already happening. We have got to the point where, for instance, an experienced academic, who has dedicated their life to painstaking research, can be discredited in seconds by a conspiracy theory-laden social media post.

The side effects from this are awful. Society is becoming increasingly polarised and politics ever more partisan. There is a real risk that global trade is starting to break down, mired by superstitions between nations rather than true economic fundamentals.

But before we start this book and address these issues, let's think long and hard about how we got here. In short, we have brought these problems upon ourselves by creating a world that defies our nature.

Let me explain. Homo Sapiens, our species, emerged around 300,000 years ago (Smithsonian National Museum of Natural History 2024). For hundreds of thousands of years, we were successful hunters and gatherers. Despite many hardships, we as a species thrived and spread to nearly every part of this planet.

We discovered how to use fire to keep us warm at night and protect us against predators. We clothed ourselves so we could live in colder climates, using the furs of animals we hunted. We developed tools that allowed us to hunt and kill animals far larger than us, including those who would have otherwise hunted us. Through these adaptations and innovations, we became the most lethal apex predator this planet has ever seen, even wiping out other human species, like the Neanderthals.

Then something quite extraordinary happened. About 12,000 years ago, we made a pivotal discovery: farming (National Geographic Society n.d.). From then on, we decided to become masters of the universe, commanding nature to serve us as we ruthlessly exploited her to maximise our 'utility'.

We tamed and bred animals to labour on our behalf, cultivated crops to ensure a steady food supply and cleared forests for our farms and cities. We dammed rivers to harness their power and irrigate our crops. We fished in the oceans for an even easier supply of fresh protein that we scooped up by the net load. We wiped out even more species with even greater ease.

Then, about 5,500 years ago, we discovered the wheel (Bellis 2024). Now, this is crazy. I actually thought the wheel was invented before farming, but it wasn't. It too was an innovation that helped us exploit this planet's resources.

Transportation and trade were revolutionised, allowing us to move goods and people over vast distances with unprecedented efficiency. Our nascent global economy expanded, which meant conflicts and war could occur more frequently and on a much larger and deadlier scale. Huge empires could now rise and fall, and diseases, like the Black Death, could spread more easily across the globe.

We also mined the land for metals to make tools, weapons and trinkets. Later on, we dug and drilled for hydrocarbons to fuel our industrialised economies. We invented vehicles that could drive without horses and conquered the skies with flying machines that could transport us further and quicker than ever before. Eventually, we split atoms, first to incinerate or threaten our foes and then as an energy source. We even blasted ourselves into space and went for a few walks on the Moon in the late 1960s and 1970s.

At around this time, a quieter revolution was underway as computer scientists grappled with the challenge of managing and storing burgeoning volumes of digital information that we create through our increasing economic activity. That eventually led to the introduction of microprocessors and personal computers like the Altair 8800 in 1975. This made computing power accessible to individuals, setting the stage for the first data explosion.[1]

By the 1990s, the Internet had arrived and created a second data explosion. This continued into the start of the millennium when we began to share pictures, videos, engage in online discussions,

---

[1] The Altair 8800, a microcomputer designed in 1974 by MITS, featured the Intel 8080 CPU. It gained rapid popularity after being showcased on the cover of the January 1975 issue of *Popular Electronics* and was sold by mail order.

shop for things we probably did not need and consequently left even larger digital footprints everywhere we went.

When social media and smartphones arrived, our Internet activity accelerated, creating yet another data explosion. Companies such as Google, Facebook and Amazon quickly rushed to capitalise on this trend, amassing and analysing data on an unprecedented scale. This was the Big Data Revolution and it would go on to influence every facet of our lives.

From personalised advertisements to predictive healthcare and government decision-making, the impact of Big Data is ubiquitous. It is the lifeblood of AI and machine learning today and has fundamentally transformed our industries, our everyday lives and our global economy.

The result is that we are absolutely swamped in data. There is so much data that we are drowning in it. We no longer understand how our world works. It's too much of a cognitive overload for our brains because we haven't evolved fast enough as a species to handle this level of complexity.

Our ability to assess the risks we face is poor because the world has become too complicated for us to understand. This, I believe, is the greatest threat to human survival. The only way we can defend ourselves, therefore, is to be prepared and be well armed.

What could be the greatest weapon in our arsenal? I believe the answer is data visualisation. In this book, I will make a passionate plea for why we need more data visualisation.

If you have come here to read a guide on how to do data visualisation, then this is the wrong book for you. There are far more intelligent authors out there who can help you achieve this goal. I would start with 'The Visual Display of Quantitative Information' by Edward Tufte. It's a great book and has served me well in my own journey.

As for this book, it is not a guide on how to do it. Rather, it is a reason why we must do it.

Chapter 1

Data Visualisation Is Written in Our DNA

As the dig entered its sixth month, Hormuzd Rassam's team had unearthed thousands of clay tablets. Most contained mundane economic records. But his instincts, honed through years of excavations at Nimrud and Nineveh, told him they were onto something and so he persisted. On one sweltering day in July 1881, under the scorching Iraqi sun, a very special tablet was unearthed (Persia and Babylonia 2019).

Rassam could not have known what it was. It was catalogued and packed away with the rest of the tablets, destined for the British Museum. Once there, in the months that followed, scholars painstakingly deciphered the cuneiform inscriptions on these tablets.

Then they came to this particular tablet. Excitement rippled through the halls of the museum. Sir Henry Rawlinson and his colleagues were looking at something quite extraordinary.

It was an ancient Babylonian map of the world from the seventh or eighth century BCE.

Now you might wonder what this story has to do with data visualisation. It has everything to do with it. Let me explain.

The importance lies in the origins of human civilisation. In fact, this tablet is intrinsically linked to answers related to our evolution, the workings of our human minds and what drives human civilisation forward.

In this book, I passionately explain why mankind needs data visualisation and how it might save us in the world we have created. It begin with our desire for exploration and discovery, which this ancient clay tablet represents. This is true for both the Babylonians who created this map and the Victorian archaeologists who found it in Iraq.

We as human beings have a deep-rooted curiosity that pushes us to explore and understand the world we are in, driving us to uncover its mysteries and beauty. Data visualisation is very much a part of this endeavour, as it requires us to see what's hidden within data to reveal it mysteries.

You do not always know what you will find or where you will end up when you try to visualise data. It is an adventure! And that's exactly what happened when Hormuzd Rassam and Sir Henry Rawlinson uncovered those hidden secrets in that 2,800-year-old ancient clay tablet.

That tablet would eventually become known as the *Imago Mundi*, which in Latin translates as 'Image of the World'. It would rewrite what we knew at the time about the history of mankind by offering us an unprecedented look into how ancient civilisations viewed their place in the cosmos. It also raised many questions, like why did people back then feel the need to create maps?

Those people who created *Imago Mundi* also had an unquenchable thirst for voyage and discovery just like us. They wanted to understand how their world looked and functioned, which is why they created that map. It wasn't simply about navigation.

That map represented a view of an earlier economic system that had developed with mankind's first civilisations. There is also a lot more to the *Imago Mundi* than that meets the eye. To appreciate this, we need to go back even further in human history.

Picture a Palaeolithic landscape, where our ancestors once roamed, their lives dictated by the harsh environment that they lived in and where food was scare. From archaeological evidence, we know that humans first added wild grains to their diet about 100,000 years ago (Mercader 2009).

Life back then was radically different world from today. We lived as nomadic hunter-gatherers in small groups, battling for survival in an environment dominated by untamed nature, where large animals such as mammoths, sabre-toothed cats and woolly rhinoceroses roamed the earth.

This was the Ice Age. We used stone tools to hunt, prepare food and build shelters, which were essential for our survival. Fire provided warmth, allowed us to cook food and offered protection from predators, significantly enhancing our ability to survive.

However, this was still a very harsh environment. Life expectancy was low, with many individuals not surviving past 30 due to disease, injury and malnutrition. Despite these challenges, our ancestors showed incredible adaptability and developed complex language, created art and used symbols to communicate. Believe it or not, this would eventually help lay the foundation for developing modern-day data visualisation thousands of years later.

The Dawn of Maps and Abstract Thought

Around 12,000 years ago, we reached a revolutionary point in human history – the arrival of agriculture. This event is thought to have first occurred in the Fertile Crescent, irrevocably altering the course of human history and laying the foundations for the emergence of the world's first civilisations (Naithani 2021).

As wheat and barley sprouted from deliberately sown fields, so did the first seeds of economic development. These first crops, nurtured by human hands, represented more than just reliable sustenance; they ushered in a new world order, where humans became the most resourceful species the planet had ever seen.

Agriculture had brought with its emergence the world's first economic systems where resources could be marshalled to serve and sustain us, whether this came in the form of crops grown, animals tamed or raw materials like metal extracted from the ground to make tools and weapons.

After this, populations in newly formed cities grew and societal complexity flourished in ways our nomadic ancestors could scarcely have imagined.

These developments meant that we needed to comprehend and navigate an increasingly complex economic environment. This is what gave birth to extraordinary innovations such as the map and the wheel. Trade routes could develop over vast distances this way, and humans could travel further and quicker than ever with greater certainty of where they were.

What is more amazing is that this wasn't a development limited to early Indo-European civilisations. In other parts of the world, early Mesoamerican civilisations were doing the same. They were recording their territorial boundaries and trade paths in their own symbolic forms (Batalla 2009). The Inca of South America employed quipus, which was an intricate system of knotted cords that recorded numerical information (Cartwright 2016). Australian Aboriginal groups had their own methods, navigating the lands they travelled through songlines that encoded their geographical knowledge (Cairns and Harney 2004).

These diverse approaches for recording information applied by ancient societies reveal a universal human drive to visualise and interpret the world. We have always visualised data whether that has been through knots, songs or symbols, which has served as a bridge between abstract concepts and our human understanding.

These examples, along with the *Imago Mundi*, were the first innovations we had developed for data visualisation. Over time far more complex developments in information management would propel mankind even further. The most important of these is still used heavily today – the written word.

Before we discuss the miracle of writing, however, let's look back to what life was like before words were written. It is the only way we can truly appreciate how wonderful this innovation is and why we were always destined to discover it. Let's go back to that Stone Age scene again.

The Roots of Visual Communication

Imagine a caveman telling his son how he hunted and killed a mammoth. Would he give him a 10-point plan for getting the job done? Would he explain the workflow required to carry out such an activity, from sharpening the spear to taking an ethical shot? Would he give him a boring PowerPoint slideshow on how to do it?

No! The answer is no. If you are a dad, you would never do this even now. That is not how you make kids listen. You would tell your son a wild story. You would do this probably while sitting by the campfire for maximum dramatic effect, and this wouldn't be just any story. This would be the most insane, terrifying and yet exciting story you could possibly tell.

Your son's eyes would be bulging out. He would be hanging on to every word you spoke.

This is a story that he will probably remember for the rest of his life. Moreover, it could potentially save his life. Years from now, he might be hunting a mammoth himself as an adult, and the information you gave him through your own heroic saga might prevent him from being trampled or gored to death.

This is the oral tradition that I'm describing, and it has been with us since the dawn of humanity. It is what allowed the art of storytelling to develop, where valuable information could be transferred from one generation to the next, ensuring the survival of our species. These stories also enriched our language and allowed us to transfer not just words but visual imagery and human emotion to anyone who listened. Storytelling is undoubtedly the most powerful communication tool our species ever created and perhaps even more miraculous than the written word. Our ability to tell stories is literally written into our DNA. It is part of our evolution so it cannot be ignored.

Human Minds Are Pattern-Seeking Machines

One of the reasons why stories work so well is because they feed directly into our natural human ability to recognise patterns. By presenting events and characters in a sequence, a good story helps our brains connect the dots, just as our ancestors did when spotting lurking predators, following tracks and interpreting subtle signals in their environment. This fundamental ability to recognise and interpret patterns was crucial for our survival and still drives how we make sense of words, images and data today.

While our ancestors once tracked animals through muddy earth, we now trace trend lines on graphs and decode abstract symbols on maps. This is a remarkable example of how we still use ancient survival skills to meet modern challenges in this digital world. However, this pattern-seeking does carry some hidden risks.

Our minds can deceive us into finding meaningful patterns in random noise – a vulnerability that grows with the more data we create. Without careful, critical thinking, we might draw flawed conclusions from the data before us, seeing connections that simply aren't there. Data visualisations can even become tools of misdirection in the wrong hands, reinforcing our existing biases or leading us towards misleading interpretations. While these are risks that need to be addressed, we will delve deeper into these cognitive pitfalls later in the book.

For now, let's focus on the innovations that pattern-seeking spurred. What began as a skill for interpreting physical signs in nature, like animal tracks or weather patterns, eventually led us to develop complex symbolic systems. As mentioned before, this progression culminated in one of humanity's most powerful innovations, the written word.

Writing developed because there are drawbacks to solely relying on spoken words. Have you ever played Chinese whispers or Telephone (as the Americans call it)? Picture a line of eager players, each ready to whisper a secret message into their neighbour's ear. It sounds simple, right? Oh, how wrong you would be!

As the message gets passed down from one person to the next, it morphs into something wildly different from the original. By the time the last player belts out what they heard, the room erupts in laughter. 'Wait, how did "The cat sat on the mat" become "Fat bats eat old hats"?!'

This simple game reveals the fragility of oral communication. Though our minds excel at remembering stories, information tends to shift and blur without stable ways to record it. This weakness in purely spoken communication meant that we needed to discover the written word. It was an inevitable evolution in human communication, which even to this day we cannot live without. There is no way society could advance without it. In fact, I am using it right now to write this book.

Writing is a way to preserve knowledge more precisely than the spoken word. It first started with cave paintings, but then we started using symbols, letters and sentences to record information more precisely. Writing allowed us to develop grammar and new ways to express ourselves. Our language grew even richer and more densely packed with information when we started writing. It was an incredible innovation that ensured knowledge could be recorded forever, for generations to come.

Writing allowed us to communicate in a way that was unbounded by distance, time, language and even culture. For instance, thousands of years after the ancient Egyptians disappeared, humans from a completely different time in Victorian Britain could study the knowledge and beliefs of these ancient Egyptians through their hieroglyphs. Separated by thousands of years, Victorians found a way to listen to ancient Egyptians. It's incredible when you think about it.

The phrase 'the pen is mightier than the sword' is actually an understatement. Knowledge is power, especially if you can collect it and narrate it using the written word. Consider how Babylonian boundary stones etched with cuneiform inscriptions defined territories and legitimised the claims of those who controlled them, or how Egyptian hieroglyphs recorded royal achievements to reinforce the divine authority of pharaohs. Inscriptions on temples, monuments and official decrees were carefully crafted to present the ruling elite's perspective as truth, cultivating a narrative that justified governance, expanded influence and perpetuated social hierarchies. Being able to write gave enormous power and the ancients used this to their advantage.

Writing's power to influence, persuade and control is very similar to how data is used today. Organisations that gather and control fast amounts of personal information, from corporations to government, have immense power over us and how we behave. They can influence us through targeted ads, political messages or subtle changes to what we see online.

Just as how ancient empires used grand stone inscriptions to prove their right to rule, or how religious institutions guided believers through sacred texts, data is now being used in a similar manner. It can help support particular viewpoints or turn personal information into profit. What connects these past and present practices is how readily humans trust written information – whether carved in stone, printed on paper or displayed on a screen, we tend to change our behaviour based on what we see.

The reason why the written word is such a powerful communication tool is because of what it does to our brain. When we open a book, something magical occurs: the printed symbols on the page seem to dissolve, transporting us into worlds crafted entirely from an author's imagination. It's an extraordinary feat achieved through simple marks on paper.

Think very carefully about this. As you read, you see pictures in your mind and feel strong emotions, just like in real life. You might connect with a character and feel for them, which is quite special. That's called empathy. Not all animals can do this, but humans can. You might not physically feel a character's pain, happiness or sadness, but you can imagine what it might feel like. It is an emotional experience. And whether you like it or not, viewing data can also be just as highly emotional. This is something that we don't pay enough attention too. In the academic discipline of studying literature, we might question the author's intentions or the themes and issues being raised to get a better understanding of what is being presented. We should also do the same with the way data is presented.

When data is presented visually, it can spark empathy and understanding. Cold figures on population displacement become far more effective when displayed in a way that shows the human stories they represent. Take climate data or health statistics today – when we transform these numbers into clear visual stories, they can stir people to action. A powerful chart showing rising global temperatures or the spread of a disease does more than just present facts – it helps us feel the human impact behind the numbers and often pushes communities and politicians to respond. It shows how data, when presented in a compelling way, can bridge the gap between abstract figures and real-world change.

The same was true about that ancient map, the *Imago Mundi*. When it was made, it's purpose wasn't just to be a map that showed where places were. It gave a snapshot of a time when people first tried to picture and understand complicated trade connections that were created by our earliest civilisations. Like a good book, this map told a story of humanity that would have been full of feelings and mental images of the world to a person reading this map at that time. It shows us how these ancient people saw their world and their place in it, much like how a novel helps us see a world through someone else's eyes, whether it's the author or through the characters themselves.

Like a message across time, the *Imago Mundi* tells us stories about what people knew and thought, rather like how we use books today to share our own knowledge and ideas. Maps were the very first forms of data visualisation that we created and communicated with when our first civilisations began to emerge. They were also a brilliant demonstration of early human abstract thought. The real world is not flat like a map, nor full of drawn contours, strange symbols or international borders. Yet maps are still logical to our human brains.

For thousands of years, people used maps to express themselves and tell stories. Map makers would decorate their work with vivid images and calligraphy that told amazing tales. They would draw scary sea monsters popping out of large oceans. They would make mountains emerge from the flatness of the map.

When I was young, I loved reading books such as *The Chronicles of Narnia*, *The Hobbit* and *The Lord of the Rings*. I would spend just as much time looking at the maps in these books as I did reading the stories. The maps helped me understand where the characters were in these made-up worlds and made the stories feel richer and more real.

Stories, in general, are meant to do this, whether captured in a map or a book. They share important information in a way that's easy for our brains to picture and remember. They are like containers for human feelings and cultural memories, helping us move forward while reminding us of where we came from. They show how we have always wanted to understand, explore and dream about things beyond what is right in front of us.

Our minds are remarkable cartographers, continuously mapping both our inner world and outer reality. Just as traditional maps guide us through physical terrain, our brains create sophisticated neural maps that chart our relationship with the surrounding environment. These mental maps align our thoughts with sensory experiences, emotions and intentions – a process that's both instantaneous and intricate. Through the exchange of electrical signals and chemical messengers, our brains can transform fleeting thoughts into enduring memories by strengthening the connections between neurons rather like well-trodden paths becoming permanent routes on a living, breathing map of consciousness.

This mapping function of the mind is fundamental to human cognition and neural processing. It is a spectacular evolutionary design that allows humans to store and process information (Varoquaux et al. 2018).

This is how we evolved as a species. This is how we came to be. Our minds do not just store data, nor do they process it in the same way as a computer. It's not what we were designed to do.

Think about how wisdom was formed and delivered to us in the past and how it has remained in our collective memory ever since. In ancient Greece, Aesop's fables conveyed moral lessons through simple yet profound stories involving animals, while Plato's dialogues explored complex philosophical concepts through the voice of Socrates. In China, Confucius's *Analects* offered practical wisdom on ethics and governance that continues to influence Eastern thought. The Indian epic *Mahabharata*, attributed to Vyasa, wove intricate tales of duty, honour and cosmic order into its narrative.

Whether passed on through the oral tradition or recorded in ancient scriptures, these stories are a form of visualised data or information that is meant to save us or at least provide us a map that guides us on how we should live our lives. It's no different from the valuable information that the caveman father we discussed earlier gave his son on killing a mammoth by telling him a powerful story.

Stories remain in humanity's collective memory and represent a form of stored data that we draw upon, even to this day. It's your mind that deciphers it and visualises what it means. The same is true with memories, which you map across your life and which makes you who you are.

Memories are a multi-dimensional form of data, whose nature constantly changes. They capture the emotions you felt at the time they were formed and then morph and warp to influence the experiences you have in the present. They are influenced by the stories we tell about ourselves. Just like in drama, in our stories there are conflict and villains, where we cast ourselves as the hero. Moreover, we believe the stories we tell ourselves.

There are plenty of real-life stories that show how people see themselves as the heroes. Think of someone who worked their way out of poverty to become successful, or a person who stood up to discrimination and made a difference. Many of us have gone through tough breakups and cast ourselves as the wronged party.

But some stories are harder to believe. Take a criminal who claims they had no choice because of a rough childhood. Are they really the victim they think they are? Or are they just trying to justify their actions to you and themselves? These examples show how tricky it can be to separate fact from the stories we tell ourselves. Nevertheless, they represent the way we visualise the world we are in with the information we have.

The point here is that data comes in many forms and how we interpret data depends on our circumstances. Storytelling is one of the oldest forms of communicating visually that relies on a mental map of memories that we have formed. It allows us to see and visualise the information we have.

Throughout this book on data visualisation, you will see me do this. I will narrate stories, whether about myself and my own experiences, or about others who are fundamental to understanding data visualisation. This is essential. Without stories, we cannot possibly understand data visualisation and the profound impact it has on us.

So, let's draw a quick mental map of where we are now. We've covered storytelling through the oral tradition, the written word and the profound influence that maps have in helping us understand our complex world.

These innovations emerged from our need to understand our world. As economic systems grew increasingly complex, we developed maps to navigate. When our collective knowledge expanded beyond what the oral tradition could reliably preserve, we invented writing, allowing us to record information with remarkable precision. Each of these creative leaps forward came in response to an overwhelming flood of data that our existing tools of comprehension simply couldn't manage.

Fast forward to the present and we are once again drowning in data and in need of innovation. I believe that the next step of innovation lies with data visualisation.

William Playfair and the Birth of Modern Charts

So let's begin with where modern-day data visualisation started. In the eighteenth century, the first graphs were created. William Playfair, a Scottish engineer and political economist, is widely credited as their inventor. He developed and popularised several fundamental chart types, including line graphs, bar charts and pie charts. In 1786, he published *The Commercial and Political Atlas*, revolutionising how complex economic and statistical information could be presented visually (Playfair 1786).

Charts had a profound impact across many fields, from economics and science to politics and journalism, enabling more effective communication of complex information. What's incredible is how easy they are to interpret, despite their abstract nature. Think about it: in real life, you don't see bar charts sprouting from the ground or line charts streaking across the sky. Yet, these types of charts make complete sense to us.

None of these changes happened on their own. The printing press sent maps and texts travelling far beyond their birthplaces, opening up new knowledge to countless minds across the world. Libraries grew, scribes passed on their craft and schools flourished, all helping to spread learning more widely through society. As these tools and institutions developed, more people gained access to written and visual records, slowly breaking the elite's grip on knowledge. With each new breakthrough – from written words to printed pages to modern data tools – the power to understand and create meaning from information spread to ever wider circles of society.

Navigating the Era of Information Overload

Just as the printing press multiplied the spread of maps and written texts, the Internet and computational tools have now unleashed a torrent of visual data, far beyond what our ancestors could have imagined. This shift from scarcity to abundance brings its own challenges, demanding new skills and literacies.

Throughout human history, innovation has been constantly required to keep pace with our increasingly data-rich world. We began creating data through cave paintings, the oral tradition and eventually the written word. As our economies and civilisations grew more complex, we developed maps. For a long time, our books and maps served their purpose well, until the world became too complicated even for these tools. Thousands of years later, Playfair developed charts to help us handle even greater levels of complexity as the world entered the industrial age.

As mentioned before, human civilisation has experienced several significant data explosions, each triggering new methods of information management and data visualisation. From the advent of agriculture and early urban settlements, through the rise of complex societies, the Classical period, the Renaissance and Age of Exploration, the Industrial Revolution, and finally to our current Digital Revolution, we've continually developed new ways to handle increasing amounts of data.

This is where we find ourselves today. The amount of data being created has grown exponentially and we're drowning in it. The problem arises when we assume data is just information, devoid of human emotion. As I've tried hard to argue in this chapter, it really isn't. When we become emotionally detached from data as we are today, we can lose our sense of reality.

Data begets data without human attachment and before we know it, we are experiencing cognitive overload. Rather than creating more clarity about the world we inhabit, the world we know becomes chaotic. Complexity reduces clarity and we no longer know our place in the world. The danger is that we become blind to our surroundings and the risks we face.

This represents one of the greatest threats to the human race, which we have inadvertently created. Not being able to see the world around us properly in this deluge of data means we are more susceptible to misinformation or propaganda. We are at greater risk of misunderstandings or gaining warped opinions of the world.

It can lead to greater division within countries, increased geopolitical tensions and even war. In the nuclear-armed age, it only takes one bad decision to set things off.

Just as early agrarian societies needed new records to stabilise their social structures, we now need advanced tools – interactive dashboards, machine learning algorithms and immersive data experiences to navigate today's overwhelming information rich world. Developing these tools and the skills to use them is as crucial now as learning to farm or to write once was.

Today, historians, anthropologists, neuroscientists and data scientists work together to understand not only how we process visual information but how these processes have evolved over millennia.

Why Visual Literacy Is the New Survival Skill

Data visualisation has emerged out of necessity – out of the need to navigate complexity and uncertainty. Through stories, maps, written words and more recently through charts and graphs we have established pathways of understanding that help us see beyond what lies directly before us. This evolution is a testament to human ingenuity: as our world grew more perplexing and unfamiliar we found new ways to make sense of it, to share our discoveries and to foster collective growth.

Yet this is no simple endeavour. Each stage of development in how we share and interpret data carries with it a host of questions and challenges. How do we know which story is the right one or which map is the most accurate representation? How do we choose what data to show and what to leave behind? Every choice shapes how we perceive reality and how others understand it. This is why data visualisation is more than mere aesthetics or an intellectual exercise – it is a responsibility, one that requires careful thought and ethics.

If we fail to acknowledge that responsibility, if we allow data to flood our senses without the adequate means to interpret it, then understanding begins to slip through our fingers. We risk becoming strangers in our own world, uncertain of where we stand, manipulated by the illusions of others and drawn into conflicts founded on misinterpretations and half-truths.

This is the essential problem lurking in our digital age. We must now harness all the wisdom gleaned from thousands of years of storytelling, mapmaking and symbol creation and apply it to our present circumstances. Interdisciplinary fields such as cognitive psychology and semiotics now study how we perceive and interpret images, while data literacy initiatives underscore the importance of understanding the visual forms of information we encounter daily.

In this sense, visual literacy – our ability to discern meaning and intention in graphs, charts and maps – stands as vital to modern life as hunting skills were to our Ice Age ancestors. Just as they navigated harsh landscapes in search of sustenance, we must navigate a world awash with competing facts and figures. The ability to spot credible evidence, recognise misleading data visualisations and place information in the right context has become crucial to our collective well-being and possibly the survival of the human race.

Like skilled hunters reading subtle signs in nature, we need to develop sharp eyes that can sift through complexity and turn chaos into clarity. These abilities guide our decisions with greater insight and confidence in an increasingly data-rich world.

In the next chapter, we explore today's information landscape, where data flows at an unprecedented scale. As we've discovered, this torrent of information often obscures more than it reveals, creating a thick fog through which reality becomes harder to discern. This challenge echoes through every aspect of modern life, from social media feeds to scientific papers.

We will examine how this overwhelming flood of data can cloud our understanding, especially when numbers and statistics pile up without meaning behind them. But there is hope. By learning to read and create clear visual stories from data, we can begin to make sense of our complex world again.

KEY TAKEAWAYS

- Data visualisation has deep historical roots, tracing back to ancient civilisations such as the Babylonians, who created maps like the *Imago Mundi* to understand and depict their world.
- Long before written language, humans relied on oral storytelling and symbolic imagery to communicate complex ideas and share essential knowledge, with these practices ultimately influencing the evolution of data visualisation.
- The invention of writing allowed societies to record and preserve information, enabling knowledge to be passed across generations and facilitating the creation of maps, charts and other visual tools that supported navigation, trade and cultural development.

- Our minds are naturally drawn to patterns and stories, a result of ancient survival instincts. This pattern recognition helps us understand visual representations of information – from cave paintings and maps to modern data charts – although it can also mislead us if not approached critically.
- As societies became more complex, data visualisation evolved to keep pace, helping people make sense of increasingly intricate economic systems, global trade routes and cultural exchanges.
- In the modern digital era, data exists in overwhelming abundance. Without thoughtful data visualisation and interpretation, this torrent of information can obscure truth, fuel misinformation and complicate our understanding of reality.
- By developing our ability to interpret and create meaningful data visualisations, we enhance our capacity to navigate a data-rich world, bridging the gap between raw information and an understanding of how our world works – a skill now as vital as any survival instinct.

Chapter 2

Technology Makes Us Fragile

He stumbled out of the dense forest, clutching his stone axe, only to find himself amid a bustling modern city. His eyes widened with both terror and amazement as he stared at the towering steel structures that pierced the sky. Shiny metal beasts roared past him, their eyes blazing with light, while strange people in vibrant clothing moved briskly around him, oblivious to the wonder and confusion etched on his face.

The magic of the flickering screens held in the hands of these people and the strange symbols written everywhere left him feeling disorientated and lost. He had been transported to another world, one where the rules of nature he knew so well no longer applied. In his old life, survival depended on his attuned senses and intimate knowledge of the environment. In this new world, it seemed to depend on mastery of invisible systems that were far beyond his comprehension.

Yes, you guess it. That is our Stone Age man from 100,000 years ago, the one who was telling his son how to kill a mammoth. I have plopped him in our world, just for a bit of fun. Let us give him a name. We will call him Ethan. He's now a single father living in a strange new world – our world.

Ethan would probably be quite confused in our world. It's understandable. Just a few hundred years ago, people would have regarded our current achievements as nothing short of miraculous. We now enjoy an incredible quality of life, often living to our biological maximum, a luxury we take for granted thanks to modern healthcare. Throughout most of human history, people usually died young either from physical injury or sickness. Today, the only threats to our longevity seem to be largely self-inflicted: a poor diet and lack of exercise.

This shift in our circumstances has changed the way we think. Hunting, once a necessity for survival, is now seen as cruel because we can simply wander down to the supermarket and pick up meat from the fridge devoid of any knowledge of how it got there. We have made the world serve us so effectively through complex economic systems that it has allowed us to remain blissfully ignorant of how anything works. A really good example of this is money: the unit of account, the medium of exchange and the store of value that our economies run on.

Most people do not realise that money today is no longer tied to anything physical like gold. It exists as a shared belief, based on trust in governments and central banks. This system of fiat money, where currency derives its value from agreement rather than tangible assets, is deeply confusing for many. While it has enabled incredible economic growth, it also distances us from understanding the basics of value and trade.

As these systems grow more sophisticated, they mask their own fragility, leaving us detached from the mechanisms that sustain our daily lives. It creates a peculiar paradox: the more seamless our systems appear, the less we comprehend them and the more precarious our position becomes if those systems fail.

Indeed, this lack of understanding is not merely an intellectual shortcoming. It reflects a deeper vulnerability. Our forebears who hunted and foraged understood every tool they fashioned and every step of their food supply. Today, we outsource that understanding to experts and intricate machinery. As a result, we have lost touch with the fundamentals of survival. The sense of mastery over our environment has given way to complacency, which could one day be our undoing.

Systems, Networks and Hidden Fragility

Our Stone Age ancestor Ethan, if he were to view our world today, might see it as wondrous and see us as some kind of super race. Yet, the very technology that makes us look powerful to him can actually make us very fragile. Take away our tech and our systems, and we are pretty useless. Without power grids, we cannot pump clean water or preserve food. Without global supply chains, we struggle to source the raw materials of daily life. Without modern communication networks, we lose the ability to coordinate, collaborate and react swiftly to crises.

Consider what would happen if the major infrastructure that supports our economy suddenly collapsed. Supermarket shelves would empty, fuel stations would run dry and communication channels would fall silent. While we pride ourselves on our intelligence and adaptability, many of us would find ourselves shockingly unprepared. We are vulnerable without our technology. Most of us wouldn't survive in the wilderness like Ethan did. We wouldn't know how to light a fire without matches, build a shelter, cloth ourselves or even hunt an animal. We probably wouldn't survive.

Let us look at an example in history, one that also casts light on how perceived superiority can mask deep fragility. When the Spanish arrived in South America, the native people treated them like gods, awestruck by their shimmering armour and impressive weapons.

These newcomers, with their towering ships and strange animals, seemed to embody the power of divine beings. But that awe soon turned to horror as the Spanish, driven by an insatiable lust for gold, unleashed a wave of destruction. The diseases they brought from Europe ravaged South American populations and their quest for wealth left a trail of death and devastation.

Yet imagine if the South American natives had access to an early warning system – perhaps a precursor to the modern-day forms of data visualisation. If they could visually see data that showed the effects of Spanish encroachment and the diseases they carried, they may have recognised the threat sooner. They could have fortified their defences, form alliances and united to stave of invasion before it was too late.

On the other hand, what if the Spanish had better maps and navigation equipment. They would have been able to have circumnavigated the globe, sailed around the Americas and found India, filling their ships with valuable spices. If they had access to modern-day weather forecast data, GPS and charts on wind patterns and currents, then perhaps this tragedy would have been avoided.

The Spanish were neither Gods nor a morally superior race. They were simply armed with better warfare technology but had poor data visualisation tech. In a sense, both conquerors and conquered were undone by their inability to visually see the risk of their encounter, which helps seal the fate for South America. What was perceived as Spanish technological strength turned out to be a weakness for both sides.

The New Global Scale of Exploitation

Today, we possess the kind of data tools and visualisation techniques that might have altered the course of history for both the Spanish and the South American natives. We can track storms from a smartphone, model climate change scenarios and pinpoint global supply-chain vulnerabilities with ease. In theory, this should help us recognise and avert disasters before they strike. The problem we now have is that the world is too technologically complex for even these advances. The tech, therefore, doesn't really make us stronger.

We live in a constant cycle of consumption and exploitation that not only strains the Earth's resources but also put us at risk. If we continue down this path, we risk inflicting a level of devastation on our planet that far surpasses the tragedies of history, like the Spanish conquest of the Americas.

We have constantly extended our economic productivity through better technology to reach our ever-extending human desires. Every leap in productivity brings with it a leap in complexity. Each new device or system adds another layer to the global infrastructure that supports our lives.

These layers are interconnected, creating a web of dependencies so intricate that a failure in one part can cause disruptions across the whole system. As this web grows, we find ourselves relying on a precarious network of technology that not very many people understand.

In fact, these vulnerabilities can already be felt today. As I am writing these words, it is a beautiful Saturday morning in Otranto, Italy. I am on holiday, sitting on the balcony. We are right at the end of the southern heel of Italy in a region called Puglia. This area is surrounded by sparkling sea, pristine beaches and beautiful whitewashed buildings that epitomise the Puglia charm.

I am truly grateful to be here to be honest, especially after what happened yesterday. I am writing this on 20 July 2024, in the wake of what may be the most extensive global technology blackout in history. The chances are that you have probably already forgotten that it happened when reading this, but it did.

This incident, which occurred yesterday on Friday 19 July 2024, far surpasses previous tech blackouts and even the previously anticipated Y2K bug which actually never materialised. A faulty

CrowdStrike security update caused widespread disruption to Microsoft Windows systems globally.

The repercussions were swift and far-reaching. From Sydney to London, the modern world's digital underpinnings came apart. Airlines grounded flights, office workers found themselves locked out of their virtual workspaces, hospitals postponed operations and even television channels went dark. The scale was unprecedented with millions of computers potentially affected.

Users were confronted with the infamous 'blue screen of death' as machines entered an endless reboot cycle dubbed the 'doom loop'. The crisis, likely stemming from inadequate testing of an update, left CrowdStrike scrambling for solutions. IT teams faced a Sisyphean task: manually fix each affected device and then pray for a swift remedy. The cascading nature of this failure demonstrated the fragility of our technological ecosystem. A single flawed patch rippled through global networks revealing how tightly coupled and vulnerable our systems truly are.

Here is why I am grateful. First, our holiday started a week before this now infamous IT blackout. Second, we drove here. It was an intense road trip – 19 hours in total. We left Zurich at 2 a.m. and arrived here at 9 p.m. If we had left a week later and flown like most people do, our flight would have likely been cancelled, ruining our holiday.

Some might say this is just a first-world problem. But it is not because the IT bug hit emerging markets too, grounding their flights as well. This is more of a modern-age-take-technology-for-granted issue. Or rather, it is not even a problem, but a risk we do not fully understand or just ignore because we think we are invincible. In truth, it is a warning shot – one that reminds us that we exist atop a precarious mountain of digital dependencies.

Floods of Data, Deficits of Wisdom

At the heart of our modern dilemma sits an avalanche of data that is growing exponentially as our technology advances. We have fallen into a curious trap: the more information we amass, the more confident we become in our supposed omniscience. This is very similar to the way that we rely on technology and the complex systems that we have created. It has left us feeling invincible, unaware of our vulnerabilities.

This situation is even more alarming when it relates to data. Unlike the ever-expanding amount of data we are creating, we are at least somewhat aware of the risks of over-relying on technology.

For instance, climate change is a crisis we recognise, discuss and actively seek to address. But, while we worry about the carbon emissions we pump into the atmosphere, we pay little attention to the torrents of data we create thanks to our complicated technological systems.

This data does not merely document our existence; it increasingly shapes and defines it, embedding itself in our systems and creating new dependencies that we are only just beginning to comprehend. The danger lies not only in what we know but also in what we fail to foresee.

We rarely pause to examine this, convincing ourselves that the data we have is safely tucked away on hard drives and servers for whenever we might need it. This casual approach to knowledge reveals a peculiar modern attitude – we collect information like digital magpies, mistaking possession for understanding.

In truth, the sheer volume of data can obscure meaning, making it harder to see trends, connections and warnings that might otherwise be obvious. Without careful analysis, we risk navigating a world where critical knowledge is buried beneath noise. Our brains, evolved for simpler patterns, struggle to extract clarity from this chaos.

Before we continue, however, it is really important to note that this is not a new vulnerability. This is a problem that has plagued humanity since the dawn of civilisation. If we look back into the past, there are many tragic events that rhyme with what we are seeing today. We have always created data, and we have always taken it for granted. It has provided us in the past with access to incredible amounts of wisdom and collective knowledge. There are so many events where we have found, lost and had to recover that knowledge again, sometimes centuries later.

Here are two very powerful examples. The Library of Alexandria, founded in the third century, was once a beacon of learning and is believed to have declined over centuries due to neglect, political turmoil and the dispersal of its texts. Almost a millennia later, in the thirteenth century, the Mongols sacked Baghdad and destroyed the House of Wisdom, erasing countless texts and advanced knowledge that the Arabs had discovered. Let's not leave it here, however, as mere mentions of events in history. We need to understand what happened.

The Library of Alexandria and the House of Wisdom were far more than repositories of scrolls. They were the neural hubs of their time, where the collective wisdom of the known universe converged and were actively explored. These institutions represented the height of intellectual achievement for humanity at the time, fostering innovation and preserving the accumulated wisdom of humanity. These were not just isolated tragedies but significant losses that set humanity back for centuries, underscoring how fragile knowledge can be and how easily it can slip away, even when it seems secure.

Although the Lighthouse of Alexandria was one of the Seven Wonders of the Ancient World, you could argue that the Library of Alexandria was far more spectacular. It held the knowledge and musings of the greatest minds of antiquity within its walls. Scholars from across the known world flocked to this Egyptian wonder as they sought wisdom in mathematics, astronomy, philosophy and literature.

Centuries passed and as war ravaged the last vestiges of the Roman Empire, this once-prized body of wisdom faded away into the dark ages.

More centuries passed until a new civilisation emerged. Islam had arrived, transforming a once illiterate race of Arabs into one of the most advanced and progressive civilisations in human history within just a few generations. Arab scholars painstakingly collected, preserved and translated classical texts not only from Greek philosophers like Aristotle, Plato, Ptolemy and Euclid but also from Indian scholars such as Aryabhata, Brahmagupta and Charaka.

Indian contributions in mathematics, such as the concept of zero, the decimal system and algebra, as well as significant advancements in astronomy and medicine, were studied and expanded upon. These diverse sources of knowledge were synthesised in the Islamic Golden Age, ensuring that this accumulated wisdom survived, thrived and eventually influenced European intellectual progress during the Renaissance.

Individuals like Avicenna (Ibn Sina) and Alhazen (Ibn al-Haytham) not only preserved classical knowledge but also expanded upon it, particularly in medicine, mathematics and astronomy. Al-Khwarizmi, whose name gave us the word 'algorithm', made profound contributions to mathematics, including laying the foundations of algebra, which later proved essential to European scientific progress during the Enlightenment.

Centuries after Al-Khwarizmi's great works, another tragedy struck with the destruction of the House of Wisdom in Baghdad. This was the very place where Al-Khwarizmi and others had made their contributions to the world.

What happened was tragic and arguably more traumatic to the Arabs than the Crusades. Hulagu Khan, a grandson of Genghis Khan, led the Mongols in 1258 to conquer Baghdad, the capital of the Abbasid Caliphate. The city was sacked, and an estimated 200,000–1,000,000 people were killed.

When the House of Wisdom was destroyed, many priceless manuscripts and texts were lost and the Tigris River is said to have run black with the ink of books thrown into it. The loss set back global economic progress for centuries.

This is why we need to pay attention today. Those tragic events are minuscule compared to what we could experience if we are not careful with data we have now.

Simulations, Pandemics and the Cost of Inaction

We store vast amounts of data, believing ourselves immune to such catastrophic loss like those in the past that we have just described. Yet, we are just as vulnerable as past civilisations that have been sacked and plundered. A well-coordinated cyberattack or a solar flare could wipe out swathes of our collective knowledge, leaving us as bereft as the scholars were of ancient Alexandria and Baghdad.

Even without such dramatic events, we face an even subtler danger. In Alexandria and Baghdad, scholars did not just collect scrolls. They were explorers, searching deep into the knowledge contained within these staggeringly vast libraries. Today, we amass terabytes of data in the blink of an eye, but how much do we truly understand? Filling a hard drive with data makes us no wiser than filling a bookshelf with books that we have never read.

The tragedy of Alexandria and Baghdad was not just the loss of physical artefacts, it was the severing of our living connection to collective human knowledge. Today, we risk a similar disconnection not through destruction by foreign invaders but through neglect. We skim instead of study, scroll instead of scrutinise and outsource our memory to search engines and artificial intelligence. In doing so, we assume that the mere presence of data is a shield against ignorance.

This is a dangerous assumption. Data without comprehension is like a map without a legend. We might have every coordinate and contour line, but if we cannot interpret them, we are still lost. Our civilisation's challenge is not just to preserve data but also to ensure it remains interpretable and actionable. Without that, our massive digital libraries become little more than impenetrable vaults of information.

These lessons echo through the ages: true resilience comes not from hoarding information but from using it. As we build our modern temples of data, let us not forget to cultivate the wisdom they hold, lest we find ourselves, like our ancestors, scrambling to recover lost knowledge in the face of an uncertain future.

The Transformative Power of Data Visualisation

This is why data visualisation matters. The deluge of data makes it very difficult to evaluate and understand the risks we face. The complexity and our cognitive limitations might tempt us to ignore these risks. This could be the biggest threat to our human existence.

This is not an exaggeration. The loss we face if we fail to act would be far more catastrophic than the destruction of the Library of Alexandria or the House of Wisdom in Baghdad. Although those events were extremely painful, they only set humanity back a few centuries. Such a loss in the modern world would set us back to those times that may even predate the Stone Age.

If our technology fails, would you be able to hunt, kill, build a fire without matches and provide shelter for your family? It might sound dramatic, but it is not. We have, in effect, outsourced even the most basic survival skills to distant technological systems.

We have been watching the Planet of the Apes movies over the holidays in the evenings after dinner and gelato. In this movie series, humanity's downfall begins with mankind's overconfidence, hubris and arrogance. The world is ravaged by human neglect and the exploitation of natural resources. There are clear moral and ethical failings from the human societies depicted in each movie. There is also too much dependence on technology and an inability to unite, which ultimately allows the apes to take over.

Perhaps this is what we are now seeing today. Our over reliance on modern conveniences and loss of basic survival skills are vulnerabilities that could be catastrophic in a real-world scenario. What could wipe us out is our inability to see what is coming – and I am not talking about an asteroid hitting Earth, but something far more likely which we are not even bothering to track adequately. Without clear interpretation, our wealth of data is an ocean without navigational charts.

Let us return to that IT blackout I mentioned earlier. This was a risk that we knew about long before it happened. In fact, over a quarter of a century ago, back in 1999, we were furiously preparing for the Y2K bug that threatened to unleash havoc. This bug was a computer flaw that people feared would cause widespread system failures at the start of the year 2000 because many software programs at the time only used two digits to represent years, potentially interpreting '00' as 1900 instead of 2000.

Nothing happened. We were over prepared. But then we completely forgot about it, and 25 years later we experienced what we had feared, the biggest IT blackout in human history. The same was true with the pandemic. We had all the data. We knew there was a risk that it could happen. We have lived through pandemics throughout the ages. The Spanish Flu that occurred more than 100 years ago in 1918 killed more than 50 million people. We know about pandemics and yet we were still unprepared.

To compound the situation, the US government was fully aware of the potential for such a crisis long before the pandemic struck. In the years leading up to 2020, two remarkably prophetic simulations were conducted, both of which eerily anticipated the unfolding of events and highlighted these looming dangers.

The first, called Crimson Contagion, was a large-scale exercise organised by the Trump Administration between January and August 2019. It simulated the outbreak of a novel influenza virus originating in China and swiftly spreading to the United States through international air travel. The scope of this exercise was vast, engaging 19 federal agencies, 12 states, 74 local health departments and 87 hospitals nationwide.

As the Crimson Contagion scenario unfolded, it revealed significant weaknesses in the country's ability to respond effectively to a pandemic. Participants grappled with confusion over leadership roles and decision-making authority, highlighting the complex nature of coordinating a national response.

The exercise also exposed inadequate funding mechanisms for swift action, a critical factor in the early stages of an outbreak. Perhaps most alarmingly, it uncovered potential shortages of medical equipment and supplies – a preview of the challenges that would become all too real in the coming year. The simulation revealed problems in how information was shared and communicated, highlighting how challenging it is to provide consistent clear messages to the public during an emergency (Salyer 2019).

Just a few months later, in October 2019, another simulation took place. Dubbed Event 201, this exercise was conducted by the Johns Hopkins Center for Health Security in partnership with the World Economic Forum and the Bill & Melinda Gates Foundation. Event 201 focused on a hypothetical coronavirus pandemic, bringing together 15 global business, government and public health leaders to examine pandemic preparedness efforts across various sectors.

The simulation delved into several critical areas of pandemic response. It emphasised the need for public–private cooperation in both preparedness and response efforts, recognising that neither government nor business alone could effectively manage a global health crisis.

The exercise also highlighted the importance of developing systems that shared data and information in real time, a crucial factor in understanding and responding to a rapidly evolving crisis. It emphasised the need to combat misinformation and disinformation, a challenge that would become especially important in the early months of the actual coronavirus pandemic (Pearce 2019).

You cannot make this up. We knew this risk and we were still caught unprepared. In fact, the United States could not have been better prepared for the pandemic given the vast amounts of research and data they had collected during these studies. It was clear that there was an urgent need for better coordination and resources and yet very little was done.

The country saw mass lockdowns and quarantine measures not experienced in living US memory. Shelves were emptied in supermarkets as panic buying led to shortages of items such as toilet paper, hand sanitiser, masks and even flour to make bread. The US economy shut down overnight and experienced a sharp and brutally short two-month recession. At its height, mass graves were used in New York City to handle the overwhelming number of deaths. It is estimated that at the time of writing, 1.2 million Americans have died from complications due to the coronavirus disease 2019 (COVID-19) (Worldometer 2024).

Let us put this into perspective. The death toll from COVID-19 was nearly twice that of the American Civil War. It surpasses the fatalities from the Spanish Flu pandemic of 1918–1919 in the United States by 1.8 times. It is 3 times greater than the number of US deaths in the Second World War, 32 times more than those lost in the Korean War, 21 times more than in Vietnam and a staggering 403 times the death toll of 9/11. How could this have happened? We had the data – perhaps we had too much.

This is at the heart of the issue: we were overwhelmed by information. Despite thorough analysis and clear conclusions drawn from studies and simulations, the gravity of the impending crisis was lost on us. We were long overdue for a pandemic and yet we failed to fully comprehend the scale of the threat.

When I say 'we', I do not mean to place the blame solely on the US government. The global scientific community had the data, the analysis and the findings right in front of them. Governments across the world, including the United States, could have been pressured more strongly to act on these insights. If decisive measures had been taken based on the simulations, the trajectory of the pandemic could have been vastly different – in China where it began, in Italy where it spread rapidly and in countries such as the United Kingdom, Brazil, Mexico and India, all of which soon found themselves gripped by its devastating impact.

Millions of lives could have been saved from COVID-19, but they were not because of our human inability to cut through the fog of data. This is where the true power of data visualisation comes into play. It helps us see through that fog, bringing critical risks into focus that might otherwise go unnoticed.

Data visualisation is not just a tool for analysis, but it is also a powerful medium of communication with complex data. It allows leaders to grasp the full scope of problems and risks, facilitating quicker and more informed decision-making. In a crisis like the COVID-19 pandemic, this clarity was essential. Had data visualisation been more effectively utilised, scientists could have communicated the urgency of the situation to politicians in a far more impactful way.

The scientific knowledge was there, but the communication to policymakers fell short. Data visualisation bridges this gap by making information more cognitively accessible. It also strengthens the connection between policy decisions and public welfare. It does not merely present complex issues, but it also communicates them in a way that both governments and the public can understand by doing so visually. This shared understanding fosters transparency, builds trust and ensures that everyone fully comprehends what is truly at stake.

Imagine a world in which the torrents of raw data are channelled into clear intuitive images that highlight impending disasters before they strike. Picture dashboards that show hospital capacities at a glance or charts that reveal the progression of infection rates with unmistakable urgency. By conveying meaning swiftly and vividly, data visualisation can rouse leaders and citizens from complacency and spur them to act.

Data visualisation should be more than just a tool; it should be a way to cut through the noise and see the heart of the issues we face. It helps bring focus in moments of uncertainty, offering a clear view when decisions are tough. What is more, by integrating data from various sources, data visualisation ensures that every angle is considered, reducing the chance of missing something important. Ultimately, good data visualisation is not just about making decisions, but it is also about making better, more informed choices that lead to a fairer, safer and more just world.

As we stand at the threshold of unprecedented complexity, where data floods every aspect of our lives, we must learn to transform this torrent of information into genuine understanding. In many ways, we are not so different from our Stone Age ancestor Ethan, who would find himself utterly bewildered if hurled into our technological present.

He possessed the skills to survive with only the simplest tools, while we have become so reliant on intricate digital system that if they were to suddenly vanish, we might struggle even to light a fire or secure our next meal. Our survival no longer depends on raw instinct but on the delicate threads of interconnected systems that we barely comprehend.

This is precisely why data visualisation is not merely an option but also a necessity. By shedding light on what lies beneath the surface of complexity, data visualisation helps us see emerging threats before they engulf us. Just as the scholars of Alexandria and Baghdad once delved into their libraries to preserve and expand knowledge, we must now sift through our data to anticipate challenges and respond decisively. Should we fail to embrace this approach – if we continue to neglect the insights hidden within our data – we risk repeating the fate of those lost civilisations. Their knowledge and wisdom were scattered to the winds, leaving future generations to grope in the darkness of forgotten learning.

At its core, data visualisation is far more than a collection of colourful charts and slick graphics. It is a bridge between obscure statistics and enlightened action, allowing us to decode the reality behind the numbers. By bringing clarity to complex issues, it empowers leaders and citizens alike to recognise the true scale of problems and take action. In an age when so many dangers lurk just beyond our immediate perception, data visualisation can guide our sight, sharpen our wits and lead us away from predictable preventable disasters.

Ultimately, the true strength of our civilisation does not lie in the sheer volume of information we have amassed but in our willingness to interpret and apply it meaningfully. Without this critical engagement, data remains nothing more than lifeless code or indecipherable archives, destined to be lost or ignored. With it, we illuminate hidden risks, navigate uncertain futures and forge a wiser, more resilient path forward. In that spirit, we must ensure that the knowledge we accumulate remains not only intact but also alive and accessible – a vital inheritance for generations yet to come.

Let us remember that data is a starting point, not a conclusion. When we transform it into data visualisation, we bring it closer to human intuition. When we act on what we see, we breathe life into numbers and give purpose to information. By doing so, we honour the legacy of our ancestors who once fought against ignorance with ink, parchment and keen minds, and we can secure a future in which knowledge truly empowers our future generations.

KEY TAKEAWAYS

- Modern technological and economic systems mask their own fragility. Although they appear seamless, their complexity leaves us detached from their inner workings and vulnerable to sudden collapse.
- Historically, knowledge and wisdom have been lost or destroyed when societies became over-reliant on intricate systems they did not fully understand – as seen with the Library of Alexandria and the House of Wisdom in Baghdad.
- Collecting vast amounts of data does not guarantee comprehension. Without the ability to interpret and apply this knowledge – to find meaning within complexity – data becomes a burden rather than a benefit.
- Over-dependence on technology and complex networks can render us helpless if they fail. Without basic survival skills, we risk being ill-prepared should our systems be disrupted.
- Past crises, such as pandemics, illustrate that despite abundant data and forewarning, society often struggles to translate knowledge into action. Poor communication and a lack of clear data visualisation can lead to catastrophic outcomes.

- Effective data visualisation is essential. By making complex information accessible, it can reveal hidden risks, guide informed decision-making and prompt action before problems escalate.
- Good data visualisation enables leaders, policymakers and the public to understand pressing issues quickly and accurately. It helps cut through the noise of digital abundance, revealing the heart of the matter and preventing vital warnings from being ignored.
- Embracing data visualisation as a tool for insight and clarity is critical to our future resilience, ensuring that knowledge remains meaningful and enabling us to tackle emergent challenges with wisdom and foresight.

Chapter 3

Fighting Data Pollution

As Ethan trudged through the smog-filled streets, the blistering heat was a constant reminder of what they had done. Global warming was no longer a threat; it was here, just as predicted. The Maldives were now submerged beneath the sea, droughts were killing millions in Africa and bushfires raged annually as far north as the Arctic. We had been just too preoccupied to do anything, even though those data points were there. Our inability to act wasn't due to a lack of information – we were drowning in it.

So, when Ethan first arrived, if you remember, everything seemed perfect and almost magical. But there were some underlying tensions. Society had been weakened by an overreliance on technology. I've already complained about that in the last chapter. What I forgot to also mention is this technology has also flooded the world with data.

So, Ethan soon realised that the real danger wasn't the smog he breathed, but the haze of data that was now clouding the mind.

People were so overwhelmed by the constant influx of data that they became numb, unable to discern the urgent from the insignificant. In this fog of data, society lost its ability to act when it really needed to.

The problem we have today is that every device we use, every platform we visit and every moment of our lives are filled with streams of information demanding our attention. This constant barrage has made it nearly impossible to process or prioritise what matters.

It has created a sense of mental paralysis, where the only way for us to cognitively cope is to construct simplistic narratives. This creates a fertile ground for conspiracy theories, misinformation and disinformation to spread, by offering easy answers in a world that is impossible to comprehend.

If you want to fire a nuclear weapon, carry out ethnic cleansing or ridicule science and academia, then start with either a conspiracy theory or a convincing lie that people want to believe. That's how dangerous it can be, and although such techniques have been used throughout human history to manipulate society, it has become even easier to pull it off in a data-polluted world enhanced by social media.

Lies Are the First Symptom of Data Pollution

In a data-polluted world, facts compete with rumours, hoaxes and propaganda. Individuals or political regimes can intentionally flood the public sphere with contradictory and confusing information amid the data pollution.

Former Trump strategist, Steve Bannon, bluntly described this as 'flood the zone with shit' in an interview with acclaimed writer Michael Lewis (Lewis 2018). He meant that if you could overwhelm the media with noise, people would struggle to distinguish from what is real and what is fake. If you can create a cacophony in which data itself is distrusted, misinformation can thrive unchecked.

In a data-polluted world, even genuine facts can lose credibility amid the din of false or conflicting reports.

There are a variety of techniques that can be used. Independent journalism and fact-checkers can be accused of being inherently corrupt or biased. All news, including data used in news reports, becomes suspect even if it comes from reliable public sources. This strategy also helps insulated conspiracy theories from scrutiny because if all sources are tainted, then there is no authoritative refutation.

Yuval Noah Harari explained this in great detail in his book *Nexus*. He explained if populist leaders can sow enough doubt, people feel they cannot trust anything, apart from what the leader personally endorses; a tactic that has been used by Joseph Stalin, Vladimir Putin and Kim Jong-un (Harari 2024).

Conspiracy theories and falsehoods also hold well because of the illusory truth effect: when people are exposed to repeated assertions, they tend to perceive them as more credible, regardless of veracity (Bromberg 2023). Repetition creates processing fluency, which validates these false claims. One method for doing this is by flooding social media with posts that promote those false claims, which help spread dangerous disinformation.

For instance, President Donald Trump's communication style is to use constant repetition of catchphrases like 'witch hunt', 'fake news' and 'rigged election', plus a variety of conspiratorial tropes. Every time he makes a claim – whether about DEI causing plane crashes, Ukraine starting its own war, climate change being fake or 'woke' culture ruining America – he's tapping into this powerful psychological trick.

In Russia, a similar phenomenon occurs through state media, which uses a 'firehose of falsehoods' strategy – a term first coined by the RAND Corporation in 2016. TV channels and online spaces are flooded with synchronised pro-government messaging. Through constant repetition across multiple channels, certain narratives become ingrained in the public consciousness, which during Russia's invasion of Ukraine included claims that 'Ukraine is run by Nazis', 'the West aims to destroy Russia' and 'Russia's actions are always defensive'.

This propaganda system is amplified by strict media control and censorship that blocks alternative viewpoints, creating an echo chamber where repeated falsehoods gradually feel like truth to many Russian citizens.

None of this is of course new. Throughout history, societies face major changes and an overwhelming flood of information, misinformation and disinformation flourished. During the Salem Witch Trials of 1692, a community grappling with social and political upheaval turned to accusations of witchcraft, scapegoating individuals to explain their fears. What is commonly not mentioned is why this fear spread so efficiently. It was due to a brand new piece of technology – the printing press. This then amplified witch hunts across Europe, as mass-produced pamphlets and books spread terrifying tales of witchcraft, transforming local fears into widespread persecution.

In the twentieth century, the Red Scare in the United States saw unfounded fears of communist infiltration drive baseless accusations and persecution, while in Nazi Germany, the antisemitic stab-in-the-back myth and malicious propaganda enabled the regime's genocidal policies. Later, the Soviet Union itself spread fabrications – such as claims that the AIDS virus was created by the US military – to sow distrust in Western institutions.

Online platforms have also facilitated movements like QAnon, which repackages old and new conspiracy tropes into sweeping narratives of hidden elites orchestrating global affairs. Likewise, the anti-vaccine movement distils intricate health issues into misguided stories of sinister agendas and population control, to the point that respected scientists and public health experts are shunned and ignored. These examples underscore how conspiracy theories and propaganda often thrive when complexity overwhelms people's ability to verify information, leading to scapegoating, polarisation and real societal harm.

The Deadly Impact of Data Pollution

This makes data pollution far more lethal than carbon dioxide. Data pollution doesn't just confuse us, it paralyses our minds. When we're drowning in data, our brains search for lifelines and conspiracy theories offer deceptively simple answers. These false narratives often target specific groups, turning confusion into fear and fear into violence. History bears the scars of where these leads: divided societies, genocide and mass murder. This is a direct example of how data pollution could end up leading to the demise of the human species.

I ran a poll on LinkedIn with this question: Should schools in the UK be forced to teach Arabic numerals as part of their curriculum? It is of course a trick question (Figure 3.1).

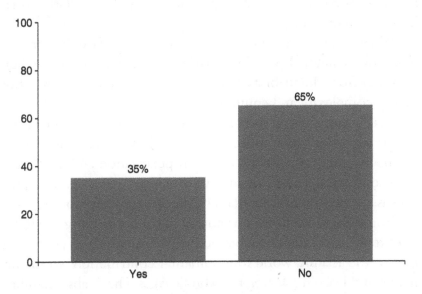

Figure 3.1 Should schools in the UK be forced to teach Arabic numerals as part of their curriculum?
Note: Poll taken by 1547 respondents between 7 December 2024 and 14 December 2024.

The numbering system we use today was introduced to Europe by the Arabs. It was originally developed in India and later adopted and transmitted by the Arabs to Europe during the Islamic Golden Age, before the Renaissance.

This chart is a striking example of how to take advantage of data pollution. It was a Friday afternoon prank, but I also did it as an experiment for this book.

I deliberately created enough ambiguity and lack of context to play on the emotions of those who participated in my bias poll. I used the term 'Arabic numerals' because there was a strong chance that it would be misunderstood and unearth some Islamophobic views. I use the word 'forced' to frame the question in a negative way. A large number of people didn't realise I was referring to the familiar numbers 0–9, which are called Arabic numerals in modern English. This misunderstanding skewed responses, with participants reacting based on cultural or political assumptions rather than informed opinions.

What I wanted to show was an aspect of data pollution in a world overwhelmed with information. We live in a society where we suffer from the inability to discern facts from misinterpretation due to complexity and confusion.

Arabic numerals, far from being a threat to British cultural identity or education, are a universal system already deeply embedded in our lives. Yet, in a society rife with polarisation and overloaded with contextless data, many survey participants perceived this question as a veiled attempt to 'Islamify' the British education system.

Ironically, this reflects a profound misunderstanding of history, as Europe's adoption of Arabic numerals centuries ago was indeed part of the Islamic world's monumental contributions to mathematics and learning during the Middle Ages. The Arabs 'Islamified' us for more than a millennia ago, and if they hadn't, we probably wouldn't have had the Renaissance.

My prank exposed how data, when divorced from its context, can amplify confusion rather than foster understanding. By doing so, it should serve as a reminder that amid today's flood of information, clarity and education are more important than ever.

It also revealed another layer of how data can mislead: not just through ambiguity or framing but also through the way our minds struggle to process unfamiliar or overwhelming information. Just as terms like 'Arabic numerals' can trigger assumptions, large numbers can similarly confuse by being too abstract to grasp.

Without relatable comparisons, numbers like '7,000,000,000,000 gallons' or '100,000 deaths' lose their meaning, becoming another source of noise in an already overloaded information world. The same mechanisms that led participants in my experiment to misinterpret a simple term are at play when vast numbers or complex data are presented without context, further illustrating how data pollution can obscure rather than reveal the truth.

This is not an exaggeration. It is a phenomenon known as 'psychic numbing' (Slovic 2007). As human beings, empathy is incredibly important, both as a communication tool and as an emotion that pulls us together as a society, through thick and thin.

When we hear about one person facing tragedy, our innate compassion is triggered, and we may feel moved to act or help through empathy. However, when confronted with statistics involving thousands or millions of people, the sheer scale becomes abstract, and our emotional engagement wanes.

This isn't due to a lack of concern but rather a cognitive limitation in processing large quantities of information. This is why data pollution can be so dangerous.

Desensitisation and the Invisibility of Data Pollution

In today's digital age, we're bombarded with an overwhelming amount of data every second – news alerts, social media updates and endless statistics. If we are not careful, this data overload can lead us to become desensitised. Critical issues such as climate change, humanitarian crises and pandemics become just another headline to scroll past. The constant influx of information creates a kind of noise that drowns out the significance of each individual data point, making it difficult to discern what is truly important.

Historically, humanity has been adept at responding to visible threats to our existence. From the looming dangers of nuclear war to the catastrophic effects of global warming, our collective imaginations have been captivated by these large-scale crises.

Hollywood, for instance, has thrived on these fears, crafting blockbuster scenarios where meteors, earthquakes, volcanoes and even intelligent apes bring about our downfall. But the threats we can't see – like data pollution – are just as deadly and rarely talked about.

Just as carbon emissions are invisible yet harmful, so too is the toxicity of data pollution. This constant barrage of data doesn't make us wiser; instead, it forces us to oversimplify, often leading to flawed conclusions. The very data meant to enlighten us has, paradoxically, become a source of confusion.

Early on in my career at HSBC, I was given a book as a young graduate. I had made a rather bold proposal to the management team to restructure a range of equities funds. I had ruffled some feathers, including those of a seasoned portfolio manager who hailed from a distinguished career in the British military.

He wasn't angry about my presentation, but he wasn't pleased either. The following day, he thrust a book into my hand and said, 'You have a lot to learn, young man'.

This book would have a profound impact on me and shaped the course of my career. To this day, I am incredibly grateful that he did this. The book was called *Fooled by Randomness* by Nassim Taleb (Taleb 2001). I went on to read a number of his books, but this book – the first I read from him – in my opinion, was his best.

Nassim Taleb is a statistician and former options trader who gained fame for his work on risk and probability. He grew up during the Lebanese Civil War, and this experience had a significant influence on how he views risk and uncertainty. The random nature of violence and the collapse of societal structure he had witnessed as a teenager made him acutely aware of our cognitive limitations and ability to understand risk.

He argued that more information often creates an illusion of understanding. In our data-drenched world, he explained, we tend to see patterns where none exist and mistake noise for signals. He warned that this false confidence leads to poor decisions and suggested that instead of trying to process ever more data, we should focus on recognising the limits of our knowledge. This means being sceptical of apparent trends, questioning our interpretations and avoiding the trap of thinking that more data automatically leads to better insights.

Data Visualisation as a Tool to Combat Misinformation

From this perspective, data visualisation should be seen as a tool to help us navigate vast amounts of information without becoming overwhelmed. When used properly, it can help us filter out the noise and focus on what is meaningful. While Taleb cautions against imagining patterns in random data, good data visualisation can show real trends and remove distracting information. The poll that I carried out on LinkedIn is the complete opposite of that.

By showing complex data in a simple way, it supports Taleb's point that we should understand our cognitive limits and focus on what's important. But if data visualisation is used poorly, it can add to the confusion in today's world. What matters is how we use data visualisation.

By showing complex data simply and clearly, data visualisation makes information easier to understand. It helps us spot important trends and insights we might miss in a bunch of numbers.

This is where data science comes in useful. As an academic discipline, it provides the tools to challenge data visualisations that are poorly presented or narrate false stories. It helps prevent data from being used to manipulate an audience into following half-truths. This is a very real risk and is a symptom of the data-drenched world we inhabit.

For instance, misleading graphs or charts can distort the truth by manipulating scales, cherry-picking data or using inappropriate visual representations. Prior to the emergence of data science, this was a very real problem, where misleading charts were often published by even highly respectable publications like *The New York Times*.

My favourite data science book was actually published just a year after I was born in 1983. It's called *The Visual Display of Quantitative Information* by American statistician and professor Edward Tufte (Tufte 1983). One of my favourite chapters in his book is *Chapter 2 – Graphical Integrity*.

It contains some breathtaking example of really poor data visualisations that we used during the early 1980s. Quite a few of these came from *The New York Times*. If you remember, I recommended Edward Tufte's book in the introduction and I did so for good reason. If you are passionate about creating your own data visualisations, this is the first book you should read.

The critiques and analysis provided by data science pioneers like Professor Edward Tufte actually changed journalism quite profoundly. *The New York Times* is actually one of the most progressive and groundbreaking news outlets in the world when it comes to data visualisation. It has since contributed significantly to the rapidly emerging field of data journalism.

In fact, one of the most famous data journalists Mike Bostock was instrumental in driving this trend at *The New York Times*. Bostock is the creator of D3.js, a groundbreaking JavaScript library that allowed interactive data visualisations to run directly in our web browsers. If you follow my work and my animated data visualisations, then you should know that most of my work is produced using D3.

While at *The New York Times*, he used this expertise to craft some of the most innovative and impactful visual narratives ever produced there, transforming how complex information is communicated to the public. His work not only advanced data journalism but also empowered designers and developers, including myself, to push the boundaries of what data visualisation can achieve.

I've heavily relied on D3.js throughout my own data visualisation journey, and in fact, most of the charts in this book which I created myself were also created using this powerful JavaScript library. Bostock's contributions have shaped not only how data is visualised but also how it is understood, making his work a cornerstone of modern data storytelling.

Cognitive Pitfalls and the Spread of Half-Truths

Despite the heroic efforts made by data scientists such as Edward Tuft and John Bostock, we still experience statistical abuse, even today. For example, there's an old joke in statistics that 83.4% of all statistics are just made up on the spot. If you haven't got the joke, just re-read that last sentence.

It all comes down to how our brains are wired. Human cognition heavily relies on mental shortcuts or cognitive biases that help us process information rapidly. While these shortcuts can be useful, they often lead us astray. One such bias is the availability heuristic, where we give undue weight to information simply because it comes readily to mind. If we hear a statistic frequently, we may accept it without scrutinising its origins or validity.

We are also prone to confirmation bias: the tendency to favour data that aligns with our existing beliefs. If a statistic supports what we already think, we are far less likely to challenge it (Kahneman 2011). This bias encourages us to filter information in a way that preserves our worldview, often at the expense of truth. Over time, this selective acceptance can reinforce false or incomplete understandings of a topic.

Overconfidence bias compounds these problems. We may assume that our interpretation of data is more accurate or informed than it really is, leading us to overestimate our knowledge or skill (Bellizzi 2022). This self-assuredness can make us even less likely to question dubious data or seek out more thorough analysis. The result is a dangerous feedback loop, where confidence grows despite the absence of reliable evidence.

Another subtle yet potent cognitive pitfall is the sleeper effect, where we forget the source of information over time (Stangor and Walinga 2014). Even if we initially encounter a statistic from a dubious or biased outlet, as we forget where it came from, we may increasingly accept it as credible. As time passes, our memory loses crucial context, making us easy targets for half-truths and misinformation.

Half-truths are particularly insidious because they present a fraction of the facts while withholding or distorting the rest. They are not outright lies, yet they convey a misleading impression. To understand how powerful this can be, consider the traditional oath in a US courtroom: 'Do you swear to tell the truth, the whole truth and nothing but the truth, so help you God?' The emphasis on 'the whole truth' acknowledges that partial truths can be as misleading as outright lies.

Imagine the statement 'There is no God but one'. To a believer, this affirms a core principle of faith. However, if someone only relays the first three words – 'There is no God' – the meaning is entirely changed. This selective editing transforms a statement of devotion into one of denial.

Half-truths poison data just as effectively as outright lies. If someone cherry-picks statistics and omits contradictory data, the resulting impression may be completely false. In this sense, half-truths are indeed lies. They leverage our cognitive biases to guide us towards incorrect conclusions, often leaving us unaware of how we have been misled.

This brings us back to the critical role of data visualisation in the fight against data pollution. In a world saturated with information, good data visualisation can help guide us through the fog of excessive data. It transforms numbers into something we can see, helping us understand what would otherwise be lost or misrepresented.

We should therefore remain vigilant. Our cognitive biases – like confirmation bias, overconfidence and the availability heuristic – can lead us to misinterpret or overly trust what we see. If data visualisation is misused or manipulated, it can perpetuate half-truths and misleading stories, exacerbating the very confusion we're trying to get rid of.

That's why the rigour of data science is essential. Data science equips us with the tools to critically evaluate data visualisations, question apparent trends and challenge those stories we are told that don't hold up under scrutiny. Data visualisation isn't just about seeing patterns, but it's also about interrogating them, ensuring we don't mistake noise for something meaningful.

Information Overload and Social Inequality

When the world is too confusing and complicated to understand, we risk experiencing information overload. We have mentioned this throughout the chapter and given several examples of this danger. It was a topic first discussed by Alvin Toffler in 1970 in his book *Future Shock* (Toffler 1970).

He described how people have become overwhelmed by excessive information, making it hard to make decisions. Now this was back in 1970 and it has got a lot worse since then with the birth of the Internet and emergence of social media, which now give us an endless supply of information that is often designed to keep us hooked.

Scientists have found that too much information can make it harder for us to focus and think deeply. It can even affect the part of our brain that helps us make decisions. This information overload is also causing problems in society. False information spreads easily on social media, which can lead to real-world problems such as health crises and political unrest (Firth et al. 2019).

The spread of misinformation, especially on social media, is a significant problem. False information about companies and products can lead to financial losses; rumours within organisations can cause confusion and reduce productivity and incorrect beliefs about medical issues can affect health decisions, such as vaccination choices.

Data overload has a hidden cost. It deepens inequality. In their book *Scarcity: Why Having Too Little Means So Much*, Shafir and Mullainathan explain how scarcity – whether of time, money or mental bandwidth – overwhelms people and impairs their ability to process information effectively (Shafir and Mullainathan 2013).

They explain that those who are financially stressed have less mental bandwidth to process the overwhelming amount of information bombarding them daily. The wealthy, on the other hand, have more resources and time to filter through data, make informed decisions and utilise tools – like sophisticated data visualisations – that help them navigate complexity.

This disparity means that information overload disproportionately impacts those with fewer resources, exacerbating existing inequalities. The rich can afford to invest in technologies and services that sift through the noise and show them what's important and what to do. Meanwhile, the poor are left grappling with an unfiltered deluge of data that makes it harder for them to make decisions that could improve their circumstances.

Information Overload and Social Inequality

Data visualisation can help solve this problem. By turning complex information into an easy-to-understand visual format, everyone can make sense of important information, no matter how rich or poor they are. This way, more people can use data to make better choices in their lives. Good data visualisation cuts through the clutter, highlighting what truly matters and enables good decision-making across all levels of society.

Another particularly alarming consequence of data pollution is ideological misinformation. After a knife attack at a children's summer dance class in Southport in 2024, far-right groups quickly circulated false claims online, identifying the perpetrator as a Muslim asylum seeker who had arrived illegally by boat.

These claims were entirely fabricated – the attacker, Axel Rudakubana, was a British citizen born in Cardiff to Rwandan parents, with no connection to immigration, yet the story was bought by many at face value. The false information ignited riots across the country, leading to further violence and deepening societal divides.

Initially, platforms such as X (formerly Twitter) attempted to combat misinformation by tagging posts. However, since Elon Musk's acquisition, the platform's approach to moderation has shifted. Misinformation is often left unchecked and the spread of false claims can contribute to violent unrest, as seen in Southport. The shift in moderation strategy has sparked debate over whether platforms are doing enough to prevent harmful disinformation.

At the heart of this issue lies trust. The overwhelming influx of data, coupled with the proliferation of misinformation, has led to widespread scepticism – not just towards social media but also mainstream media outlets. Accusations of bias and selective reporting erode public confidence.

In the fight against this erosion of trust, data visualisation has emerged as a powerful ally. For example, the *Financial Times* utilised interactive maps and charts to explain the humanitarian crisis in Gaza in 2023–2024, clearly displaying casualty figures and the scale of destruction over time. This helped readers grasp the complexity of the conflict at a glance, cutting through conflicting narratives spread online and by governments (Financial Times n.d.).

Similarly, *BBC Verify* used data visualisation to track the spread of misinformation during global crises, such as the coronavirus disease 2019 (COVID-19) pandemic and the 2024 UK riots. In one case, it mapped the flow of false claims on social media, showing how misinformation moved through networks and how it led to real-world consequences like protests. These data visualisations made it easier for audiences to understand the impact of misinformation on public perception (Leimdorfer n.d.).

Clear, data-driven visualisations like these empower people to engage with accurate information, which is critical for rebuilding trust in the digital age. This is where data visualisation emerges as a critical tool. By presenting accurate, unbiased information in clear and engaging ways, data visualisation can cut through the noise of data pollution. They can be used to help the public understand complex issues – such as economic policies, health statistics or environmental data – without overwhelming them. Effective data visualisations can debunk misleading information by making the truth more accessible and understandable than false narratives.

Cass Sunstein's book *#Republic* (2017) is particularly relevant here (Sunstein 2017). In his book, he explores how social media and online platforms create echo chambers, where users are only exposed to information that aligns with their views, reinforcing biases and increasing societal polarisation.

Data visualisation, like those used by the *Financial Times* and *BBC Verify*, can act as a countermeasure. By presenting transparent, unbiased information visually, data visualisation cuts through the noise and echo chambers, helping individuals engage with factual content that promotes a more balanced and informed view.

In our digital age, where the sheer volume of information can lead to disconnection from reality, data visualisation provides a beacon of clarity. Our perspectives are undoubtedly influenced by our cultural backgrounds and personal experiences, but well-crafted data visualisations can offer common ground, allowing us to see beyond our individual biases.

If you haven't realised this already, data visualisation is one of the most powerful communication tools we have in the twenty-first century. It empowers us to interpret and understand the world in ways that raw data alone cannot achieve. While we might not be facing an immediate mass extinction event yet, the risk of misinterpreting the complex world around us is real and potentially dangerous. If there's one thing data visualisation can do, it is to bring us together and unite us. Surely that's worth fighting for?

But how can we truly harness this potential? To understand this, we must reflect on those who have pioneered the craft of data visualisation, showing how to transform data into a universal language of comprehension, empathy and progress. One such figure was the late Hans Rosling, a Swedish physician, academic and public speaker who dedicated his life to clarifying the world through data.

Rosling became known globally for his captivating presentations that combined statistics with innovative data visualisations. He demonstrated how life expectancy and wealth changed over time, showing that much of the world had become healthier and more prosperous. Rather than burying audiences under spreadsheets of numbers, he used animated bubble charts that allowed people to witness historical progress at a glance. With these simple yet dynamic tools, Rosling helped viewers understand that the world, despite its problems, had improved in many ways they never realised.

One of Rosling's most famous tools was his bubble chart, featured in his book *Factfulness* (Rosling et al. 2018) and in his TED Talks. Each bubble represented a country, with its size, position and movement over time depicting population, income and health metrics. By animating these bubbles across decades, Rosling brought clarity and optimism to a data-rich narrative that was often misunderstood. People could see how formerly poor nations steadily improved infant mortality rates, grew their economies and expanded access to education. Instead of conjuring vague, fearful impressions of a troubled world, the Factfulness Bubble Chart gave a balanced perspective rooted in real data.

The key to Rosling's philosophy was that understanding the facts is the first step towards constructive action. By seeing which countries were lagging behind, policymakers, activists and citizens could focus their efforts more effectively. This is the true power of data visualisation when applied with integrity. It encourages engagement, problem-solving and collaboration.

In a world afflicted by data pollution, Rosling directly tackled the misconception and false impression people had about the world we live in. He challenged how we see the world by confronting our biases with data by using data visualisations. His mission was simple but powerful: replace fear and stereotypes with facts, showing how countries across Asia, Africa and Latin America have made dramatic gains in health, education and quality of life. Although he sadly passed away in 2016 from pancreatic cancer, the work he did had a profound impact on the world.

For instance, consider the data visualisations created during the COVID-19 pandemic by organisations like the Johns Hopkins Coronavirus Resource Center. Their dashboards presented key metrics – infection rates, death counts, testing data, and vaccination progress – in clear, easy-to-understand formats. This accessibility allowed millions of people worldwide to comprehend the gravity of the situation, enabling governments to allocate resources more effectively. These data visualisations helped strike a balance between being clear and providing detailed information that help guide government policies, influence individual choices and support international aid efforts, helping save lives.

The Moral Responsibility of Data Visualisation

The threat data pollution poses to humanity is immense. It can create an environment where trust erodes, governance can be undermined, while social unrest and inequality can worsen due to the actions of bad actors who seek to exploit the confusion created. This can obscure the urgent truths we need to confront, such as climate change, biodiversity loss and the fragility of global health systems. Yet the remedy is in our hands. We can equip ourselves with tools to navigate this increasingly complex data-rich world by improving our data literacy and improving how we communicate with data by visualising it in a way that offers great clarity on these urgent issues. We can use data visualisation to discern truth from falsehood, grasp the significance of intricate trends and help us emphatically connect with experiences that might be far removed from our own.

Ultimately, data visualisation is a form of storytelling that can bring us together on complex issues that we might otherwise struggle to comprehend. When done right, it crosses linguistic and cultural barriers, enabling all of us to share a common understanding of the world's challenges. They often say mathematics is a universal language that is unbounded by time, culture and linguistics. Data shares that same characteristic when we visualise it in a way that unites us in a common understanding or what is truth and misinformation.

That is how data visualisation can save humanity – by helping us see what truly matters and by uniting us in our pursuit of a better world.

KEY TAKEAWAYS

- Excessive data, or data pollution, overwhelms people and makes it difficult to prioritise important information, leading to confusion.
- This overload of data encourages the spread of conspiracy theories, misinformation and disinformation, as simplistic narratives appear more accessible and comforting than complex truths.
- Historical examples, such as the Salem Witch Trials and the anti-vaccine movement, show how misinformation thrives when people struggle to process complexity, resulting in scapegoating and societal harm.
- Data pollution leads to the misuse of data visualisation, either unintentionally or deliberately, by presenting information without proper context or clarity, and this can profoundly mislead audiences.

- Cognitive biases, such as confirmation bias and the tendency to become desensitised to large numbers, compound the dangers of data pollution, making it even harder to discern facts from distortions.
- Trust erodes as misinformation spreads unchecked across digital platforms, often exacerbating social unrest and undermining public confidence in reputable media and institutions.
- Data visualisation, when done ethically and with care, can counteract data pollution by providing clarity and context. It can help people understand complex issues and guide better decision-making, bridging cultural and ideological divides.

Chapter 4

AI and Data Visualisation Become Allies

I woke up at 4 a.m. Travelling from Europe to North America always messes up my sleep, leaving me wide awake at odd hours. A few hours later, I found myself walking through Boston on a bitterly cold winter's day, making my way to the conference. Little did I know that within an hour I would learn about something that would change my life and the world as I knew it forever.

It was Thursday, 15 December 2022, and I was on my way to the MIT AI and Quant Conference. When I arrived at the registration desk, I found the whole place had been plastered with laminated letter-sized paper, each bearing an oversized QR code. They were everywhere. There must have been about a thousand of them, just in case you didn't know where to aim your iPhone. Someone's enthusiasm had evidently gotten the better of them.

'Scan the QR code for the conference agenda', the registration lady told me flatly. It was obviously too early in the morning for her.

I helped myself to a lovely big mug of hot black filtered coffee, which is somewhat of a luxury for me. It's actually incredibly difficult to find a place in Zürich that serves plain filter coffee.

A young chap rocked up, evidently high on caffeine and suffering from jet lag just like me. He looked at the printed QR codes splattered across the room and said half-jokingly, 'You have to love MIT's attempt at going digital.'

I laughed. It was actually quite funny. They had probably used about half a tree and a tonne of plastic to do this.

He introduced himself as a statistical arbitrage hedge fund manager from San Diego who had flown in on the red eye that morning.

'So, what do you think of that new thing from OpenAI?' he asked. 'It's pretty incredible, isn't it?'

I didn't have a clue what he was talking about. 'What thing?' I replied.

He stared, his eyes widened in disbelief, as if I had just stepped off a spaceship from another galaxy. What he then told me blew me away. I felt like Ethan the caveman.

We didn't need to scan those QR codes. The agenda had already been set. Every speech, panel discussion and fireside chat focused on a single, inescapable topic that day – ChatGPT.

A New Technology Gold Rush

The transformation of our world since then has been nothing short of astounding. Generative artificial intelligence (AI) has disrupted our entire global economy on a monumental scale. We are merely a few years into this brave new world, yet the fervour it has ignited within the investment community echoes the excitement of the late 1990s dot-com bubble.

Generative AI can crunch through mountains of data in seconds, spotting trends and oddities in data that a human might miss even

AI and Data Visualisation Become Allies

after weeks of research. For example, it's already being used by the retail industry to quickly identify a subtle shift in customer buying habits or flag an unusual pattern in manufacturing defects on the factory floor (Spencer 2024; Davis 2023).

This raw computing power, however, raises a question: Do we still need charts, graphs and dashboards when AI can spit out answers in seconds?

This is where my fear kicks in because people like me might become redundant and obsolete. This was not the way I imagined my career ahead to be. I make my living creating data visualisations that are supposed to bring clarity into this world. But what's the point of having me if a robot can do that instead?

As fantasy and sci-fi author Joanna Maciejewska lamented in a now famous post on X: 'I want AI to do my laundry and dishes so that I can do art and writing, not for AI to do my art and writing so that I can do my laundry and dishes.'

The good news is that, for now, AI still needs to listen to us. It's meant to help us, not replace us. And, with any luck, there will be a healthy dose of government regulation to protect our jobs from AI, at least to some extent. Besides, as a species, we still have an immense amount to offer the world. Well, I would say that, wouldn't I? I'm human.

But in all seriousness, the greater risk isn't robots destroying us – it's us destroying Earth first. This could stem from a more immediate and perhaps subtler threat posed by AI rather than the apocalyptic scenarios imagined by science fiction films like *The Terminator*.

The innovation behind ChatGPT is incredible. It was built on something called Transformer architecture – something I knew nothing about at that Boston conference. It's difficult to explain how it works, but I will give it a go.

Imagine a team of experts, each with their own speciality, analysing the same passage of text. Even though they're all looking at the same words, each expert notices different clues, patterns or relationships. They share what they find with each other, and by combining their unique insights, they arrive at a coherent interpretation that seems surprisingly intelligent.

This is, in simple terms, how ChatGPT's 'attention' mechanism works. In a Transformer model (the architecture behind ChatGPT), there are multiple 'attention heads'. Think of each attention head as one of those experts, zeroing in on specific connections between words or phrases.

For example, in the sentence 'the cat sat on the mat', your attention head might focus on how 'cat' relates to 'sat', while another might connect 'cat' to 'mat'. By pooling these different perspectives, the model gains a broad understanding of the entire sentence and does so far more efficiently than if it treated each word in isolation.

There are risks, however. For instance, Nick Bostrom gave an example in his book *Superintelligence*, where an AI system whose only goal is to make 'as many paperclips as possible' accidently turned the entire world, including people, buildings and all of the Earth's resources, into paperclips (Bostrom 2014).

The solution here is to either put some guardrails on AI to prevent these issues or feed the model with even more information so it is less likely to make these mistakes. The real risk is not AI taking over the world, but rather us becoming overreliant on AI. That is what makes us vulnerable.

The Cognitive Cost of Technological Reliance

As already discussed, it is our increasing reliance on technology and complex systems that our economies rely on makes us fragile. Take these away from us and we would struggle to survive in the way our ancestors did.

Similarly, AI might free us from routine and onerous tasks, but it can also deskill us and make us more vulnerable.

AI can already write code snippets, draft essays, summarise research papers and generally remove the need for much active thought. This might not only free us to engage in higher-level thinking, but it could also mean we practise less of the intellectual effort required for logical reasoning, linguistic precision, critical reading and structuring our knowledge. The danger is that we become intellectually dependent on AI.

Generative AI worsens this issue by presenting its output as authoritative, often without a transparent methodology. The chain of custody for knowledge breaks down because nothing is verified, interpreted and critically evaluated by us anymore – we outsourced it to AI.

This means we are at risk of becoming dependent on a black box. The problem is not just forgetting how to do long division by hand – it is also about losing a deeper understanding of why mathematical principles, scientific methods and engineering designs function as they do.

We were already heading in this direction long before generative AI appeared. Modern society is defined by its highly specialised roles: a cardiologist understands the intricacies of the human heart, an electrical engineer ensures grid maintenance and an options trader navigates the complexities of financial markets.

The average person now grasps only a tiny fraction of the knowledge required to sustain humanity in this highly specialised society. If we outsource this specialist knowledge to AI, then perhaps there really is no point in education at all.

I must be honest: data visualisation will not magically solve the challenges posed by our overreliance on AI. However, it can help make information more accessible and easier for us comprehend, which could weaken this reliance.

Data visualisation could encourage active learning, foster better communication across academic disciplines and provide a clearer understanding of economic systems we might otherwise take for granted. In doing so, it could help us maintain and even strengthen our critical thinking skills, reducing the risk of us becoming passive participants in a world governed by technology and AI that we no longer fully understand.

We are visual creatures, often grasping ideas more quickly through images than by reading a wall of text or data. Consider how easily we can spot a sales spike on a line graph or how a heat map of website clicks instantly reveals where users are focusing. This is why data visualisation is so important, especially now, with the arrival of AI.

It is not just our ability to spot and interpret stories within data visualisations that makes them valuable, but it is also the emotional connection we form when we uncover those stories through our visual comprehension. This human element – our capacity to feel and intuit – could actually be a powerful complement to AI's analytical capabilities.

We could even use AI to create data visualisations that improve our understanding of the world. Instead of just processing data, AI can help us see the world with data visualisation by enhancing how we interact and interpret data.

Fighting Misinformation with AI

We could even use AI to challenge and expose those who spread misinformation. Existential risks like global warming would be made undeniably clear through compelling data visualisations produced by AI that cut through the noise and enabling anyone to grasp the severity of the situation. AI could foster unprecedented transparency, making it impossible for governments, media outlets or social platforms to manipulate the narrative.

In a business setting, AI could revolutionise how organisations understand and act on their data. Imagine a dynamic, interactive dashboard that updates in real time, showing seasonal trends with line charts, comparing regional performance through geographic heat maps and forecasting future sales with clear graphs. By transforming vast datasets into intuitive data visualisations, AI could help a CEO and their management team identify inefficiencies, streamline operations and make more informed decisions.

AI could also be applied in government settings to reduce inefficiencies and cut costs, ultimately saving taxpayers' money. For instance, AI could help identify inefficiencies in healthcare or defence, optimise procurement and streamline research and development. By speeding up processes and improving the management of large projects, data-driven AI would make better use of public funds while maintaining a high standard of service and communicating these issues using data visualisation.

In this sense, AI could become data visualisation's greatest ally. Its potential even extends to other important areas, such as combating misinformation and conspiracy theories. It could use a combination of knowledge, logic and data visualisation to present evidence that helps people grasp complex truths and challenges preconceived beliefs.

In fact, there was recent study by MIT and Cornell University that actually explored how conversational AI could engage conspiracy theorists in a dialogue to address and refute these beliefs (Costello et al. 2024).

In the study, 2190 self-declared conspiracy theorists in the United States were engaged in personalised written conversations with GPT-4 Turbo.[1] Participants described their favoured conspiracy theories and GPT-4 Turbo generated dialogues to challenge and debunk these beliefs. The study had two groups: a treatment group that used AI and a control group that discussed neutral topics. In the chart shown in Figure 4.1, black dots represent the treatment group, while white dots represent the control group.

---

[1] GPT-4 Turbo is an advanced version of OpenAI's GPT-4 model. It's designed to be faster and more cost-efficient while maintaining high performance in natural language understanding and generation tasks.

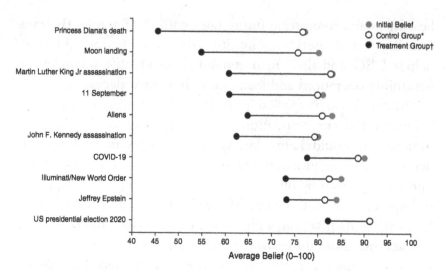

Figure 4.1 Average belief in selected conspiracy theories; 100 = definitely true. United States, 2024. *Conversation with the AI about a neutral topic. †Conversation about their favoured conspiracy theory

Source: Adapted from Costello et al. (2024).

The treatment group showed, on average, a 20% decrease in their belief in conspiracy theories. Meanwhile, approximately 25% of participants changed from strongly believing their favourite conspiracy theories to feeling uncertain about them.

Overall, using AI to debunk conspiracy theories had a huge impact on the participants' belief systems, causing them to reevaluate their convictions. The effectiveness of this approach stems from the ability of AI to personalise counterarguments and provide evidence tailored to each conversation – a feat that has been difficult to achieve at scale until now.

Imagine deploying such a tool on social media platforms to counter falsehoods in real time. It could have prevented, for instance, the circulation of false claims about the knife attack incident at the children's summer dance class in Southport in 2024, which we covered in Chapter 3.

Posts could have been fact-checked instantly, false information corrected with counter posts and overtly harmful content immediately removed before it had a chance to spread. Moreover, this could have been done on a large scale, very quickly and effectively.

Defending Against Extremism and Manipulated Visualisations

Misinformation is often used by extremist groups to manipulate and recruit followers, amplifying hate speech and fostering division.

AI could address extremism at its roots. Just as it can debunk conspiracy theories through personalised counterarguments, AI could directly tailor responses to address the motivations and misconceptions that drive extremist thinking. By intervening early, AI could play a critical role in preventing radicalisation before it takes hold, potentially preventing future terrorist attacks.

AI could also guard against the misuse of data visualisations, a tactic often employed by extremist and fringe groups to support their agendas. When data is manipulated or poorly presented, data visualisations can mislead the public and lend credibility to false information.

AI can help prevent this by critiquing and challenging such misuse. It can analyse datasets to identify misleading or false data visualisations and flag issues such as poorly labelled axes, missing sources or inappropriate chart types that distort the message.

It could also be used to enhance and improve data visualisation. Imagine if you could train an AI model to be the ultimate data science professor.

Let's revisit Edward Tufte's book *The Visual Display of Quantitative Information* once more, the book that we mentioned in Chapter 3, and also the introduction of this book. Alongside his critiques and examples of poor data visualisations, Tufte also provided a framework for best practices in data visualisation, which is still followed and widely respected by the data science community today. If you could train an AI model on Tufte's best practices, it could be used to apply these principles automatically as you build and create your data visualisation.

Let's take one of Tufte's key concepts that he introduces in his books – the *data-ink ratio*. He argued that every mark on a chart should serve a meaningful purpose directly tied to data rather than being mere decoration. By removing unnecessary elements – such as redundant gridlines or excessive labels – data visualisations become clearer, more accurate and easier to interpret. The goal, therefore, is to maximise this ratio to maximise the amount of ink used to present data and minimise the amount used for what he called *chartjunk*.

Chartjunk includes unnecessary embellishments such as 3D effects, distracting images or overly decorative elements. His aim was to prioritise clarity over decoration, thereby enhancing the communicative power of data visualisation by making it more efficient.

To illustrate this, let's consider an example from his book. Figure 4.2 shows a data visualisation originally published by *The New York Times*. *The New York Times* back in the late 1970s did not adhere to the same rigorous standards for data visualisation that it follows today.

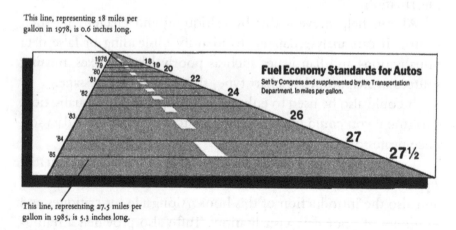

Figure 4.2 A distorted chart with chart junk

Source: Reproduced from Edward R. Tufte, 2000/Graphics Press Inc.

AI and Data Visualisation Become Allies

This data visualisation breaks Tufte's principles quite badly. You can see quite clear that both the data-ink ratio and chartjunk are clearly an issue. But the biggest problem here is graphical distortion.

Even I have been guilty of graphical distortion, which is quite easy to do without realising. Data visualisation is a process of continuous learning and you often only note your mistakes after you publish your work. My advice is to never be too harsh on yourself or others when mistakes are made. Just try to learn from them and don't be afraid to republish. But what if I could have run this past an AI model, specifically trained on data visualisation? I would probably have learnt this lesson a lot quicker and avoided this mistake.

Let's take another example. In Figure 4.3, Tufte also brings in this concept called the *Lie Factor*.

$$Lie\ factor = \frac{\text{Size effect shown in the graphic}}{\text{Size of effect in data}}$$

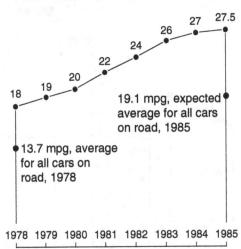

Figure 4.3 Revised version of the same chart that is shown in Figure 4.2

Source: Reproduced with permission from *The Visual Display of Quantitative Information* by Edward R. Tufte/National Association for Healthcare Quality.

This shows the distortion in scaling, which is actually the main issue with this data visualisation, other than the chart junk. If there is no distortion, then the *Lie Factor* would give a value of 1, which is a perfect score. As Tufte explains in his book, any *Lie Factor* that rests above 1.05 or below 0.95 should be cause for concern.

In this example, he actually measured a Lie Factor of 14.8, which demonstrates an enormous amount of distortion. He goes on to provide a solution that can incorporate some graphical design but removes the distortion. Take a look below and note the huge difference in quality.

Here is another example that Tufte uses in his book, which again he has taken from *The New York Times* (Figure 4.4). What you have here is an example of design variation that ends up distorting data, making it difficult to interpret.

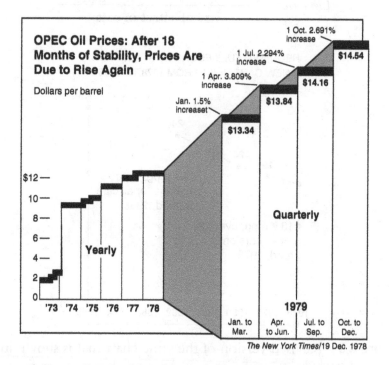

Figure 4.4 A distorted bar chart with a 3D effect

Source: Reproduced with permission from *The Visual Display of Quantitative Information* by Edward R. Tufte./National Association for Healthcare Quality.

This is how he explains the problem:

> The confounding of design variation with data variation over the surface of a graphic leads to ambiguity and deception, for the eye may mix up changes in the design with changes in the data. A steady canvas makes for a clearer picture. The principle is then: Show data variation, not design variation.

AI as a Sparring Partner and Impartial Critic

Now just imagine if you could train AI on this text from Edward Tufte. In fact, imagine you could train it on Tufte's entire works and the works of other great data scientists. You could use AI as an intelligent 'data visualisation consultant', offering critiques, layout suggestions and subtle improvements in line with what is considered data visualisation best practice.

By systematically using its feedback, it could reduce clutter, boosting clarity, emphasising comparisons and integrating textual explanations. You could consistently produce high-quality data visualisations that respect both the aesthetics and the ethical standards championed by data scientists. The key is an iterative, human-in-the-loop approach: use AI as an advisor and cross-check its proposals against your domain knowledge.

AI could, therefore, make an enormous contribution to improving the quality of data visualisation. Unlike humans, AI doesn't usually trigger defensiveness or emotional responses when it provides feedback. It simply identifies weaknesses, allowing you to refine your work without the discomfort of personal criticism. I already use AI for this purpose and it has proven invaluable for me.

Beyond critiquing data visualisations, AI can also act as a powerful collaborator. It can analyse datasets, flag inconsistencies and suggest ways to clean and refine data. AI can even help create more accurate and unbiased data visualisations by tailoring design elements to the data and the audience's needs automatically at the beginning of the creation process. By acting as a sparring partner,

AI can push us to create better, more effective data visualisations while reducing the emotional strain often associated with human feedback.

Liberating and Democratising Data

In recent years, I've explored how AI tools can enhance my own workflow. While the technology is still evolving, tools such as ChatGPT and Claude have already proven useful for analysing and refining datasets. I've even used it to write snippets or code or identify problems with my own code.

Previously, I relied on Python – a coding language – to clean and process data, which could take hours to write and debug. Now, AI not only generates Python code automatically, but also uses advanced algorithms to complete these tasks extremely quickly, saving time and improving the quality of the final output.

There is another powerful use for AI, which I haven't mentioned yet. It's something that I am doing more frequently these days. With the right AI tools, you can extract data points from nearly anything. You can even extract data from pixelated charts that appear to have no available underlying dataset.

Advanced algorithms can analyse a chart's structure, interpret its axes and narrative and use mathematical calculations to reconstruct a spreadsheet from the drawn lines or bar heights of a chart. This technology has become so sophisticated that it can replicate almost any dataset. If there's a pixel on the screen, it can be analysed and converted into usable data.

I've been doing this myself for years using Python, but AI now achieves these tasks at a speed my code can't match. It is not only faster, but I must admit that it's likely more accurate as well, producing results with a level of precision that surpasses my own efforts.

This has profound implications for the data industry. If AI can accurately extract data from any chart – even without access to the

AI and Data Visualisation Become Allies

underlying dataset – it challenges the concept of proprietary data. Some financial data vendors, for instance, have strict licensing agreements and closely monitor how their data is used, raising concerns about misuse or breaches of fair use policies. However, with AI's ability to reconstruct datasets directly from charts, enforcing these claims becomes increasingly difficult.

The consequences of this shift are significant. It's now easier than ever for anyone to analyse and replicate data from a data visualisation, even if it is animated. While I believe this is acceptable as long as proper credit is given to the original creator – it's simply good manners – the reality is that the concept of proprietary data is rapidly becoming obsolete. As this transformation unfolds, the data industry will need to adapt to a world where raw data can no longer be easily hidden or controlled.

As AI technology continues to advance, it has the potential to liberate and democratise data in ways we cannot yet fully imagine. This democratisation process could have far-reaching effects on industries and fundamentally change how we interact with information. While this new world presents challenges, it also offers unprecedented opportunities for transparency, innovation and collective knowledge-building.

AI is a liberator of data. However, as we embrace this new era of accessibility and replication, establishing ethical guidelines and best practices will also be very important. Issues such as privacy, intellectual property and the nature of information ownership in the digital age will have to be taken very seriously.

Mosaic Theory and the Risks of Weaponising Data

Beyond privacy and intellectual property concerns, there are also significant national security implications. AI's ability to process datasets at previously unimaginable speeds presents not only opportunities but also serious threats. In this new digital era, data could increasingly be weaponised.

A concept I encountered during my career in asset management was mosaic theory. It involves piecing together information from multiple sources to form a more complete understanding on a topic that wasn't available from any single source. The key here is the process of joining the dots – connecting disparate pieces of information to arrive at novel conclusions. AI, as a sparring partner, has the potential to assist in this process. It can provide vast amounts of information at incredible speed, challenging us to think critically and come up with ideas that we might not have managed to do before.

However, there is a dark side to this. Search queries, website visits, location history and app usage can be used to piece together a remarkably detailed picture of an individual's interests, habits and intentions. This information could then be exploited in ways that we might be uncomfortable with.

Data visualisation plays a role here because it makes it easier to 'connect the dots'. Although this can be incredibly powerful for legitimate uses – helping, for instance, a financial analyst quickly spot trends or anomalies – it can also be abused. An organisation or government with less ethical intentions could use data visualisation to identify and exploit individual vulnerabilities using mosaic theory.

There is another problem with data visualisation and this involves deepfakes. Deepfakes are highly realistic, AI-generated videos or images that manipulate a person's likeness. These technologies have already been used to spread misinformation, defame individuals and manipulate public opinion, demonstrating the potential for AI to be weaponised in ways we are only beginning to understand.

For example, deepfake technology can place a celebrity's face on someone else's body or create fabricated messages to spread false information. One of the most well-known demonstrations involved actor and comedian Jordan Peele in 2018. Using advanced deep learning and facial mapping, Peele created a convincing digital replica of Barack Obama. This virtual Obama, powered by Peele's voice mimicry, appeared to speak words the former president never said. The experiment highlighted the alarming potential of AI to manipulate public perception by co-opting a public figure's image and voice.

Deepfake technology typically relies on generative AI models like Generative Adversarial Networks, which simulate lifelike representations by training on vast datasets of video and image inputs. This technology predates tools like ChatGPT, but as generative AI continues to advance, it could further accelerate the creation of deepfake videos, making them even more realistic and harder to detect.

This technology also introduces the possibility of *deepfaking* data visualisations. Just as AI can generate highly convincing deepfake videos, it could be used to manipulate data or imagery to present a narrative that is difficult to verify or disprove. By altering datasets or fabricating charts, malicious actors could weaponise data visualisation to mislead audiences.

The reality is that when we look at a chart, we might glance at the source but rarely take the time to verify it. There's often an assumption that whoever created that chart has accurately sourced and presented the information. While it's true that digging deeper can expose fraudulent data – and even AI can be used to uncover such inconsistencies – the damage is often done before it is investigated.

This makes it all the more essential to ensure transparency and accountability in how data visualisations are created and shared. The potential of AI to revolutionise data visualisation is immense, but without safeguards, it could also amplify the spread of false information, blurring the line between truth and deception in the digital age.

Privacy, Intellectual Property and Open Data

As more data flows freely, there's a heightened risk of misuse ranging from privacy violations to more complex security threats.

Striking the right balance between data availability and safeguarding personal or sensitive information will be one of the key challenges for both governments and corporations in the coming years.

This is already happening, especially with social media companies. Meta (formerly Facebook) paid a record-breaking $5 billion fine in 2019 as part of an Federal Trade Commission settlement for violating privacy rules and misleading users about data handling. Similarly, Twitter (now X) faced penalties for its own data handling issues. In 2022, Twitter agreed to pay $150 million to settle claims that it deceptively used phone numbers and email addresses for advertising purposes after telling users it was for security reasons.

In China, Didi Global was fined $1.2 billion in 2022 over breaches of data security laws, marking one of the largest penalties in the world. TikTok faced a €345 million fine in 2024 for failing to protect children's privacy in the European Union, and Instagram was fined €405 million for similar violations.

Ultimately, the democratisation of data could spark a new wave of innovation, but it will need to be well regulated to prevent abuse and exploitation. A balance must be struck where regulation does not stifle research or hinder entrepreneurs from driving progress in areas such as artificial intelligence, climate science and even space exploration.

The ability to share and build on existing knowledge is one of the great promises of this data-driven era, but it must be matched by responsible data governance to prevent the erosion of trust in this new landscape.

Yet despite these challenges, the democratisation of data, paired with AI's transformative potential, holds immense promise. AI doesn't just make data more accessible, but it also has the power to elevate data visualisation, enhancing its role in how we understand and interact with information. Far from eroding its value, AI can assist us in generating new data visualisations, critiquing their accuracy and refining how they are presented. As our data-saturated world grows ever more complex, the partnership between human

AI and Data Visualisation Become Allies

interpretation and machine intelligence can cut through the noise, highlighting what truly matters.

Enhanced by AI, data visualisation can clarify socio-economic trends, expose truths hidden beneath propaganda and guide critical decision-making. It can allow us to grasp once-incomprehensible global phenomena and inspire collective action. Rather than narrowing our vision, AI-driven data visualisations can broaden it, giving us the tools to think more critically about the data we consume and create. Instead of reducing us to passive onlookers in a world of inscrutable algorithms, they invite us to become informed, discerning participants in shaping our future.

By embracing this new era responsibly, we reaffirm the enduring relevance of human creativity, expertise and ethical judgement. The partnership between AI and data visualisation offers a powerful counterbalance to the intellectual passivity that unchecked technology might otherwise engender.

It reminds us that while AI excels at handling complexity at staggering speed, it is human interpretation that ensures this complexity remains grounded in values and wisdom. In this way, data visualisation doesn't become a relic of the past but a guiding light for the future, with AI as its most powerful ally in navigating a rapidly changing world.

AI can actually ensure the survival of the human species rather than its demise if used properly. It can also use data visualisation as a powerful communication tool to ensure we humans make the right decisions in this complex data-saturated world.

KEY TAKEAWAYS

- Despite AI's ability to process vast amounts of data quickly, data visualisations remain essential as they provide visual clarity and create emotional connections that help humans understand complex information.

- AI can enhance data visualisations by tailoring them to individual needs, improving data quality and suggesting better ways to display information.
- AI can also protect against misleading data visualisations by identifying manipulation techniques and applying best practices from experts like Edward Tufte, who emphasises minimising 'chartjunk' and maximising the data-ink ratio.
- Modern AI can extract data from any chart or visualisation, challenging the concept of proprietary data and democratising access to information that was once controlled by large corporations.
- While this democratisation creates opportunities for transparency and innovation, it also raises concerns about privacy, intellectual property and data security that will require balanced regulation.
- At its best, the partnership between human creativity and AI's analytical capabilities can empower citizens, expose hidden truths and enhance our ability to make informed decisions in an increasingly complex world, and data visualisation is part of that story.

Chapter 5

Data Is Inherently Bias

It was a relatively mild 40° that day – in the shade, of course. Opening the door onto my hotel room balcony, the intense Kuwaiti heat struck me full force, instantly fogging my glasses.

So much for getting some fresh air. With everything happening at home, I couldn't focus even though I was half a world away.

My phone buzzed. Khaled was calling. He wanted to cook me this fish called zubaidi – one of my favourite fish actually, known as pomfret in English. My mother is originally from Goa, a former Portuguese colony in India, where this fish is very popular.

The Kuwaiti zubaidi are particularly special, caught in the Shatt al-Arab waterway, and they are huge. The Iraqis cook it really well, although I wouldn't mention this to Khaled. They grill it over charcoal and serve it with saffron and raisin rice, washed down with black tea infused with cardamom that they also do on the charcoal to circulate the tea leaves. It's amazing. One of my favourite meals.

Before I could respond though, Fadi called. He seemed unimpressed by Khaled's dinner plans. I'm not sure he is the fish type.

'Ya'ni, we'll go to this hotel after work,' he said, 'see this, shisma... Kuwaiti exhibition where there is harakat, then we smoke shisha and drink tea. Ya'ni Khaled's fish can wait.'

Truth be told, I was having trouble focusing on either invitation. News had just broken that HSBC was cutting 10% of staff from their $280 billion asset management division – a proper Roman-style decimation. Back in Britain, my own position felt precarious. The thought of returning home to unemployment loomed large.

I ended up driving to this hotel with Fadi and Khaled, with music blaring out the window. He pulled up to the front of the hotel and an angry little Indian man came up to us and said, 'Sir, you can't park here!'

Fadi looked surprised and replied: 'Lech? habibi, shoof! Fi makaan...ya'ni... there is space for sure.'

We didn't stay for long. The exhibition was last month. Fadi misread the leaflet. We smoked shisha instead and I explained to them what was happening. What I told them was better than Arab politics and fish.

The Great Financial Crisis

All this happened back in September 2008. The world was witnessing one of the most catastrophic financial meltdowns in history – the Global Financial Crisis. Lehman Brothers had just collapsed and financial markets were in turmoil. Suddenly, we in the asset management industry didn't look so smart anymore. In fact, many of us didn't really understand what was going on. Events were moving too fast.

Our banking industry had made flawed and overly confident interpretations of data that had misled the public, investors and even entire governments. Nothing worked. Bond markets were frozen, equity markets crashed and we even saw high street-style bank runs in the United Kingdom, reminiscent of the Great Depression.

Money was literally flowing out the door. Investors were redeeming. HSBC Global Asset Management literally saw 80 billion dollars of its assets under management disappear within weeks. But that was nothing compared to what the banks were experiencing. Without central bank intervention, we were looking at the potential collapse of the entire financial system.

There were banks literally on the brink of collapse. Then suddenly bailouts happened overnight. They included Citigroup, Bank of America, JPMorgan Chase, Wells Fargo, Morgan Stanley, AIG, Bear Stearns and Washington Mutual. In the United Kingdom, the Royal Bank of Scotland and Lloyds Banking Group were also rescued.

It was brutal and the economic impact was devastating. The crisis had a profound impact on my life. At the time, I was working for the Sovereigns and Supranationals team. Our team was responsible for roughly $120 billion in assets under management for central banks, ministries of finance and sovereign wealth funds. Most of them were located in Asia and the oil-rich Gulf states, including Kuwait.

Subprime Mortgages: A Lesson in Hubris

In the years leading up to the crisis, house prices in the United States had skyrocketed. Fuelled by easy access to credit, Americans were buying up as much real estate as they could. Banks were cashing in and began offering mortgages to people with increasingly risky profiles, creating what became known as the subprime mortgage industry.

Now this isn't meant to be a history lesson – there are far better books that explain in detail why this crisis erupted. However, it's an incredible point in history that I lived through during the early part of my career. It is also a great case study on why data and the way we visualise it is always going to be inherently biased. I know that you are probably thinking I'm shooting myself in the foot with this statement. After all, this book is supposed to argue the case that we need data visualisation. But stick with me. You will understand why this is important if you read on.

The Global Financial Crisis had a profound impact on my life and how I view data, which eventually would lead me on a mission that I could never have imagined taking. Filled with evangelical zeal I had to pursue this career path because I truly believe that the fate of humanity hangs in the balance if we cannot conquer data that we have created in this complex world. Data is so open to abuse and if not handled properly it can be potentially devastating.

When Data Visualisation Fails Humanity

The amount of pain and suffering the Global Financial Crisis wrought is unforgivable. We in the banks were meant to be the fiduciary custodians of wealth and health for the nations that we served, not bonus-hungry jackrabbits. Ordinary people lost their homes. Marriages ended. People who were so heavily in debt that they saw no end in sight, committed suicide. As I said, this was unforgivable.

It was a humbling experience for me. In short, what started this crisis was our typical human ability to overestimate our intelligence, which wasn't helped by our overpriced suits and fancy watches. It was a classic case of poor financial engineering that few people really understood, which we all assumed was rock solid.

Banks like Lehman Brothers and Bear Stearns saw an opportunity to sell more mortgages to a higher-risk group of home buyers to plump up their revenues. They didn't even pause to think about the risks, and lots of money was made and huge bonuses handed out (see Figure 5.1).

The risks were there all along, staring us in the face, laid bare by decades of accumulated data. This wasn't an unforeseen

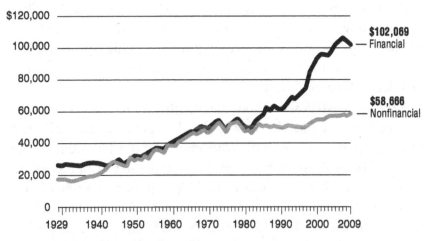

Figure 5.1 Financial sector pay was overly inflated
Source: Reproduced from The Financial Crisis Inquiry Report, 2011/U.S. Government Publishing Office/Public Domain.

catastrophe that caught us off guard. Our greed was so boundless that banks turned subprime loans into complex financial products, like subprime mortgage-backed securities (MBS). They didn't just dabble in these risky ventures – they built an entire industry within the banking sector around them. This is how they rationalised handing out subprime mortgages, lending money to people who were never in a position to repay it.

The Flawed Assumptions Behind MBS

There's nothing inherently wrong with MBS – they play a vital role in the mortgage market, helping to provide access to affordable home ownership. The problem wasn't with MBS as a concept;

it was the staggering volume being issued, particularly those filled with toxic subprime mortgages. By 2006, a staggering $600 billion in subprime loans were originated, accounting for 23.5% of all mortgage originations (see Figure 5.2). This wasn't a minor anomaly – it marked a major and troubling shift in lending practices (Born et al. 2011).

In theory, MBS should bundle together a nice, diversified selection of home loans. The idea is that by spreading the risk across various borrowers, you limit your exposure if a few homeowners default. The problem is that diversification doesn't work if the entire portfolio is junk. It's like throwing a bit of junk into a pile of other junk and thinking you've suddenly cleaned things up. It won't save you when you hit the end of a credit cycle and face mass defaults on junk loans that have been dressed up as high-quality bonds.

As I've said, there's nothing wrong with MBS as an investment or asset class. Investors buy them and in return they get paid based

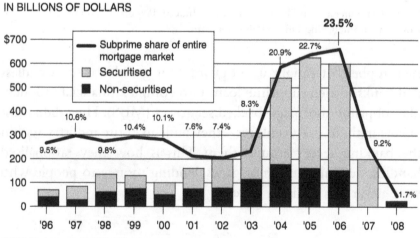

NOTE: Percent securitised is defined as subprime securities issued divided by originations in a given year. In 2007, securities issued exceeded originations.
SOURCE: Inside Mortgage Finance

Figure 5.2 Subprime mortgage origination
Source: Reproduced from The Financial Crisis Inquiry Report, 2011/U.S. Government Publishing Office/Public Domain.

on homeowners making their mortgage payments. The real risk was what happened when homeowners en masse decided they couldn't or wouldn't keep up with those payments. The issue wasn't the MBS structure itself, but the toxic loans stuffed inside them and the dodgy ratings they carried.

The financial models used to assess different tranches of MBS were, in short, flawed. They were based on historical data that painted far too rosy a picture of the housing market – a deliberate mistake to keep the MBS conveyor belt churning, so banks could move more mortgages off their balance sheets and lend more. To see how this worked, have a look at Figure 5.3. MBS seemed safe because they rested on the belief that house prices would keep going up. No one seriously factored in the possibility of a nationwide slump, which created a dangerous sense of complacency. The world saw rising house prices as the norm, even a sign of economic progress.

Here's how the money-making machine worked: the more mortgages banks could bundle into MBS and offload, the more capital they freed up to lend and the more profits they generated. When they ran out of prime mortgages, they didn't slow down – they turned instead to the subprime market, feeding a self-perpetuating cycle driven by greed.

Convincing investors to snap up MBS wasn't difficult. All it took was an attractive yield and a shiny credit rating. But those credit ratings were fundamentally flawed.

MBS were sold in tranches, with ratings ranging from triple-A (the safest) to double-B (moderate risk) and down to unrated junior tranches (the riskiest but offering higher returns). Agencies like Moody's and Standard & Poor's handed out triple-A ratings to tranches loaded with subprime loans, claiming – or pretending – that the risk was either diversified away or safely contained within the lower-rated tranches. This misplaced confidence lulled investors into believing these securities were far safer than they truly were.

Residential Mortgage-Backed Securities

Financial institutions packaged subprime, Alt-A and other mortgages into securities. As long as the housing market continued to boom, these securities would perform. But when the economy faltered and the mortgages defaulted, lower-rated tranches were left worthless.

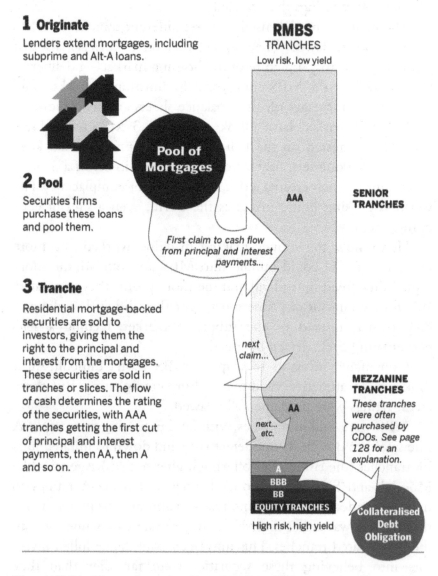

1 Originate
Lenders extend mortgages, including subprime and Alt-A loans.

2 Pool
Securities firms purchase these loans and pool them.

3 Tranche
Residential mortgage-backed securities are sold to investors, giving them the right to the principal and interest from the mortgages. These securities are sold in tranches or slices. The flow of cash determines the rating of the securities, with AAA tranches getting the first cut of principal and interest payments, then AA, then A and so on.

RMBS TRANCHES
Low risk, low yield

SENIOR TRANCHES
First claim to cash flow from principal and interest payments...

MEZZANINE TRANCHES
These tranches were often purchased by CDOs. See page 128 for an explanation.

EQUITY TRANCHES
High risk, high yield

Collateralised Debt Obligation

Figure 5.3 How the subprime MBS industry worked
Source: Reproduced from The Financial Crisis Inquiry Report, 2011/U.S. Government Publishing Office/Public Domain.

The problem is that you can't turn excrement into gold, no matter how you slice it. You also can't tranche excrement into different grades of excrement. And if you mix it with gold, you just have gold with excrement mixed with it. It doesn't diversify away. The excrement is still there.

This is why the so-called 'low-risk' triple-A MBS tranches were probably not triple-A. To put things in perspective, even the United States government doesn't have a triple-A rating anymore – it lost it in 2011. So, how could the rating agencies label a tranche triple A if it was full of subprime loans?

There was without a doubt a huge conflict of interest: these credit agencies that rated these securities were paid by the very investment banks that sold these MBS. This then allowed commercial banks to lend even more mortgages to people that would never be able to pay them off. All of this depended on biased data – skewed assumptions, selective reporting and misleading data visualisations.

In 2007, the first cracks began to appear. As adjustable-rate mortgages reset to higher interest rates, an increasing number of homeowners found that they could no longer afford their mortgage payments. Foreclosures soared, especially among subprime borrowers. House prices, for the first time in years, began to fall. In the end, many of these subprime MBS turned out to be worthless. Panic spread and the financial crisis began.

Biased Data at the Heart of the Crisis

The problem here was data. It was biased and deliberately so. This is what the commercial banks, investment banks and credit rating agencies needed to make these MBS attractive to investors. As mentioned, they first used risk models that assumed house prices in the United States would never crash. Well, why not? If you can continue selling mortgages forever at an increasing rate, then house prices would also rise forever.

They also didn't incorporate the widespread possibility of default, which was arguably the fatal error that ultimately led to the Great Financial Crisis. What's worse was that data visualisation was partly to blame. Risk heat maps, bar charts and various dashboards that were used to display financial metrics on the mortgage market failed to reveal the underlying fragility that was present.

Here's an example in Figure 5.4. This was taken from a pitchbook made and presented in January 2005 by a well-known investment bank. It shows how data visualisation can be used to dress up a toxic portfolio. There's a slide in there showing a bar chart of projected yields based on hypothetical performance scenarios.

It all looks very polished – clean lines, solid bars and a comforting upward trend – albeit almost impossible to understand. This was a terrible data visualisation and a subtle weapon of misdirection. Bankers are almost as gifted at making terrible charts as they are at inventing three-letter acronyms for their financial products.

The chart is based on the laughable assumption of a 0.0% cumulative default rate (CDR) in one scenario and a mere 0.2% CDR in the other. These assumptions are wildly optimistic, particularly considering that subprime retail mortgage-backed securities (RMBS), which make up more than half of the collateral, are inherently risky. You can see the portfolio breakdown in the two heavily labelled pie charts shown in Figure 5.5.

This was a classic case of data visualisation being used to hide risk rather than reveal it. It was a sleight of hand, designed to convince investors they were entering a safe deal when in reality they were stepping onto a financial ticking time bomb. The entire portfolio in this example was investment-grade rated, with 30% of it given a triple-A rating.

In this sense, data visualisation didn't just fail humanity – it betrayed it catastrophically. Those working in banks and credit agencies used these charts not to inform but to mislead, painting a false narrative of stability to churn out more MBS, sell more mortgages to the most financially vulnerable in society. It was an unforgivable abuse of trust.

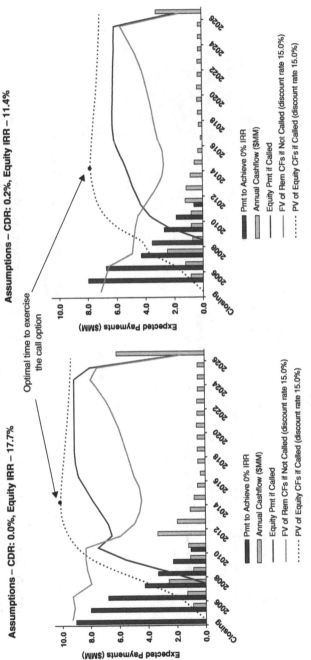

Figure 5.4 A slide from a pre-Financial Crisis investment bank pitchbook

Source: Reproduced from Adirondack 2005-1 CDO Pitchbook, Clinton Group, 2005/Yale University Library/Public Domain.

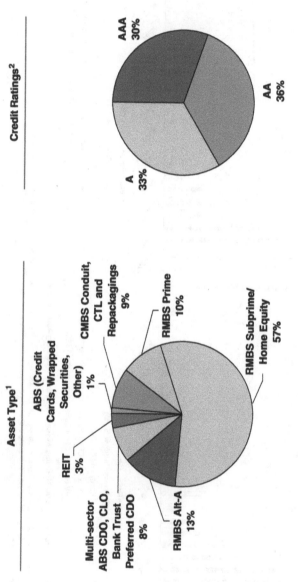

Figure 5.5 A slide from a pre-Financial Crisis investment bank pitch book

Source: Reproduced from Adirondack 2005-1 CDO Pitchbook, Clinton Group, 2005/Yale University Library/Public Domain.

What we saw during this era was a cascade of half-truths, presented in thousands of poorly designed pitchbooks that allowed America's mortgage market to grow in an unsustainable and reckless way. Few were willing to challenge the status quo. Instead of providing insight, data visualisation was used to spread a false narrative, create a deceptive sense of security and obscure the very risks it should have revealed.

Before we proceed, it's important to unpack what is meant by the term 'biased data' – a concept that underpins everything discussed so far in this chapter. For example, biased data played a pivotal role in the Great Financial Crisis, as banks used it to sell MBS packed with highly risky subprime loans.

We, therefore, need a framework for what we mean by 'bias data' to understand the danger it poses in a data-saturated world.

There is the textbook definition of bias data, but there is also the more philosophical understanding, which I believe is incredibly important. In fact, this definition will shape the rest of this book. It is a core component of my own set of beliefs and my relationship with data visualisation. It's also a belief system that might be considered controversial to some as it flies in the face of certain areas of traditional academic ideas, particularly in data science.

So let me be completely clear: I believe that all data is biased, which means, therefore, that all data analysis is to some extent flawed or incomplete. Now I understand that for some this might be a bitter pill to swallow. But it by no means suggests that data analysis is useless or worthless – far from it. But it cannot be completely trusted and should be challenged with rigor. Nothing in this universe is certain, including data.

This might seem like a strange statement to make, as data when displayed beautifully usually demonstrates precision and completeness. But I promise you all will make sense if you stick with me.

Before we continue, let's start with the traditional view of why data is biased because there are many ways that data can be biased. In the case of the Financial Crisis, what we described was selection bias in the way data was presented to maximise the number of mortgages sold and MBS issued.

This selective cherry-picking of data was done to maximise revenues for the banks. Not all data was captured, and it is clear that decisions were made on what to include and what to exclude. What was so dangerous here was that we almost saw the collapse of our entire global financial system because of this biased data. Greed drove large financial institutions to pull the wool over our eyes and manipulate us into thinking the abnormal was perfectly normal. What is even more frightening is that many of those individuals in those financial institutions, from credit rating agencies to commercial banks, even believed the lies they told. We deceive ourselves not because of false data but because of biased data.

It doesn't end there, of course. There are many other forms of biased data that we should be wary of. There is also measurement bias, where methods to measure data are skewed towards a particular outcome. This can happen, for instance, in a survey where questions are framed in a certain way to get a particular response. Do you remember the example we used in Chapter 3, where a LinkedIn poll asked: '*Should schools in the UK be forced to teach Arabic numerals as part of their curriculum?*'

The question was designed to evoke a more emotional response than an objective one. This was an extreme example, but measurement bias is literally everywhere. Here's another example – inflation!

The way we measure inflation has never been entirely accurate. We start with a basic definition – a sustained increase in the general price level of goods and services – and treat the resulting headline figure as fact. Yet this figure is built on assumptions that do not always fully reflect reality.

Inflation and Evolving Economic Forces

Take the US Consumer Price Index, for example, which is used to adjust payments like Social Security benefits. Analysts have found that it overstated inflation by about 1% due to substitution bias – the tendency of consumers to switch to cheaper alternatives when prices rise – and quality adjustment bias, which tries to account for changes in product quality over time. These seemingly small errors resulted in billions of dollars in overpayments and unnecessary taxpayer costs, illustrating how flawed measurements can have significant real-world consequences on society (Reed and Rippy 2012).

One fundamental issue is that inflation itself is dynamic and influenced by various forces. Demand-pull inflation occurs when too many buyers chase too few goods, driving prices higher. Easy credit can amplify this, creating the illusion of affordability, until it abruptly vanishes. On the other hand, cost-push inflation arises from external shocks, such as supply chain disruptions or energy crises, which force prices upward in ways that monetary policy often cannot control. This limits the effectiveness of central banks in combating this type of inflation.

These diverse influences make inflation inherently complex to measure, especially as the factors driving it can differ dramatically across periods. Yet we often treat inflation data as if it is comparable over time, ignoring the distinct forces shaping it in different eras.

Take the late 1970s, for example, when inflation was primarily driven by oil shocks – a textbook case of cost-push inflation. The United States' heavy reliance on imported oil made it particularly vulnerable to supply disruptions, causing energy prices to spike and ripple through the economy. Central banks were largely powerless to counter these pressures, as monetary policy cannot resolve supply-side constraints.

Contrast this with the post-pandemic period, where inflation arose from a complex mix of demand-pull and cost-push forces. On the demand side, unprecedented government spending during the pandemic, pent-up consumer demand and ultra-low interest rates led to a surge in spending. Meanwhile, severe supply chain disruptions and rising energy prices, exacerbated by the invasion of Ukraine, added cost-push pressures.

These factors created a fundamentally different inflationary environment, making comparisons with the 1970s misleading.

Yet at the same time, we continue to draw charts depicting the level of inflation over long periods of time. News outlets published, for instance, reports about inflation reaching levels not seen since the 1970s. While this makes for a striking headline, it tells an incomplete story – one that is inherently biased.

The bias lies in treating inflation as a single, unchanging phenomenon, when in reality it is shaped by different forces in different eras as we have shown. This doesn't mean the comparisons are deliberately misleading – they're not – but they inevitably simplify a complex topic. However, we still need these comparisons because, as humans, we are storytellers. We rely on narratives to make sense of the world, and these comparisons provide a framework for understanding broader trends, even if they carry inherent flaws.

Acknowledging this bias is not about rejecting these comparisons outright but about recognising their limitations. They help us grasp the contours of economic change, but we must remain aware that the story they tell is only one perspective – a starting point rather than the full picture.

GDP and the Shifting Nature of Data

This problem extends to gross domestic product (GDP) as well. Our primary measure of economic output struggles to account for how economies evolve. The US economy of the 1970s as mentioned before was heavily reliant on imported oil and scarcely resembles today's more energy-independent, technology-driven US economy. Yet we continue comparing them in our charts.

Relying on economic indicators such as GDP and inflation to understand complex systems over time have their shortcomings. The factors driving GDP and inflation evolve as economies transform, introducing biases that make comparisons across different periods more challenging.

Looking to the future, the drivers of GDP and inflation may deviate even further from today's norms. Emerging factors such as climate change, environmental priorities or breakthroughs in technologies such as artificial intelligence could reshape the global economy in ways current measures cannot capture. As we move into an era defined by unprecedented technological and environmental challenges, it becomes increasingly clear that traditional metrics such as GDP and inflation need to be adjusted to understand the full complexity of our evolving world.

Why Accepting Data Bias Matters

What we measure will never be entirely accurate. There will always be some degree of measurement bias. While we cannot eliminate it, we can remain open-minded and aware of this bias when making observations and crafting stories around data.

This matters because we shape policy around what we measure. Interest rates and other traditional tools may lose their bite as the economy transforms. Each measurement we rely upon influences the economy and, in turn, the economy changes in response to these measurements. It is akin to the observer effect in physics: by observing and acting upon data, we alter the system we are trying to understand and change the dataset.

These measurement bias can also appear anywhere – it is not limited to economics. For instance, in 1998, NASA's Mars Climate Orbiter disintegrated because one team used pounds instead of newtons in their calculations (Grossman 2010).

Beyond measurement bias, there are countless other forms of bias that can be found in data. There is sampling bias, where the chosen data do not represent the whole population. More subtle is interpretation bias, where our cultural backgrounds, personal beliefs and world views shape how we read and understand data. Even presentation bias, such as using misleading charts, can distort the truth, sometimes without anyone intending harm.

No data is free of bias. Human perception always creeps in. Our unique perspectives, shaped by culture, religion, upbringing and personality, colour the way we see the world. The same applies to how we read data. Understanding this is critical if we are to use data effectively. We must acknowledge that bias exists and approach data with a sense of humility and caution. Only then can we strive towards more honest and constructive data visualisations that help us make better decisions for society and the planet.

Recognising that all data is inherently biased does not mean abandoning data altogether. On the contrary, it means embracing the uncertainty and complexity that come with it. Quantum mechanics has shown us that uncertainty is woven into the fabric of reality. Similarly, when we measure complex economic and social systems, we encounter limits to what can be precisely known or predicted. Data can guide us, but it cannot grant absolute certainty.

This perspective should be appreciated when we use data visualisation. Rather than presenting data as the final word, it should be treated as the starting point for inquiry. Data visualisation done well can reveal patterns, show unexpected relationships and challenge false assumptions. It can help steer humanity towards more sustainable and ethical choices by making hidden biases visible and prompting us to question what lies behind the numbers. It can show us that data is bias.

In the chapters that follow, we explore these biases more deeply and consider methods to mitigate their effects. By understanding how data is shaped and influenced, we can design data visualisations that respect complexity rather than erase it. We can acknowledge uncertainty and show it honestly, inspiring critical thinking and meaningful dialogue. Used in this way, data visualisation does not just describe the world as it is – it helps us imagine a better world, guiding us towards truth, empathy and a more hopeful future.

I used to say, 'data never lies', but the truth is more nuanced. Data can both inform and mislead – a reflection of its inherent complexity. This isn't a reason for despair but a call to action. Recognising the biases and limitations in data allows us to question conclusions and use data more thoughtfully. When done with care and integrity, data visualisation becomes a powerful tool to foster understanding, bridge divides and navigate the uncertainties that accompany all measures of the world around us.

It is not just about acknowledging that data is biased, although this is a vital point to understand. It is also about recognising that the very nature of what we measure – the underlying variables shaping our world – changes over time. The shifting conditions, evolving structures and altered relationships between factors can make direct comparisons between past and present data feel like comparing apples with pears.

When we talk about time-series data, for instance, and try to compare a value from the early 1800s to one in 2024, we risk ignoring how the world has changed in profound ways between those two time periods. Factors that once influenced these numbers may have faded away, been replaced or altered beyond recognition.

The problem becomes greater the further back we look. With every passing year, the environment generating the data changes. This is especially problematic in time-series data, where the inherent assumption is that we can treat the past as a reliable baseline for the present.

By overlooking the evolution of the explanatory variables we use, we risk building flawed stories that lead us astray. This is a critical issue for data visualisation because failing to show the context of shifting variables can turn a chart into a misleading museum piece – a neat line that pretends the world never changed.

Yet this challenge does not diminish the importance or potential of data visualisation. On the contrary, once we understand these biases, we can strive to create data visualisations that are honest about uncertainty and respectful of complexity. We can design charts, graphs and dashboards that acknowledge how the underlying forces shaping the data have evolved, prompting users to question the validity of simple comparisons. The great promise of data visualisation is its ability to help us navigate these shifting sands.

This honesty in data visualisation is not a luxury. In an age of existential threats – climate change, resource scarcity and geopolitical instability – grappling with complex, shifting data is essential. If we want to preserve humanity, we cannot rely on static views of the world. We must embrace the evolving nature of our measurements. We must challenge assumptions and remain open to new explanations. Only then data visualisation can move beyond simple storytelling to become a tool for collective survival – one that reveals biases, acknowledges uncertainty and helps us chart a path forward through the turbulence of our changing world.

By acknowledging that data is always shaped by bias and that the factors influencing it change over time, we can embrace a more thoughtful and meaningful approach to data visualisation.

KEY TAKEAWAYS

- Data is never neutral or purely objective; it always carries some form of bias due to the way it is selected, measured, presented and interpreted.
- The world changes over time, altering the underlying conditions that generate data.
- Recognising inherent bias in data does not render data analysis useless. Instead, it calls for a more critical, humble and context-aware approach where uncertainty and complexity are openly acknowledged.
- Data visualisation, when done with honesty, can reveal hidden biases and prompt critical thinking, helping society navigate uncertainty, understand complex systems better and make more informed decisions.
- The ultimate goal is to move beyond treating data as absolute truth. Instead, we should see it as a guide – continually questioning assumptions, refining narratives and striving for interpretations that genuinely serve humanity.

Chapter 6

Economics Is a Dismal Science

The young economist stood before the Royal Society, and his hands were trembling as he gripped the edges of the wooden podium. The year was 1798 and Thomas Malthus was about to become the most hated man in London.

The candlelight flickered across the faces of Britain's intellectual elite as they leaned forward in their velvet-cushioned chairs, eager to hear the latest triumph of human reason. Instead, Malthus was about to tell them that their dreams of endless progress were nothing but a beautiful lie.

'Gentlemen,' he began, his voice gaining strength as he spoke, 'I regret to inform you that humanity faces an insurmountable wall. Like a ship sailing toward the edge of a map, we race toward a future where our numbers will overwhelm our ability to feed ourselves. The mathematics is ...' he paused, swallowing hard, '... is unforgiving.'

In the third row, Thomas Carlyle's quill scratched furiously across his notebook. He had come expecting another celebration of mankind's inevitable march towards perfection. Instead, he was witnessing the birth of what he would later venomously dub 'the dismal science' – a field that dared to suggest that human prosperity might have limits (Carlyle 1841).

What neither man could have known that evening was that they were participating in a deeper truth about human knowledge itself. Like the quantum particles that would puzzle scientists a century later, the economy refused to be pinned down by neat predictions. Every model, every forecast and every confident assertion about the future would turn out to be a shadow on Plato's cave wall – useful, perhaps, but never quite capturing the full complexity of reality.

Yet in this very limitation lay a profound wisdom. Just as future generations would learn that even light itself follows probability rather than certainty, economists would come to understand that their greatest strength lay not in prophesying the future but in plotting the countless paths it might take.

The Enduring Legacy of Malthus's Mistake

If data is inherently bias, then the same should also be said about theoretical economics. This is not about singling out this area of academia without good cause. This is my world and one that has occupied my mind ever since I enrolled as an undergraduate economics student more than 20 years ago at Bath University.

I wasn't a great student to be honest. But the subject seduced me and led me on a journey spanning those 20 years that I mentioned, ultimately bringing me to my love of data visualisation. One of the first lessons you learn in economics is the *Economic Problem*: man's wants are infinite, but the world's resources are finite.

Malthus plays a leading role in explaining this problem. He predicted widespread poverty and starvation as population growth outpaced food production (see Figure 6.1). But this theory did not come to pass – thank goodness. His assumptions were wrong. Malthus had oversimplified the problem, leading him to misunderstand how innovation would transform the world: growth in agricultural production actually surpassed global population growth.

Yet, what makes Malthus so fascinating is how he embodies both the strength and weakness of economics itself. His concerns were legitimately grounded in the *Economic Problem* – the fundamental scarcity that defines our world. Yet like many economic theories, his failure came from oversimplified assumptions that

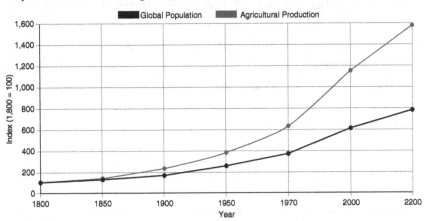

This data visualisation shows the relationship between population growth and agricultural production since 1800.

Sources:
- Population data: Our World in Data based on UN Population Division & historical estimates from McEvedy and Jones (1978)
- Agricultural production: Federico, G. (2005). Feeding the World: An Economic History of Agriculture, 1800–2000
- Recent agricultural data (post-1960): UN Food and Agriculture Organization (FAO)

Note: Agricultural production index combines various metrics including land productivity, labour productivity and total output. Values are indexed to 1800 = 100 for comparison purposes.

Figure 6.1 Population growth vs agricultural production (1800–2020)

failed to capture the complex ways innovation reshapes our productive capacity. This tension between mathematical models built on simplified assumptions and the intricate reality of human progress is why economics earned its reputation as the 'dismal science'. Yet without economics and without Malthus's contribution to it, we would understand far less about the world we inhabit and the economic systems that stich our societies together.

It's worth noting, however, that Malthus wasn't entirely wrong. Parts of the world have indeed grappled with resource scarcity, food shortages and environmental degradation linked to population pressures. But the real challenge that emerged in the centuries following his prediction wasn't about global food supply failing to meet demand, rather it was about the maldistribution of resources and wealth.

The forces of imperialism and colonisation fundamentally distorted the global balance of power. Wealthier nations, through conquest and exploitation, accumulated vast resources while subjugating other regions. This created a world not of absolute scarcity, as Malthus feared, but of artificial scarcity – where abundance and poverty coexisted due to unequal access to resources and systemic imbalances in global economic power. And this is a legacy that persists today.

The Lewis Model and the Promise of Industrialisation

Malthus also wasn't alone in making oversimplified assumptions. Throughout economic history, theoretical blunders have emerged from similar oversights. The Lewis model, proposed in 1954 by Sir W. Arthur Lewis, particularly troubles me. It presented a seductive but flawed blueprint for transforming traditional agrarian economies into modern industrial ones (Lewis 1954).

At its core, the model rested on a compelling premise: underdeveloped economies possessed a vast surplus of agricultural labour that could be redirected into more productive manufacturing sectors. Lewis argued this reallocation would naturally drive economic growth, eventually pushing wages upwards as the labour surplus diminished.

The model's elegant simplicity masked fundamental misunderstandings about agricultural economies and human behaviour. Like Malthus before him, Lewis crafted a theory that looked pristine on paper but failed to capture the complex realities of economic transformation.

The Lewis model was so influential that it earned Lewis the 1979 Nobel Prize in Economics (shared with Theodore Schultz). The Nobel committee specifically cited his work on development economics and specifically this dual-sector model. But every time I go to Brazil, I'm reminded of the failings of this model. Let me take you there to explain why.

'Vem aqui!' my father-in-law called out as I struggled with the massive sack of grain we'd bought from the farmer's store. The morning's rain had turned the dirt road into a mudslide, our car slipping and sliding the whole way up the hill. But Uncle Antonio stayed calm through it all, greeting other farmers as we passed, assuring me I was doing fine despite my white-knuckled grip on the wheel.

I set the grain down by the chicken coop, watching as Uncle Antonio shows my two-year-old daughter at the time how to feed the chickens. Just opposite stood his cocoa-processing shed, cleverly built with a sliding roof that could open to the sun, speeding up the drying of the beans spread across its wooden floor.

This farm was a testament to Brazil's agricultural riches. The soil was so fertile that forgotten seeds would root and grow without effort. Familiar fruits like mango, papaya, coconut and guava grew alongside fruits you'd never find in European or American supermarket: cashew fruit that stained your clothes with its sweet juice, creamy cupuaçu, tree-trunk sprouting jabuticaba, bright pitanga, giant jackfruit, tangy acerola, cajá, sugar cane and delicate araçá.

I couldn't help thinking, 'the Lewis model'. I feel a tinge of guilt when my wife laments that life is better on the farm than the cities. She's probably right.

She grew up in rural Brazil – one of the 12 children – very Catholic. We often joke that her father's ambition was to have his own football team plus one substitute. They lived on that farm for a while and had little money. But they were never poor. They never went hungry on that farm, and although life could be tough, they were safe and happy. They had each other.

Every single one of her siblings, including my wife, left that rural setting for life in one of Brazil's many large cities. Were they better off? That's difficult to answer. The promise of urban prosperity masked a more complex reality. As millions of Brazil's rural workers flooded into cities seeking jobs, they encountered a harsh truth: formal employment and affordable housing were scarce. This mass migration gave rise to vast urban slums – the favelas.

The reality sharply contradicted the *Lewis Model*. Instead of transitioning into productive industrial jobs, many found themselves trapped in the informal economy, perpetuating rather than escaping poverty. Perhaps even becoming poorer.

While Brazil achieved impressive industrial growth, the wealth has been concentrated in the hands of a small elite, entrenching and even deepening inequality. Yes, conditions improved over time, but the transformation fell far short of the theoretical promise. Brazil really ought to be a developed country by now. What looked elegant in economic models proved messy and often painful in practice, failing those who most needed economic uplift. Their story exemplifies the limits of theoretical economics – the gap between pristine models and the complex realities of human lives.

Economic theories are essentially stories – sophisticated narratives that attempt to explain the complex patterns of markets, human behaviour and resource allocation. But unlike traditional storytelling, these narratives arm themselves with data, mathematical models and predictive frameworks. Beneath their quantitative rigor, however, lies an inescapable truth: every theory rests on assumptions, simplifications and values shaped by its time.

Consider Adam Smith's *invisible hand* or Keynes's prescription for government intervention during recessions. These aren't just theoretical frameworks – they're powerful narratives about how economies should function, built from observations and concerns of their eras. Like all good stories, they help us make sense of the world. But also, like stories, they're subject to reinterpretation and revision as new evidence emerges.

The problem with economic theory is that it must grapple with the messy reality of human behaviour – our irrationality, our emotions and our unpredictability. They attempt to impose order on chaos, to find patterns in randomness. But perhaps their greatest value lies not in their absolute truth but in their power to help us understand and navigate an inherently unpredictable world.

An Invented Lecture and the Power of False Stories

Eager historians among you will have noted something wrong about the story at the start of this chapter: it wasn't true. I lied.

Thomas Malthus never delivered a lecture on his theory at the Royal Society as I suggested. His ideas were first published in his famous 1798 work, *An Essay on the Principle of Population* (Malthus 1798). It would have been impossible for Thomas Carlyle to be sitting in the third row of that mythical lecture – he would have been only three years old. They lived in overlapping but distinctly different periods and never met: Thomas Malthus (1766–1834) and Thomas Carlyle (1795–1881).

Even if Carlyle had read Malthus's famous essay, it likely wasn't what triggered him to call economics the 'dismal science'. That label emerged from a more complex journey he took through the field of economics.

This illustrates the dangerous power of storytelling. You can lie, twist reality and make people believe you. You can rewrite history and alter reality itself to suit your own purposes. More insidiously, you can come to believe and evangelise the very stories and lies you tell. What makes this particularly treacherous in data visualisation is how data can be weaponised to legitimise falsehoods.

We see this deception play out daily. Politicians rattle off misleading statistics to win voters. Companies creatively massage their financial statements to seduce investors. Toothpaste brands make unsubstantiated claims about whiter teeth. Washing powder companies conjure images of scientists in labs perfecting their formulas, while providing scant evidence of actual improvement.

Carlyle's criticism of economics cuts to the heart of this problem. He saw how economic theories could reduce complex social issues to impersonal forces, stripping away moral and cultural considerations. His frustration wasn't just with the field of economics' conclusions but with its overly mechanistic approach – how it could take the rich tapestry of human experience and flatten it into simplified models, just as manipulated data can distort reality. His label of economics as the 'dismal science' wasn't merely about its pessimistic predictions but about its potential to dehumanise the very subjects it studied (Carlyle 1841).

The problem is that you could probably make this criticism about many fields of science. True, economics sometimes masquerades as a science, but at least economists are broadly honest about this. We know those econometric models we create, test and publish can be wrong. Theory can tell the truth sometimes and then lie at other times.

The problem is that science itself is no different and perhaps worse. Scientists can become so convinced of their methodologies and rules that they forget these are human constructs, not universal truths. Apply these same errors to data science and the rules we've created over centuries for data visualisation and you begin to see the danger in making this a rule-based field. Rules only work if the universe wants to follow them and it's God's will.

Let's examine some economic theories that have fallen apart and explore the role data visualisation played in both their rise and demise. This investigation matters because when economic theories fail, they often have devastating consequences. Yet paradoxically, without these truths in economics transforming into false illusions, our species couldn't progress. These failures served as humbling experiences that exposed the limits of our cognitive abilities. We are not as invincible or as smart as we like to think we are.

Data visualisation lies at the heart of this story. It remains one of the most powerful tools theoretical economists wield to communicate their ideas. The same data visualisations that can make a flawed theory appear compelling can also later reveal its fundamental weaknesses. They serve as both sword and shield in the battle between economic theory and reality. Data visualisation is not meant to provide the answers, it's there to help find them and allow intellectuals to communicate and debate.

One of my favourite examples that I remember learning was the collapse of the Phillips Curve after more than a hundred years. It had a profound impact on economics as a discipline and a huge impact on the future course of economic policy and theory.

In the post-war era, A.W. (Alban William) Phillips was not your typical economist. Born in New Zealand, Phillips lived many lives: electrical engineer, farmer and Japanese prisoner of war in Indonesia. His path to economics was unconventional and his impact on the field would be both profound and, perhaps, unintended.

In the 1950s, while studying at the London School of Economics, Phillips brought an engineer's perspective to economics. Instead of favouring dry mathematical abstractions like his contemporaries, he sought tangible, observable connections between unemployment and wage inflation. His engineering background led him to approach economic data differently – searching for patterns and systemic relationships as he would in a physical system.

His 1958 paper analysed over a century of British economic data and revealed a striking pattern: when unemployment fell, wages rose quickly as employers competed for scarce workers. When unemployment was high, wage growth slowed or declined. This inverse relationship, immortalised as the *Phillips Curve*, suggested a stable trade-off between inflation and unemployment (Phillips 1958). You can see his original curve in Figure 6.2, which was published in his paper.

The findings electrified the economics world. Here, seemingly, was a roadmap for policymakers: they could lower unemployment by tolerating more inflation, or fight inflation by accepting higher unemployment. The concept appeared almost magical – an economic lever for governments to pull.

Yet Phillips himself remained ambivalent about his discovery. Having witnessed the complexities of real-world economics firsthand,

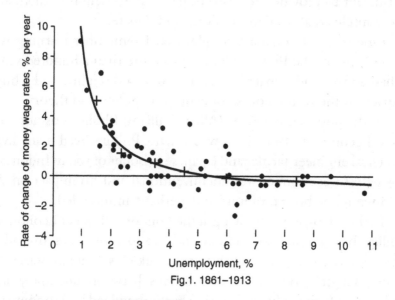

Figure 6.2 The Phillips Curve
Source: Phillips, 1958/John Wiley & Sons.

he knew no economic relationship could be this simple. But the curve's elegance proved seductive, and by the 1960s, it had become gospel in economic policy. Governments believed they could fine-tune the economy with this new tool.

The 1970s shattered this illusion. As stagflation – the toxic combination of high inflation and high unemployment – gripped the world, the Phillips Curve's promise crumbled.

Economists like Milton Friedman and Edmund Phelps argued that the relationship Phillips observed was merely temporary. In the long run, they warned, attempting to exploit this trade-off would backfire, spawning inflation without reducing unemployment. Their work in the late 1960s revealed a more complex reality, introducing the concepts of the *natural rate of unemployment* and the *expectations-augmented Phillips Curve*.

Friedman's pivotal 1967 speech, *The Role of Monetary Policy*, challenged the conventional wisdom on the Phillips Curve. He argued that the Phillips Curve trade-off was merely a short-term illusion. At the heart of his argument was the 'natural rate of unemployment' – a level determined by real economic factors, not monetary policy. Friedman warned that any attempt to push unemployment below this natural rate through inflationary policies would ultimately fail. People would adjust their expectations, recognise inflation's persistence and demand higher wages to compensate. The result would be rising inflation without any lasting reduction in unemployment (Friedman 1968).

Phelps, working independently but reaching similar conclusions, emphasised the role of *adaptive expectations*. He showed how workers and businesses would eventually factor expected inflation into their decisions, understanding that higher inflation wouldn't translate into real wage increases or sustained lower unemployment. His insight was crucial: inflation expectations would adjust over time, making the original Phillips Curve relationship unreliable in the long run (Phelps 1967).

Together, Friedman and Phelps created the *expectations-augmented Phillips Curve* shown in Figure 6.3, demonstrating that only unexpected inflation could temporarily lower unemployment. Their work fundamentally altered central banking, shifting focus from manipulating employment levels to controlling inflation – a transformation in macroeconomic policy that would define decades to come.

The Phillips Curve highlights the cognitive biases that plague our species – our compulsion to see patterns in noise and infer causation from correlation. We're wired to seek cause and effect, even when data is random. These perceived patterns become trapped in narratives we eventually accept as truth.

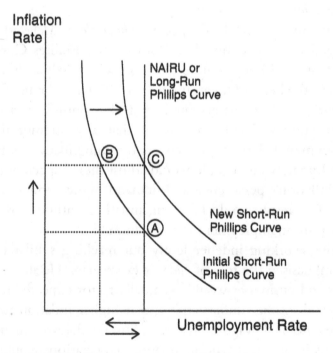

Figure 6.3 NAIRU or the long-run Phillips Curve
Source: Asacarny/Wikimedia commons/CC BY 2.5/https://commons.wikimedia.org/wiki/File:NAIRU-SR-and-LR.svg, last accessed on 27 January 2025.

When A.W. Phillips first observed the inverse relationship between unemployment and inflation, the pattern seemed irresistible. Finally, policymakers had a clear framework to follow. It was seductively simple. Central banks and politicians saw what they wanted to believe – that adjusting one variable could predictably impact another, in splendid isolation from external shocks like an oil crise.

As I've persistently argued, all data is inherently biased and prone to misinterpretation. The longer a pattern persists, the more secure we feel in its truth, even if we've merely been lucky. But luck inevitably runs out. The Phillips Curve held for decades – until suddenly it didn't.

Paradoxically, the longer a pattern persists, the greater the danger of its eventual collapse. Like tossing a coin and getting heads repeatedly, tails become inevitable. This is the peril of pattern-seeking in our noisy, data-saturated world. We grow complacent about risks, finding false certainty in the patterns we observe.

Consider one of data visualisation's most famous examples which has persistently gone viral on social media. During World War II, the Royal Air Force sought to improve their aircraft's survival rates. Engineers analysed returning planes and found bullet hole clusters concentrated in the wings, fuselage and tail sections (see Figure 6.4). The solution seemed obvious: reinforce armour in these areas.

But statistician Abraham Wald saw what others missed. These planes had survived despite being hit in these areas. The crucial data lay in what wasn't visible – the planes that never returned. The areas without bullet holes – the cockpit, engine and fuel systems were actually the most vulnerable. These were the parts that, when hit, ensured planes never made it home.

This revelation led to a complete strategic reversal: armour needed to be added where surviving planes showed no damage. This observation saved countless lives. Sometimes, it's the invisible data that reveals our true vulnerabilities.

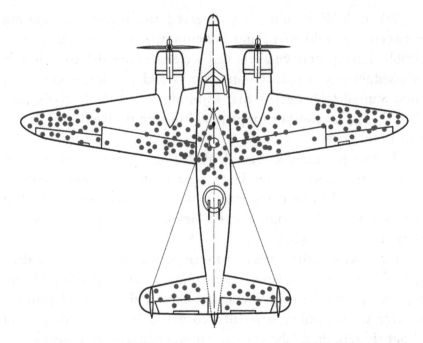

Figure 6.4 A method for estimating plane vulnerability from damaged survivors

Source: McGeddon/Wikimedia commons/CC BY 4.0/https://commons.wikimedia.org/wiki/File:Survivorship-bias.svg, last accessed on 27 January 2025.

This is often the problem with theoretical economics. Because we're dealing with complex systems, we must make assumptions or keep some variables static to build a workable model. In economics, the term *ceteris paribus* is used to describe when other variables are assumed to remain unchanged in the model or analysis being presented.

For instance, an economist might say that demand shifted along the supply curve, *ceteris paribus*, meaning all other factors remain the same. This term is part of the language of economics, allowing us to focus on the effect of a single variable without interference from others rather than acting as an on–off switch for a variable.

The challenge is that this isn't what happens in real life. Variables often move simultaneously, each with its own level of sensitivity –

what economists call elasticity. An inelastic response means a variable changes less than proportionally to another variable's change. For example, the demand for necessities like petrol is inelastic: you still need to buy roughly the same amount of petrol, even if prices rise; otherwise, you cannot drive. You take the price hit and don't alter your level of demand for petrol.

On the other hand, an elastic response means a variable changes more than proportionally. An example would be luxury items like a Swiss watch. If prices rise in the grey market, demand may drop sharply because people can easily cut back on Swiss watches. The point here is that variables are constantly shifting, sometimes in the same direction and sometimes in opposite directions, at varying levels of elasticity.

Elasticity is about causation, not just correlation. Unlike correlation, which shows whether two variables tend to move together, elasticity measures how much one variable directly causes a change in another. For example, if the price of a product goes up, and as a result, demand drops significantly, that's an elastic response – a clear cause-and-effect relationship.

Sometimes, variables don't influence each other at all, making them uncorrelated. In the asset management industry, where I've worked for most of my career, this is incredibly valuable because it means that two investments are unlikely to have been affected by the same risk factors, meaning that in combination, there are diversification benefits. Negative correlation, in particular, is very valuable because it means those investments and their returns can offset each other, enhancing the benefits of diversification.

You need to distinguish, however, the difference between correlation and elasticity: while correlation describes how variables move in relation to one another, elasticity measures a direct, causative response of one variable to a change in another.

For example, when portfolio managers invest in options, delta measures how much an option's price moves in response to a change in the underlying asset's price – this is basically a measure of elasticity. The point here is that concepts such as correlation and elasticity aren't confined to economic models; they're actively used in real life across finance.

In fact, the same modelling techniques we use in finance are also applied in economics to build models that explain complex relationships in the real world. For example, the study of econometrics focuses on using statistical methods to build models with multiple variables that might explain an economic factor like demand – this is known as multivariate analysis in statistics.

Don't be put off by the jargon here. Multivariate simply means that a model is built using several variables. These variables can be adjusted, lagged (i.e. shifted in time) and can be tested to determine if they have a causal effect on what you are observing.

For instance, you might look at how natural gas prices affect heating costs, which in turn impact disposable income, savings and investment. Testing these models to ensure they work effectively is a rigorous academic discipline in itself, requiring deep statistical knowledge and experience. Going into the details here would take too long for this book. However, it's worth noting that this complexity is one of the reasons econometrics is among the most challenging areas of economics to master at an undergraduate level.

The problem is that models can work for a very long time, until they don't. Remember we said that data is inherently biased. So, the factors that may have influenced, say, inflation in 2022, might be very different from the factors that influenced inflation back in the 1970s. This is precisely why the Phillips Curve collapsed. It worked for a hundred years, until it didn't.

Seeing patterns and then theorising on their meaning is, however, a very human endeavour. We are genetically designed to do this. Pattern recognition helped us track our prey when we were in pursuit. We also used pattern recognition to navigate at night by looking at the stars. In the modern world, noticing a pattern can lead to a hypothesis, which can then be tested to build a statistical model.

There are many more examples like this in economics. Consider David Ricardo's theory of comparative advantage – the cornerstone of free trade arguments since the early nineteenth century. Its elegant simplicity suggests that nations prosper by focusing on what they do best relative to others. Back in the nineteenth century, Portugal made port wine, while England produced cloth, and both benefited through trading with each other. The mathematics was impeccable and the logic sound (Ricardo 1817).

Number of men working for a year required to produce a given quantity of cloth and wine traded

	Cloth	Wine
England	100	120
Portugal	100	80

Source: Adapted from David Ricardo, The Theory of Comparative Advantage.

Here we have a deceptively simple table comparing cloth and wine production in England and Portugal taken from Ricardo's original paper. The numbers show how many men working for a year were needed to produce certain quantities of each good: cloth and wine.

Portugal is clearly better at making wine: it only needs 80 men to produce wine while England needs 120 men to produce the same amount. When it comes to cloth, both countries are equal, needing 100 men each. Since Portugal can make wine with fewer workers than England, while being just as good at making cloth, it makes sense for Portugal to focus on wine production. This simple example helped Ricardo show why countries benefit from specialising in what they're relatively better at producing and then trading with each other, which is their comparative advantage. Through specialisation, both countries can trade to achieve a greater combined output than if they tried to produce both goods independently.

But is life really this simple? Can centuries-old economic theories about wine and cloth tell us how to handle today's complex global trade relationships? When a country specialises in what it does best, some industries grow while others shrink. This sounds efficient on paper but try telling that to workers who have lost their jobs to fierce competition from countries like China.

This tension between theoretical economics and the geopolitical events we are experiencing today explains why countries often ignore Ricardo's advice. When President Trump imposed tariffs on Chinese goods and when Europe recently took steps to shield its car industry from Chinese electric vehicles, their decisions were driven by strategic and political considerations rather than adherence to elegant economic theories.

Ricardo's theory tells us that free trade makes the whole economic pie bigger. But it doesn't tell us how that pie gets sliced up, or what to do when the benefits of trade flow to some groups while the costs fall heavily on others, such as those who lose their jobs and cannot find employment in another industry. This is why modern trade policy often ends up being a messy compromise between free trade's promised benefits and protectionism's appeal as a shield for vulnerable industries and workers.

Here's another example. Imagine you've just won $10,000 in the lottery. According to Milton Friedman's Permanent Income Hypothesis, you wouldn't rush out and spend it all at once. Instead, you'd be sensible and spread that money out over time, perhaps saving most of it for later. Why? Because Friedman believed people make spending decisions based on their expected long-term income, not just what's in their pocket right now.

It's a bit like planning your monthly budget based on your annual salary rather than getting excited and overspending every payday. Friedman thought we're all pretty rational about money – we save during good times to help us through the lean times, keeping our lifestyle stable rather than living like kings one month and paupers the next.

But here's where theory meets reality and things get messy. Think about what happened when the US government sent out stimulus checks during the coronavirus disease 2019 pandemic. According to Friedman's theory, people should have saved most of that money since it was just a one-time payment. Instead, many Americans rushed out to spend it. Why? Because real life isn't as tidy as economic theories suggest.

Here's another example, which is perhaps a bit more familiar. It's a scene you might recount. The door swings open and a group of women enters, led by a striking blonde who immediately magnetises every male gaze in the room. John Nash's friends straighten their postures, each mentally calculating their odds, preparing their best lines.

But Nash remains still, his brilliant mind whirring with a different kind of calculation. 'Hold on,' he says, his voice cutting through the competitive tension. 'If we all pursue the blonde, we block each other's paths. None of us succeeds. Even worse, we insult the other women by treating them as second choice.'

He leans forward, the mathematics of human behaviour crystallising in his mind. 'But what if we each approached a different woman? What if we coordinated our actions instead of competing? We'd each have a chance at happiness.'

In this seemingly mundane moment, Nash glimpses something profound – the concept that would become known as the Nash equilibrium, where every participant, knowing the strategies of the others, has nothing to gain by unilaterally changing their own strategy. He would later go on in real life to win the Nobel Prize in Economics.

Like the famous Prisoner's Dilemma, where suspects must choose between betrayal and loyalty, Nash's bar scene revelation reveals a universal truth: the path to optimal outcomes often lies not in blind competition but in understanding the strategic choices of others.

This is game theory, a beloved tool that economists and political scientists have used for decades. It assumes players make careful, strategic decisions based on what others might do. Yet anyone who has witnessed panic buying during a crisis knows how quickly strategic thinking gives way to herd mentality. During the 2020 toilet paper shortage, game theory would have predicted rational stockpiling based on actual need. Instead, we saw emotional contagion leading to empty shelves and stockpiled garages.

The famous scene in *A Beautiful Mind*, where John Nash logically deduces a strategy to maximise the payoff for himself and his friends, offers a captivating portrayal of the Nash equilibrium. However, this scene, while brilliant, reflects the thinking of an exceptional mathematician rather than the average person. In reality, most people's decisions are driven more by emotions than by the kind of detached logic Nash employed. There is a huge difference between how economics predicts theoretical rationality and real human behaviour.

This is a flaw in economics: it assumes that humans are rational and make well-informed decisions based on perfect information. The uncomfortable truth is that we don't. Sometimes we're rational, but we are just as often impulsive and irrational. That's why the stock market rises and then crashes in a panic. That's why we have toilet paper shortages during pandemics. The invisible hand that serves our economy doesn't marshal resources very efficiently. And there is an overall woeful lack of risk management across our economies. It's a reality that has given rise to the field of behavioural economics, which seeks to understand the quirks and biases that shape real-world decisions.

This pattern of theoretical failure isn't unique to economics. Every field that attempts to model human behaviour faces similar challenges. But what makes economics special – and yes, sometimes dismal – is its profound impact on human lives. When we mistake our models for reality, people can suffer. Yet without them, how can we make sense of the complex economic system that we have created and help those that need it most?

Economic theories are like a map of an ever-changing, complicated world – useful for navigation while acknowledging that the territory itself keeps shifting and that you might be about to enter an unknown part of the world. The key is maintaining humility about their limitations while recognising their value in helping us understand the world and the challenges that we face.

This brings us back to data visualisation and the role it plays in our lives. The same charts that made the Phillips Curve so convincing later helped reveal its flaws. Data visualisation serves not just as a tool for proving theories but for questioning them as well.

Perhaps that's the real lesson of the 'dismal science'. It's not dismal because it predicts grim outcomes, as Carlyle suggested, but because it constantly reminds us of the limits of human understanding. In this acknowledgement of uncertainty lies not despair but wisdom. After all, recognising what we don't know is often the first step towards genuine progress in the search for answers.

Perhaps that's what makes both economics and data visualisation profound endeavours. They exist in this space between theory and reality, between clean models and messy truths. When we plot our expectations against actual outcomes, each scattered point of data and divergent trend tells a story of human complexity.

Sometimes our perfectly straight regression lines bend under the weight of an unknown truth, waiting to be discovered. This is where data visualisation becomes more than just charts and graphs – it becomes a map for trying to chart the unpredictable, irrational human systems that shape our world, which economics is forever trying to untangle.

KEY TAKEAWAYS

- Economics, termed the 'dismal science', grapples with fundamental problems of scarcity and complexity, revealing that human prosperity and resource allocation rarely fit neatly into theoretical models.

- Historical figures such as Thomas Malthus and W. Arthur Lewis show how elegant economic theories can fail when confronted with the messy realities of technological change, uneven distribution of wealth and human behaviour that defies simplification.
- Models like the Phillips Curve appeared to provide stable relationships between inflation and unemployment, only to collapse when conditions changed and unexpected factors challenged the assumptions underpinning the theory.
- Economic theories are best understood as narratives informed by data and mathematics, yet their underlying assumptions and simplifications are shaped by the time, place and world view of their creators.
- While quantitative frameworks offer valuable insights, economics confronts the unpredictability of human behaviour, often deviating from the rational and consistent decision-making traditional models assume.
- Data visualisation plays a double role: it can lend powerful support to flawed theories by making complex ideas seem intuitive, yet it can also help expose those flaws when reality fails to align with the patterns and predictions the visualisations present.
- Recognising that economic models are not absolute truths but tools for understanding encourages humility and adaptability, reminding us that our best maps of human systems must continuously evolve as circumstances and knowledge change.
- Ultimately, both economics and data visualisation find their value in acknowledging uncertainty and imperfection. By striving to understand complex truths rather than clinging to misleading patterns or oversimplified rules, they guide us towards more realistic perspectives on the world we inhabit.

Chapter 7

Risk Should Be Seen Not Heard About

Night was giving way to morning as Abraham de Moivre continued his work in his dimly lit London chamber. The only sound was the scratch of his quill against the parchment. It was 1733 and the French mathematician's desk lay buried beneath stacks of mathematical tables and masses of probability calculations.

Since fleeing Paris as a young Huguenot refugee, he had immersed himself in the mathematics of chance. And now, as he plotted yet another set of numbers, something began to emerge from his work. He saw a pattern that would change our understanding of randomness itself.

As Peter Bernstein describes in *Against the Gods: The Remarkable Story of Risk*, Abraham de Moivre's quest was more than an

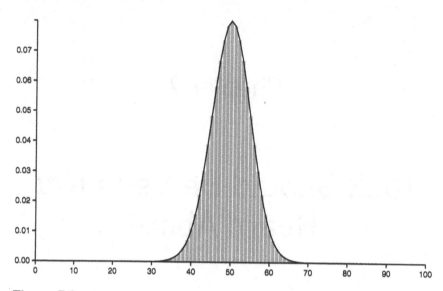

Figure 7.1 Binomial distribution and its normal approximation
Source: A.W. Phillips, 1958/John Wiley & Sons.

intellectual pursuit – it was one of humanity's first real attempts to understand and quantify uncertainty (Bernstein 1996).

While carrying out his mathematical investigation into probabilities, he noted that as the number of trials increased, outcomes began to cluster predictably around a central value.

A curve emerged that rose symmetrically on either side of the mean, with fewer occurrences as the data moved outwards. It resembled the shape of a bell and suggested something fundamentally profound. It seemed that even randomness had a form and structure. I've tried to recreate approximately what this might have looked like in Figure 7.1, assuming de Moivre made a hundred trials. But it's worth noting, de Moivre never actually plotted this curve – he just calculated it.

The Universal Allure of the Normal Curve

This is the normal distribution curve, and what de Moivre discovered represents the symmetrical beauty of so many things that we find in nature and our universe. For instance, the heights of people in a population trace this same curve, clustering around an average with fewer individuals at the extremes. IQ scores mirror this shape, as do the weights of newborns and blood pressure readings.

Beyond humans, this curve appears in nature too – in the lengths of bird wings, the sizes of seeds and even the velocities of stars within galaxies. Engineers see it in random noise in signals. Understanding that curve allowed them to reduce interference and design better systems.

The discovery of the normal distribution curve during de Moivre's time conformed perfectly to the Newtonian world view, where the universe was seen as an ordered system governed by immutable laws. This curve represented what you might call *beautiful data*: symmetry, balance and predictability. It captivated some of the greatest mathematical minds of the era.

For many, it seemed to prove God's existence – a testament to intelligent design. To them, the symmetry of the curve was divine order made visible. But this belief reflected both awe and a sense of certainty that we understood more about the universe than we really did.

The truth is there are aspects of existence that lie beyond human comprehension and likely always will. If you believe in God, you must accept that we are mere spectators, travelling through time, guided by forces beyond our full understanding. Even if you follow Einstein's theories and view time as part of a block universe, we catch only glimpses of the cosmos as we move through time. Still, we gaze at the stars and wonder, seeking order and meaning. It's no surprise we were seduced by the elegance of the normal distribution.

Many scholars shared this fascination, and one man – Carl Friedrich Gauss – elevated the admiration of the normal curve to new heights. He uncovered its hidden beauty in astronomy, using it to explain small errors in the measurement of celestial bodies. In doing so, Gauss transformed what was once a mathematical curiosity into one of the most powerful tools in science.

Centuries later, with the rise of quantum mechanics, the story of normal distribution continued. Deterministic Newtonian physics gave way to a universe governed by probabilities. What de Moivre and Gauss once saw as a symbol of perfect order also helped describe the uncertainty in subatomic particles. The normal distribution remains central to our understanding of a universe that is both ordered and chaotic. Yet what fascinated Gauss and others was its perceived order and hints of intelligent design.

Gauss refined the mathematical framework of what we now call the Gaussian distribution with extraordinary precision. Building on de Moivre's work, he created a practical tool for measuring probabilities, error and uncertainty. His method of least squares brought unprecedented accuracy to science. This was as profound in its time as perfecting pi.

However, while Gauss derived the mathematical formula for the normal distribution, there is no direct evidence he ever plotted the bell curve. In his era, visualising mathematical concepts was rare. Scientific culture believed understanding lay in equations, not images. Data was expressed in mathematical terms alone, limiting their appreciation of visual representation's potential.

A Self-Imposed Fog: When Scientists Shunned Visuals

In hindsight, this focus on formulas constrained their ability to grasp how powerful data visualisation could be. By neglecting visual tools, the scientific community laboured in a self-imposed fog, especially with probability. Visualisation could have guided researchers towards mathematical truths, offering clarity on the complexity hidden in data. Yet for much of the nineteenth century, this critical tool remained largely ignored.

William Playfair's pioneering use of line graphs, bar charts and pie charts in the late eighteenth century began to challenge this purely mathematical view, albeit it was not enough to influence de Moivre or Gauss. Playfair believed that numbers had stories to tell, and those stories became most vivid when visualised. His revolutionary approach, however, was ahead of its time. Many scientists dismissed data visualisation as unnecessary for serious inquiry, clinging to the idea that understanding lay solely in equations.

Practical challenges compounded this reluctance. Producing detailed graphs in the early nineteenth century required skilled engraving and significant printing costs. Scientific journals, constrained by resources, reserved visuals for fields such as anatomy or geography where images were deemed indispensable. Data visualisation, by contrast, was seen as a luxury rather than an essential tool.

The bell curve remained hidden in pure mathematics until an extraordinary breakthrough in the nineteenth century. Adolphe Quetelet wasn't content with abstract theory – he wanted to show people what this mathematical beauty actually looked like.

In his 1835 work *Sur l'homme et le développement de ses facultés*, he did something remarkably simple, yet revolutionary. He imagined an urn filled with black and white balls in equal numbers. By calculating what would happen if you drew 999 balls repeatedly, he demonstrated how the most likely outcomes clustered symmetrically around an even split. The extreme results – drawing mostly black or mostly white balls – became increasingly rare, creating the distinctive bell shape. This was probably the first time people could see what mathematicians had only imagined in published form, as shown in Figure 7.2 (Quetelet 1835).

But it was Francis Galton who truly brought the bell curve fully to life. In his 1889 book *Natural Inheritance*, he introduced the quincunx, a device that dropped metal balls through a grid of pins, causing them to bounce left and right until they settled at the bottom (Galton 1889).

The result was a pile shaped like a bell curve. The mathematics hadn't changed, but for the first time, people could watch randomness create order before their very eyes. By combining theory with physical demonstration, Galton turned the abstract into something tangible, making the beauty of the bell curve accessible to all.

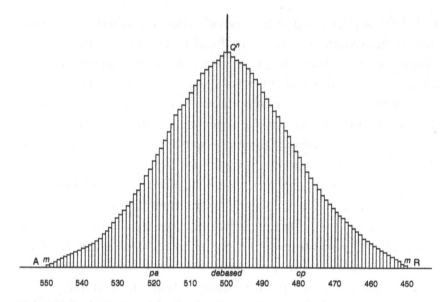

Figure 7.2 The binomial distribution visualised: Adolphe Quetelet's bell curve (1835) (This chart visualises the binomial distribution of outcomes from repeatedly drawing balls from an urn, showing the earliest depiction of the bell curve.)

Sources: Sur l'Homme et le Développement de ses Facultés, ou Essai de Physique Sociale by Adolphe Quételet (1835)/Bachelier, imprimeur-libraire, quai des Augustins.

You can see this below, from these illustrations, taken from his published work. Figure 7.3 show a distinct bell curve rotated vertically.

This is from Francis Galton's *Natural Inheritance* (1889), and Figure 7.3 is one of the earliest visualisations of the normal distribution, applying it to physical measurements and demonstrating its practical use in studying variation and heredity.

However, the delay in adopting data visualisation came at a cost. Decades of potential discoveries were lost, as science operated without tools that could reveal complex relationships and patterns at a glance. By the time data visualisation gained acceptance, the scientific community had missed opportunities to advance knowledge more rapidly.

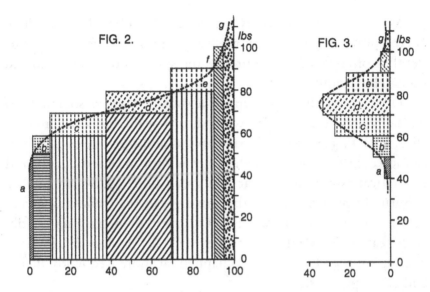

Figure 7.3 Galton's early normal distribution visualisations
Sources: Francis Galton's Natural Inheritance (1889)/Macmillan and Company.

Furthermore, like many mathematical proofs and truths, there were counter-truths that contradicted the validity of the bell curve. In finance, the bell curve led to a catastrophic misunderstanding of risk – an oversight that could have been avoided if these counter-truths had been visualised. In fact, that's why, in statistics, we now talk about the skewness of data distributions. We also examine the shapes of non-normal distributions with fat tails. We know that there are probability distributions that do not conform to the 'normal' because we can see them.

This frustration with abstraction wasn't limited to mathematics either. In economics, the problem took on a different form. I realised this during my time as a student. Economic theories were everywhere – beautifully drawn supply and demand curves, production frontiers and utility graphs – all perfectly idealised but based on little more than assumptions and equations. They were elegant, but where were these data? Where was the proof that these curves reflected reality?

My economics lecturers would fill blackboards with these curves, presenting them as if they were immutable laws of nature. Yet they often failed to capture the messiness of the real world and human behaviour.

How could they have made a subject I loved so much so dismal? Sorry to repeat the word dismal again, but Economics is alive. It's living because it's based on us and how we behave. You cannot constrain human behaviour within idealised curves and theoretical assumptions. Fear and greed don't follow an orderly pattern like planets orbiting the Sun. Instead, they follow an asymmetric pattern – rising slowly with greed, then crashing rapidly with fear. This asymmetry creates 'fat tails' in the distribution, making supposedly rare events happen far more frequently than a bell curve predicts.

We are the economic actors and our stage is the marketplace – messy, chaotic and gloriously human. No theoretical curve can capture that. But data visualisation can.

And yet, despite my frustration with abstraction, I couldn't entirely resist its allure. I was captivated by econometrics, algebraically constructing supply and demand curves and running Monte Carlo simulations.

For my ADHD brain, these tools felt therapeutic, offering a sense of order and focus. It was ironic, really. The very abstraction I questioned often felt like a refuge amid the chaos. But over time, I began to see these tools differently, not as ends in themselves but as starting points to bridge the gap between theory and reality. Data visualisation became my way to make sense of both worlds.

I'm not suggesting that I instantly realised this at first. I was also seduced by the bell curve as I said and, moreover, I even visualised it. But it was the start of a journey that got me to where I am today, and for that reason alone, I am forever grateful to economics. In fact, it is a subject that I still love today thanks to data visualisation.

So, let's begin that journey.

The Monte Carlo Moment: Random Numbers as Graffiti

Now don't lose me here. Please don't. Whenever I utter the words 'Monte Carlo simulation', people look at me in bewilderment. It's nothing complicated. In fact, it's surprisingly cool and the first form of data visualisation I ever experimented with beyond Playfair's charts. A Monte Carlo simulation is like the graffiti of mathematics — raw, unrefined and sometimes chaotic but incredibly effective at revealing the truth hidden in complexity.

To explain how it works, let's talk about graffiti. In fact, let's talk about the greatest graffiti artist who probably ever lived — Banksy.

In 2005, Banksy pulled off one of his most audacious stunts at the British Museum by covertly installing his own artwork titled 'Peckham Rock'. The piece, designed in a cave painting style, depicts a prehistoric figure pushing a shopping cart — yes, our friend Ethan is back.

Using his signature stencil technique, Banksy created this artwork on a piece of concrete, mounted it on the museum wall and even added a fake information label to make it appear as a genuine artefact. The piece went unnoticed by museum staff for three days before its discovery, demonstrating both the speed and precision of Banksy's work. The secret behind the speed and quality of his work is that he sprayed over stencils that allowed him to rapidly create the image he wanted with great precision. The British Museum was so impressed that they later described it as 'one of the most successful cases of museum infiltration in history.'

Monte Carlo simulations in statistics work just like Banksy's graffiti — instead of spraying paint over a stencil, you are spraying random numbers over a mathematical constraint. Just as Banksy removes his stencil to reveal the artwork, these Monte Carlo simulations do the same, revealing hidden mathematical truths with surprising speed and precision.

That is effectively what you do with a Monte Carlo simulation. Without complex mathematics and equations, you make the truth appear in front of your very eyes by just spray-painting numbers on it. It's the lazy way to do mathematics because although you see the truth, you don't necessarily understand why you see it. The benefit is that it vastly reduces the amount of brain power you need to see what you need to see. Rather than construct complex equations, you use the randomness of numbers to see visually what was previously not visible.

Look at this Monte Carlo simulation I've illustrated in Figure 7.4. It looks complicated, but it's not. I made a bell curve appear with $10,000 random numbers with a piece of JavaScript that took no more than 15 minutes to write.

This Monte Carlo simulation uses 100,000 random numbers using the Box–Muller transform. It calculates the probability density function for each number.

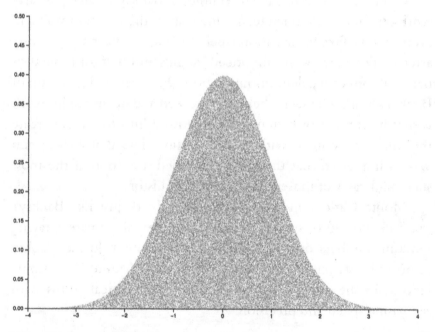

Figure 7.4 The bell curve revealed with a Monte Carlo simulation

Push Monte Carlo simulations to their max and you might see things that even the most brilliant mathematicians could never describe algebraically. As I said, it's a fast, brutal and lazy way to get to the truth. And it also got me in trouble.

In my final year of university, I took a module in financial analysis and part of the coursework was to derive the efficient frontier. This is a mathematical holy grail in portfolio theory that shows which mix of investments would give the best returns for different levels of risk. While my classmates were sweating over complex equations, I took my spray-can approach.

The professor on that course threatened to mark me down. I derived this efficient frontier with a Monte Carlo simulation, saving myself days of work. We had to answer a series of questions based on our findings. In the end, he let me off as he couldn't technically tell me I was wrong. I got the answers right, and I had presented him with my methodology.

That was my first data visualisation victory. I didn't know it at the time, but decades later it would have a profound impact on my career, even though I would later discover it was wrong, all because of that deceptive bell curve. I will come on to that in a bit.

The point is that my fascination with data visualisation had begun. Look at the chart shown in Figure 7.5, and you will see what I call a Monte Carlo simulation (data graffiti) for the efficient frontier. Here, I have created a million random portfolios containing different weights of US equities, European equities, emerging market equities, Treasury bonds, high-yield bonds, gold, Bitcoin, real estate, emerging market debt, commodities and cash.

The asset class weights for each portfolio in this simulation were randomly assigned, adding up to 100%, with annualised returns and standard deviations (measuring risk) calculated from historical data from 2010 to 2023.

The efficient frontier is represented by the thick black line at the outer edge of this distribution. It is meant to show the optimal balance between risk and return when constructing an investment portfolio.

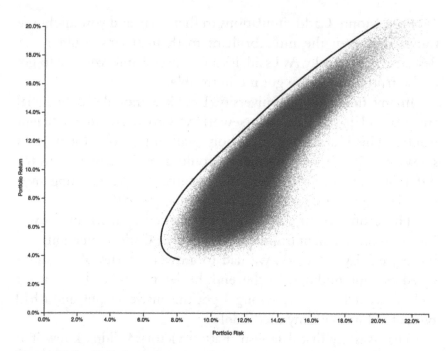

Figure 7.5 Efficient frontier shown using a Monte Carlo simulation

This fundamental concept was developed by Harry Markowitz's groundbreaking Modern Portfolio Theory, first presented in his seminal 1952 paper *Portfolio Selection* (Markowitz 1952). Markowitz's innovative work in financial economics would later earn him the Nobel Prize in 1990, cementing his long-lasting influence in the investment industry. Meanwhile, his work would be taught all around the world in university courses, like the one I took.

Calculating the efficient frontier using Markowitz's methodology is not easy. Investors need to carefully adjust the weight of each asset class to achieve minimal risk for a desired return level. This approach begins with constructing a covariance matrix to understand how investments interact with one another and then proceeds with a solution to a quadratic optimisation problem. This mathematical framework incorporates real-world investment rules – namely, that all available money must be invested and that investors can only take traditional buy-and-hold positions.

Right, have I lost you? Good! That's exactly how I felt as an undergraduate. That is why I didn't bother with any of this. It was long and tedious work. These days it is a lot easier to do it in coding languages such as Python or R, but that wasn't available to me back then. So, I ran that Monte Carlo simulation that got me into trouble.

My chart was beautiful. As I said, it was my first data visualisation victory. But while it looked elegant, there was a fundamental flaw in how it worked. There is a clue in the graphic I've shown you. Can you see how the Monte Carlo simulation creates a kind of distribution? The outliers to the left form the efficient frontier, while the Monte Carlo simulation as a whole seems to follow a normal distribution. You can just about see it, although it is rather swashed and distorted behind the efficient frontier curve.

That is the problem with the efficient frontier. Markowitz's theory assumes asset returns follow a bell curve. You cannot blame him for doing this. Mathematicians had been speaking elegantly about the normal distribution centuries before Markowitz. As mentioned before, it was a wondrous mathematical truth that could be found all the way from a subatomic level in quantum mechanics to explaining probabilities as mundane as the heights of people.

The problem is that human behaviour completely disrupts this. Our behaviour creates a greater number of outliers – events that occur far beyond the average. Our actions are not independent or uniformly distributed. We act disproportionately to certain triggers, such as fear and opportunity. This is why markets can rise gently for years and then suddenly crash. Our tolerance for risk can collapse, causing us to take drastic and risky actions when we panic. We can be completely risk adverse one moment and then completely risk adventurous the next.

As explained earlier in this book, models can collapse spectacularly without warning even after persisting for centuries.

We saw this with the Phillips Curve in economics and the same holds true in mathematics. Truth may be elegantly expressed – like the normal distribution curve – yet it can still fail us when applied to the wrong environment. In finance, such failures have resulted in losses amounting to billions and even trillions of dollars. Ultimately, this problem arises from a fundamental flaw within utility theory in economics.

Here is an example. When I was at school, my economics teacher brought in a jumbo pack of mini Mars bars. Our task was simple: we had to eat as many as we could. For each one eaten, we recorded our level of utility on a spreadsheet, rating it on a scale from 0 to 100.

The results were predictable. Our utility was close to 100 with the first mini Mars bar and then declined sharply with each one after that. The lesson was intended to illustrate the law of diminishing marginal returns and it made sense. However, in reality utility – both positive and negative – is not so uniform. Positive utility may diminish but negative utility can be far more intense, like vomiting Mars bars into a wastepaper basket in your economics class.

Negative utility does not mirror positive utility – you feel it far more intensely – which is why utility theory is flawed. Each unit of utility is not uniform as economic theory suggests, and the best place to observe this is the equity market.

Market gains tend to provide only modest psychological rewards, even as profits accumulate, each additional increase brings diminishing satisfaction. Market downturns, however, trigger a far more intense emotional response.

The psychological impact of losses is significantly stronger than that of equivalent gains, as our natural aversion to losing money generates genuine distress and anxiety. This asymmetry between the pain of losses and the pleasure of gains explains why stock market returns are not normally distributed.

To understand this better, consider an experiment conducted by Kahneman and Tversky (1979). Participants were given a choice:

receive $100 or flip a coin to either win $200 or end up with nothing. Most selected the guaranteed $100. In a second scenario, participants were asked to choose between losing $100 outright or flipping a coin to either lose $200 or lose nothing. This time most chose the coin toss (Kahneman and Tversky, Prospect Theory: An Analysis of Decision Under Risk 1979).

What this experiment illustrated was loss aversion. People tend to prefer avoiding losses rather than securing equivalent gains. It profoundly affects how financial markets operate and how risk is perceived. Our risk tolerance can shift drastically – we may feel secure and complacent when markets rise, forgetting the dangers, but when markets crash, we panic and make hasty decisions to stem our losses. We move abruptly from long-term strategies to short-term panic.

The result is that extreme events, such as financial crises, occur far more frequently than the normal distribution would predict. When we panic, we tend to panic together, producing many more negative extreme events than a normal distribution would suggest. The outcome is what statisticians refer to as 'fat tails' in the distribution.

In statistics, under a normal distribution a five- or six-sigma event is so unlikely that it is considered virtually impossible except over extremely long-time horizons. Yet in reality such occurrences appear in financial markets far more frequently, driven by fear and greed. Take Black Monday in 1987 for example – the stock market crash was a 20-sigma event, something that should have been statistically impossible. Yet, it happened.

Therefore, Markowitz's theories underestimated the probability and impact of significant market movements, potentially creating portfolios that were not robust to real-world risks. Of course, we know that now but not after experiencing a huge amount of financial pain.

Subsequently, this has led to better – though not perfect – financial models that account for the unpredictability of market behaviour. These models include the Value at Risk (VaR) and Conditional Value at Risk (CVaR) models, which aim to better capture the complexity and messiness of real market behaviour. While the details are beyond the scope of this book, I learned about these models almost a decade after I left university, within the asset management industry where I worked.

Beyond adopting advanced risk measures such as VaR and CVaR, the asset management industry has progressively shifted from constructing portfolios based solely on individual asset classes to focusing on allocations to risk premiums. This modern approach exposes investors to various types of returns linked to different risk factors – such as equity, credit and liquidity risks – that are not necessarily correlated.

By combining these uncorrelated risk premiums, portfolio managers can achieve greater diversification and build more efficient portfolios than traditional methods allow.

This type of portfolio construction also heavily relies on data visualisation. Visual tools enable portfolio managers to comprehend and communicate complex relationships between multiple risk factors, enhancing their ability to identify patterns, correlations and potential risks that may not be apparent from raw data alone. It allows them to visualise the multidimensional aspects of risk.

By focusing on diverse risk premiums and employing advanced statistical techniques, this approach accounts for non-normal distributions and the higher likelihood of extreme market movements. This results in portfolios that are better equipped to manage the unpredictability and messiness of real market behaviour.

I observed this evolution first-hand in the asset management industry nearly a decade after leaving university, where dynamic models based on risk premiums became the norm. Today a lot of the work I do in data visualisation focuses on helping these investment teams see risk better and communicate this well to their clients.

The tendency to underestimate risks also becomes even more pronounced when we follow the crowd, driven by fear of missing out.

When we see others making money, we are tempted to join in, creating momentum that pushes prices even higher, often beyond reasonable valuations.

There's a famous story about Joe Kennedy, who was JFK's father. As he sat in a New York taxi in 1929, he listened to his driver enthusiastically sharing stock tips. That evening, he started selling his stocks. When cab drivers are giving market advice, he reasoned, the market is running on pure excitement rather than value. Months later, it crashed. It was the start of the Great Depression.

Herding behaviour creates feedback loops that distort outcomes. A feedback loop means that behaviour in the market feeds back on itself. For example, if people see others buying stocks, then they are more likely to buy as well, pushing prices even higher. This cycle continues, leading to significant price distortions and again messing up normal distribution as we know it.

This behaviour isn't limited to humans. In a study by B.F. Skinner, pigeons were conditioned to perform certain actions by receiving food rewards (Skinner 1948). The pigeons developed superstitious behaviours, believing their actions influenced the delivery of food, even when it was random. This is akin to how investors may falsely attribute market movements to their actions, leading to irrational investment decisions. When we see others panic-selling stocks or flocking to a trend, we join in, amplifying these behaviours. This clustering breaks the independence assumption of the bell curve, making deviations from the mean far more extreme.

The instincts we inherited from our ancient ancestors still shape how we invest today. We still behave like Ethan the caveman in the markets. We grow complacent about risk when things go well yet feel the pain of losses so intensely that we make rash decisions, often selling in panic or trying to recoup losses through risky bets. We tend to fixate on the first piece of information we learn, like a stock's previous high price, making it hard to accept new market realities. These quirks of human nature push markets far from the neat patterns that a bell curve predicts.

Markets and wealth distribution don't follow the smooth pattern of a bell curve. Instead, they form far more extreme shapes, where a tiny number of people hold most of the money and influence. These patterns don't spread out evenly but are heavily skewed towards the few at the top. This imbalance is self-reinforcing: the rich get richer because they can invest, grow their resources and access exclusive opportunities, while influencers gain more power as their audience expands and trust deepens.

This dynamic creates inequality and concentration, replacing the balance and symmetry you'd expect from a bell curve. Again, you get fat tails where a single person amasses an enormous fortune in an almost impossible manner. This happens far more frequently than you'd expect in a system that's evenly distributed. It's a shift from fairness to extremes, driven by forces that reward success disproportionately.

Data visualisation helps us see what numbers alone can't show. It reveals patterns we might miss and makes complex risks easier to understand. Instead of just assuming everything follows a bell curve, we can actually see how markets and risks exist in the real world.

Think of the 2008 Financial Crisis – heat maps and network graphs showed how banks were connected, helping regulators spot where trouble in one bank could spread to others. Or during coronavirus disease 2019, real-time dashboards helped track how the virus was spreading, showing patterns that simple statistics missed.

By making data visual, we can see when extreme events happen more often than they should, or when risks cluster together in dangerous ways. This helps us make better decisions because we are seeing the world as it really is, not just how our mathematical models say it should be.

In essence, human behaviour completely shatters the assumptions of the normal distribution. Real-world phenomena are messy, interconnected and irrational. Understanding these complexities requires data visualisation to see through fog or complexity. The bell curve, though mathematically beautiful, is too simplistic for the chaotic realities of human behaviour.

This doesn't mean the normal distribution is irrelevant. Its discovery was transformative, rippling through every field of human inquiry. In physics, it explained the behaviour of gases and energy distribution in thermal systems. In biology, it showed patterns of genetic inheritance. In astronomy, it refined calculations of celestial motion. But in finance, its elegance proved deceptive because it never accounted for human emotion.

The bell curve's symmetry can lull us into a false sense of security, suggesting that extreme events are rarer than they actually are. Financial markets have repeatedly shown that catastrophic shocks occur far more often than the normal distribution predicts. It's not just finance either: climate risks also follow fat-tailed distributions, making devastating outcomes more likely than a bell curve would suggest.

By embracing data visualisation, we can reveal these complexities. Rather than trusting neat, theoretical assumptions, we can observe patterns as they emerge and identify subtle warning signs before they escalate into crises. Visual tools help us see what would otherwise remain hidden in abstract equations, enabling us to interpret data in context and adapt as our world grows ever more interconnected.

This matters because humanity stands at a crossroads. Climate change is reshaping the planet, pandemics test our resilience and markets can fracture under unexpected stress. Old models that assume stability and normality fail to capture the sheer unpredictability of these challenges. We must see our predicament clearly, in full colour and contour, rather than through a blurred lens of comfortable assumptions.

Data visualisation paves a clearer path forward. It allows us to anticipate extreme events, recognise when to act and focus our energies where they will count most. Leaders and policymakers can then make informed decisions, guided not by oversimplified ideals but by evidence presented in ways that clarify risk and opportunity. In translating complexity into accessible, meaningful images, we give ourselves the chance to respond wisely and avert catastrophe.

Ultimately, the greatest value of data visualisation lies not in confirming preconceived notions but in helping us understand the true range of possibilities. The more we rely on visual insight to guide us, the less likely we are to stumble blindly into disaster. In this sense, data visualisation is not just about refining our grasp of risk, but it is also about giving humanity the means to survive the unimaginable. It is a path to both knowledge and endurance.

The story of the normal distribution is not only a testament to human ingenuity but also a reminder of its limitations. While it remains one of science's most powerful tools, we must remember that not all of nature's patterns conform to its elegant shape. As Peter Bernstein reminds us in *Against the Gods*, mastering risk isn't just about measuring it, but it's also about understanding the limits of the tools we use. In an age of increasing uncertainty, this lesson is more important than ever.

KEY TAKEAWAYS

- Despite its beauty and mathematical sophistication, over-reliance on the normal distribution can breed complacency. Human behaviour, particularly in financial markets, frequently produces 'fat-tailed' events that occur far more often than the bell curve predicts.
- While the normal distribution works well for certain natural phenomena, human decision-making is driven by fear, greed and irrational impulses that distort outcomes. Real-world risks cluster and compound, defying the neat symmetry of the bell curve.

- Traditional economic and financial models assumed normal distributions of returns and risk. This led to underestimating the frequency and severity of extreme market events, contributing to financial crises and economic shocks.
- Data visualisation helps us recognise when assumptions fail. By mapping real outcomes and patterns, we can see where risks concentrate, where distributions skew and where rare events loom more frequently than theory would suggest.
- Recognising the limits of the normal distribution and embracing visual methods to explore data ensures we remain alert to the messy, unpredictable nature of human systems. Data visualisation guides us beyond comforting abstractions, forcing us to confront reality on its own terms.
- In an era of unpredictable markets, global pandemics and environmental crises, the lessons from the normal distribution's shortcomings are clear. We need data visualisation to understand our true range of vulnerabilities and make more informed, resilient decisions for the future.

Chapter 8

The Dark Side of the Dial Tone

In the dim glow of their dorm room, Steve Wozniak and Steve Jobs leaned over their prized creation: a small, clunky device that looked like something only a couple of ambitious college kids could dream up. They called it the *blue box*, a contraption that emitted a series of tones capable of tricking the phone system into thinking an operator was on the line. They had spent hours testing it, calling far-flung places for free. But that night, they wanted to push the limits. Wozniak's eyes gleamed mischievously as an idea formed in his mind.

'Let's call the Vatican,' he said, grinning.

Jobs looked at him, incredulous but intrigued. It was one thing to outsmart the phone system for the thrill of making free calls but to dial up the Pope. The idea was so outrageous that it bordered on the absurd, yet it was strangely compelling.

'All right,' Jobs replied, a smile spreading across his face. They would go all out on this one.

Wozniak picked up the receiver and dialled. As the line began to connect, he settled into character, his voice dropping to a solemn, commanding tone. 'This is Henry Kissinger,' he said, putting on his best impression of the American Secretary of State. 'I'm calling on behalf of President Nixon. It is urgent.'

A rapid burst of Italian came from the other end as the operator struggled to make sense of the call. Wozniak pressed on with the ruse, maintaining an air of calm authority as he insisted on speaking directly to His Holiness. He hinted that the fate of international diplomacy hinged on this conversation. Jobs fought back a laugh, but Wozniak stayed composed, his voice steady as the increasingly flustered operator promised to escalate the matter.

Minutes passed and on the other end the sound of shuffling and hushed voices signalled that someone high up was taking the call seriously. The person explained that they would need to wake the Pope. Wozniak and Jobs exchanged a look, barely able to contain their excitement. They had actually convinced the Vatican to wake the Pope in the dead of night.

But just as it seemed like they were about to speak to the leader of the Catholic Church himself, something must have given them away, a hesitation or a trace of youthful enthusiasm that did not quite fit the role of a seasoned diplomat. The line went silent and then, with a curt click, the call was disconnected.

They sat in the quiet of the dorm room, wide-eyed, exhilarated. They had not got through to the Pope, but they had got close enough.

The two future tech titans, who would one day co-found Apple and usher in a new era of personal computing, along with John Draper, had stumbled upon a powerful hack that cracked open the global telecom network.

Draper had introduced them to the Captain Crunch whistle, a toy found in cereal boxes that emitted a 2600 Hz tone – the same frequency used by phone systems to indicate an open long-distance line. Using this, they created a blue box, which is a device that could mimic the tones used by operators to control the phone network. With it, they could navigate long-distance lines undetected, bypassing tolls and plunging into a hidden world of technological mischief and exploration.

The blue box was invented by an 18-year-old student called Ralph Barclay. In the engineering library of Washington State College, he stumbled upon a November 1960 issue of something called the *Bell System Technical Journal*. An article called 'Signaling Systems for Control of Telephone Switching' explained how AT&T's long-distance telephone network worked, and how long-distance switching machines sang to each other with single-frequency and multifrequency tones, plus how 2,600 Hz was used to indicate whether a telephone had answered and much more. He used this to create the blue box that allow his dorm to make free long-distance calls (Lapsley 2014).

The blue box was just one of many ingenious devices used by the 'phreaker' underground community that emerged in 1960s and 1970s. They were a network of tech-savvy hobbyists who delved into the telephone system's hidden workings.

While the *blue box* mimicked operator tones to manipulate long-distance calls, other devices emerged with unique capabilities: the *black box* exploited collect call systems so the recipient would not be charged, the *red box* simulated the sound of coins dropping in pay phones and the *cheese box* rerouted calls through multiple exchanges to obscure their origin. This last trick was heavily used by bookies to secretly reroute their calls to remote locations, enabling them to run illegal gambling operations, which were outlawed due to their association with organised crime and corruption (Lapsley 2014).

Perhaps most notorious though was the *silver box*, a device capable of simulating the tones used by operators to control advanced phone line features and private branch exchanges.

Unlike other phreaking tools, which primarily enabled free calls or anonymous routing, the silver box granted access to internal system functions. With it, users could redirect calls, manipulate lines and step deeper into the network's infrastructure.

The phreakers shared their discoveries through underground newsletters and late-night conference calls using loop lines or a loop around. These were pairs of telephone numbers that telecom companies used to test circuit, which were repurposed by phreakers to host large conference calls. They formed a loose community of technological explorers at the dawn of the personal computing age, before Internet chat rooms existed (Lapsley 2014).

Although their exploits began as curious experiments, they had a profound impact on what would become the future of cybercrime and counterterrorism operations. If you are interested in learning more about this fascinating period in telecommunication history, then have a read of *Exploding the Phone* by Phil Lapsley (Lapsley 2014).

Of course, none of this was new. Across the Iron Curtain, the East German Stasi, masters of surveillance and state control, had been exploiting similar principles long before the phreaker community emerged. Engineers in their secretive Hauptabteilung III division developed devices capable of intercepting calls, monitoring conversations and even tapping into Western phone networks. While their methods served the aims of espionage and state security rather than mischief, they revealed just how vulnerable the world's phone systems were to manipulation (Anderson 2024).

Where Jobs and Wozniak saw a world of possibilities, the Stasi saw the ultimate surveillance tool, a means to monitor dissidents, gather intelligence and control their population. Their technical expertise in telecommunications surveillance surpassed even that of their Soviet allies.

It was clear something had to be done and the telecommunications industry had to act. Their solution was a new signalling protocol called Signalling System No. 7, more commonly known as

SS7. To appreciate what this means, we need to understand what is meant by 'signalling' in telecommunications.

When you place a phone call, two things happen: first, signals are sent through the network to set up the call, telling the switches where to route your connection. Then, once the call is established, your voice travels along a separate channel. In older systems, these signalling messages shared the same path as voice calls, which made it easier for hackers or spies to trick the network, like the pheakers did.

SS7 changed this by introducing out-of-band signalling, meaning the instructions for routing calls were sent along a different route to the voice channels. If you remember that was a big problem with the old system. A 2,600 Hz tone was used to interrupt the signalling process along the same line, allowing phreakers to take control of calls by mimicking the network's internal commands.

SS7 seemingly solved this problem, making eavesdropping harder and preventing unauthorised access. On paper it was the perfect fix.

The Vulnerabilities in a Trust-Based System

However, SS7 came with its own set of issues. Although it separated signalling from the main voice lines, it also lacked robust security measures. There were no strong authentication checks to confirm that a command really came from a legitimate provider, nor were there strict encryption standards to protect the data. This was partly because the telecom world at the time was built on trust between just a handful of mobile phone operators.

Mobile phones were of course still in their infancy, but they were also a disruptive form of technology that later evolved into the smartphone that we have today. Naturally, their arrival meant that the number of these mobile networks rapidly expanded. Therefore, nobody at the time could fully anticipate what weaknesses they SS7 signalling network had.

Intelligence agencies such as the NSA and GCHQ, however, soon found that SS7's out-of-band signalling could still be intercepted and manipulated. Later, criminals and terrorist groups learned to use these same vulnerabilities to track individuals, intercept text messages to bypass two-factor authentication (Thomson 2017).

This last point is particularly unnerving. If you can intercept the text message containing a verification code, you can drain a bank account within minutes. Two-factor authentication is meant to add a layer of security beyond a password, often a code sent by short message service (SMS), but if that SMS can be silently diverted then two-factor authentication is pretty much useless.

Much of SS7's design came from an era when landlines and long-distance calls were at the forefront of telecom technology. It was not intended to help track mobile phones from one cell tower to another when their owners went abroad. But this is what SS7 was adapted to manage, enabling mobile phones to roam on other mobile phone networks so people could travel and still receive calls and messages without interruption. Roaming meant sharing device location data and call-routing instructions between multiple carriers, each trusting the others to handle the information correctly. It was a system built on goodwill, not ironclad security.

This trust-based architecture soon revealed itself to be a structural weakness. Today, there are over 1,200 mobile operators worldwide and not all can be fully trusted. Some operate in countries where corruption is rife, state surveillance is routine and freedom of expression is strictly curtailed. Here, weak regulatory oversight and unchecked criminal activity create opportunities for rogue operators to access the SS7 signalling network. Compounding this risk, individuals within some telecommunications companies have been known to sell illicit access to the SS7 signalling network on the black market, further undermining its security and exposing the entire system to vulnerabilities.

The problem is that if you can persuade the network that you are a legitimate telecom operator or piggyback on the access granted to a real provider, you can send the same commands they do. You can find out which tower a phone is connected to, reroute texts or calls and piece together someone's movements.

Over time, hackers refined these techniques. They stopped caring about long-distance toll fraud and instead focused on personal data and valuable financial information passing through mobile phones. Governments used these vulnerabilities for surveillance, companies employed them for industrial espionage and cybercriminals turned them into a lucrative racket. It was a Pandora's box that SS7 had inadvertently cracked open.

Clear visual evidence began to expose these flaws about a decade ago. At the Chaos Communication Congress in 2014, researchers Karsten Nohl and Tobias Engel demonstrated how visualising SS7 traffic flows could uncover signalling anomalies and reveal systemic weaknesses. Their findings highlighted vulnerabilities that allowed attackers to intercept calls, track mobile devices and manipulate messaging systems (Leyden and Rockman 2014).

The revelations sparked a wave of reforms across the telecommunications industry. Mobile operators began introducing stronger authentication checks for SS7 network access, implementing enhanced encryption protocols to safeguard messages and collaborating with cybersecurity experts to monitor for unusual activity (Saadatmandi 2015).

Real-world incidents also soon showed just how serious this danger had become. In 2017, attackers in Germany exploited SS7 to intercept two-factor authentication codes sent by SMS. They bypassed security measures and drained victims' bank accounts within minutes (Thomson 2017).

In 2016, Norway's Telenor network faced a major disruption that left over a million customers – nearly a third of its user base – without service for hours. The incident was caused by irregular SS7 signalling messages originating from an external operator conducting security tests, which overwhelmed Telenor's network systems. This event underscored how vulnerabilities in the SS7 signalling network could destabilise entire telecommunications systems, even unintentionally (McDaid 2016).

Perhaps the most alarming example was the Greek wiretapping scandal of 2005. Attackers gained access to the Greek phone network via SS7 and secretly listened to top government officials including the Prime Minister for months (Prevelakis and Spinellis 2007).

Data visualisation has been essential for revealing the hidden vulnerabilities of the SS7 signalling network. Mobile phone operators use visualisation techniques to monitor the vast flow of data within their telecommunication systems. By mapping spikes in signalling requests or unusual roaming queries geographically, they can quickly detect suspicious activity and identify where attackers originate from. This allows operators to pinpoint security weaknesses, address problems early and block SS7 attacks before they occur.

However, this isn't perfect, and SS7 attacks still frequently get through. Part of the problem is that intelligence agencies actively exploit SS7 vulnerabilities because it is an excellent tool for surveillance and tracking, particularly when monitoring terrorist activity. While this may serve a greater purpose, such as protecting national security, it remains a deeply controversial practice. It undermines public trust in communication networks and raises concerns about abuse of power and violations of privacy for ordinary citizens.

Privacy, in its most fundamental sense, is the ability to think, communicate and evolve without external coercion. For our species to thrive, we must preserve the capacity for introspection and experimentation. Privacy ensures that individuals can form and test new ideas, free from the paralysing fear of constant oversight. When intellectual exploration and moral reasoning occur in private, they can mature before being presented to a broader audience. In open, democratic societies, this process is essential for cultural richness.

However, we must also defend our freedoms from those who seek to undermine society, such as terrorists. The challenge lies in achieving this without sacrificing civil liberties and privacy. True security does not require us to abandon the principles that allow societies to flourish; rather, it demands careful, deliberate measures that protect both safety and the individual's right to think, communicate and explore freely. If we fail to strike this balance, we risk eroding the very freedoms we aim to preserve.

As I've mentioned throughout this book, it's not the amount of data you collect that matters. There is already far too much data pollution in this world, which potentially holds more valuable information than aggressive surveillance techniques ever provide. Moreover, lapses in intelligence analysis usually occur due to failures caused by cognitive biases rather than a lack of collected data. But we will come back to this later in this chapter.

For now, I want you to listen to this story.

Detective Sarah Harrison stared at the wall, her fingers tracing the red string that connected Marcus Flynn's mugshot to the bloodied crime scene photo. Her partner, DS Tom Whitaker, stood beside her, arms crossed, his weathered face lit up by the harsh fluorescent lights of their incident room.

'Look at this web we've woven,' Sarah muttered, tapping the crossed-out photograph of their first suspect that was now eliminated after a concrete alibi emerged. 'Three months of investigating and Flynn keeps appearing in the middle of every lead.'

Tom stepped closer and examined an old newspaper clipping linked by string to the suspect. It was about a similar case from five years ago. 'Perhaps we've been looking at this wrong,' he said, reaching up to reposition the string connecting two surveillance photos. 'What if Flynn isn't the spider at the centre of this web, but the fly that led us to something bigger?'

Sarah's eyes widened as she followed the connections that Tom had created. The wall of evidence suddenly seemed to whisper its secrets, and the hairs on the back of her neck stood up. After all these months, they might finally have cracked it.

It is a pretty familiar scene if you like detective series. At the heart of it is a form of data visualisation that really deserves more credit and it should be familiar to you. It is, in fact, an incredibly important form of data visualisation used in counterterrorism. What you will note is that it's not about the data that has been collected but rather how you visually link and map the pieces together.

Intelligence agencies and analysts need to sort through vast amounts of raw information – transaction logs, phone records, social media posts and more – to spot warning signs. They have to somehow tie these scattered fragments together and to do so they often use a special form of data visualisation – the network graph.

When we begin this chapter, we told you a brief story and some history about the 1960s and 1970s phreaker community. Their remarkable success came from their ability to visualise and comprehend the telephone network. From trial and error they linked and mapped the network by figuring out how the signing system worked so they could use it to their advantage. By doing this, they understood the workings of the phone system and gained unprecedented control over what was meant to be a secure communication network during the Cold War. They had built their own network graph.

The network graph is a very powerful form of data visualisation that shows how things or people are connected. Take a look at the data visualisation illustrated in Figure 8.1. This is an example of a terrorist network, taken from an academic study carried out by Yao-Li Chuang and Maria R. D'Orsogna from California State University.

The dots, called nodes, represent terrorists. The black lines are called connectors. They show the relationships between the terrorists, such as who talks to whom, who shares ideas or who works together. These network graphs can help reveal patterns, such as who is the most connected or influential within the group.

Acquiring the data and cleaning it to create these network graphs is just as interesting. An analyst might examine thousands of

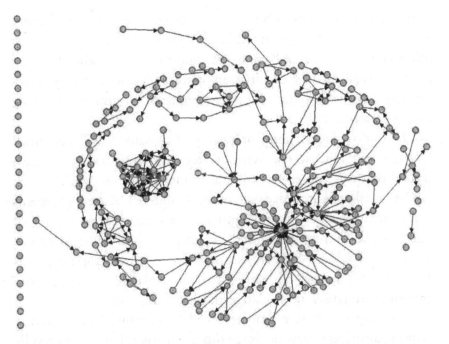

Figure 8.1 Visualising a terrorist network by identifying key actors and connections. The material will be used in the above-mentioned book, in print and electronic formats, for educational and illustrative purposes. Full credit and acknowledgment will be provided as follows.
Source: Maria R. D'Orsogna, 2019/arXiv.

phone calls linked to suspected extremist groups to create a network chart just like this.

For example, imagine an analyst examining thousands of phone calls linked to a suspected extremist group. Each record – a person phoning another at a certain time – is not very revealing on its own. When you visualise these calls as a network of points linked by lines connected to nodes, patterns reveal themselves.

Some individuals may appear as hubs because many calls pass through them as the network diagram we have shown shows. These might be leaders who coordinate different members of the group, or messengers who connect otherwise isolated clusters. These central figures often hold the group together or connect otherwise isolated members. Removing them – whether through arrests, surveillance or elimination – can break the network apart, making it harder for the group to operate or coordinate (Chuang and D'Orsogna 2019).

This is where it gets interesting. The same two academics, Chuang and D'Orsogna, who created this network graph have argued that this can reveal 'tipping points' in the network, which can be calculated through mathematical models. There are moments when small changes, like a slight rise in extremist messaging or shifts in community dynamics, can cause radical ideas to spread quickly and widely. If analysts know where these tipping points occur, they can step in earlier to stop isolated incidents from growing into larger, more dangerous network graphs.

Focusing on these connectors and community leaders, rather than monitoring everyone, is far more effective than mass surveillance. Moreover, it doesn't lead to the same level of privacy issues.

Concrete examples help make this clearer. Consider tracking suspicious financial transactions for a terrorist cell operating in a city. The raw data might list only dates, amounts and account numbers. Visualise this information on a map with points showing transaction locations and colours indicating amounts, and you might see that unexplained money flows cluster around a certain neighbourhood at regular intervals. This could suggest the location of a safe house or meeting point. Knowing this, security forces can investigate the area, check local closed-circuit television footage and possibly prevent an attack. The network collapses because the source of the network has gone, reducing the risk of another terrorist attack occurring.

Network graphs are not the only type of data visualisation used in counterterrorism. Geospatial data visualisations can also predict where future threats are likely to occur. Suppose recent attacks have happened near major rail stations. At the same time, intercepted communications suggest increased extremist interest in another similar transport hub. Mapping this intelligence against known safe houses or suspected meeting places reveals patterns. The authorities can then position their resources more effectively, placing patrols near that station before any incident unfolds.

Open-source intelligence – otherwise known in the intelligence community as OSINT – also benefits from data visualisation. This is information gathered from publicly available sources such as news articles, social media, websites or public records. It's used to investigate or understand situations without relying on secret or classified information, reducing the need for heavy handed surveillance.

Consider how extremist propaganda spreads online. Without a visual map, it may be difficult to see which videos, messages or posts gain traction. By plotting the path of a certain piece of content through social networks – noting who shares it, how it travels from one group to another and which topics trigger the most responses – analysts can identify where extremist messaging takes root. They can then intervene, for instance, by working with platform operators to remove or counter the harmful content before it influences more users.

All these approaches depend on algorithms and predictive models, but their value lies in how well their findings are visualised. For example, a model might reveal a link between specific behaviours and increased terrorist activity. However, without clear visuals – like a chart showing spikes in suspicious activity on certain dates or a map highlighting areas of rising tension – it becomes harder for decision-makers to respond swiftly. In a crisis, they need straightforward, accessible data presented in a way that guides their actions effectively. That's why data visualisation is so important.

Used responsibly, data visualisation can save lives while preserving the freedoms it seeks to protect. However, even with strict ethical standards, there is the issue of how analysts interpret and act on the intelligence these tools provide. No matter how advanced, data visualisations are shaped by human influence. The insights they offer are filtered through the analysts' own cognitive biases, beliefs and assumptions. This is where Richards J. Heuer Jr.'s work in *Psychology of Intelligence Analysis* becomes especially relevant (Heuer 2018).

Heuer highlights the ways in which cognitive biases and mental shortcuts can distort how intelligence professionals interpret complex information. His emphasis is on understanding the human element of intelligence work, reminding us that analysts are not passive receivers of data but active interpreters shaped by their experiences and expectations. Data visualisation can play a vital role here by acting as a cognitive aid that helps counter these biases.

For instance, consider confirmation bias – the tendency to seek and value information that supports an analyst's existing beliefs. It can completely shape their perspective. Without a visual guide, an analyst might focus narrowly on pieces of intelligence that confirm suspicions about a certain individual or group. A well-structured network diagram, however, can reveal overlooked connections or significant outliers. The analyst can then see patterns that contradict prior assumptions, prompting a more balanced view of the entire intelligence picture. By visually presenting all relevant data points, rather than just those that fit a familiar narrative, data visualisations encourage analysts to question their assumptions and think more broadly.

Heuer emphasises the importance of structured thinking and systematic methods, which data visualisation tools make possible. These tools turn messy data, like long lists of phone records or financial transactions, into clear data visualisations such as timelines, charts or maps. For example, instead of combing through spreadsheets, an analyst can use a timeline to identify a sudden spike in calls around a particular event or a map to see clusters of suspicious activity in specific locations. This visual organisation helps simplify complex problems, allowing analysts to compare different explanations or theories side by side.

Take financial crimes as an example. An analyst might overlay data on suspicious transactions onto a city map and compare it with known movement patterns of suspects. This makes it easier to see which explanation fits the data best, whether the transactions align with the suspects' locations or suggest a different route entirely.

Heuer also highlights the challenge of incomplete or unclear information. Data visualisations can help by showing where the gaps are, like missing links in a network or unexplained deviations in financial flows. When these inconsistencies stand out on a graph or map, they prompt analysts to investigate further, gather more information or test new ideas. This process encourages deeper, more methodical analysis, improving the chances of reaching accurate conclusions.

There is another aspect here, which we have already discussed in this book. Data visualisation isn't just about deploying information, but it is also about a powerful storytelling tool and one of the most powerful forms of human communication. A data visualisation is much easier to share and understand than a dense technical report. An intelligence analyst and a policymaker might have varying levels of technical expertise, but both can understand a data visualisation, which can help them understand evolving threats quickly.

A clear, focused chart or map can communicate complex information at a glance. As Heuer emphasises, effective communication is crucial in intelligence work. Data visualisation serves as a common language that bridges the gap between those who specialise in gathering and interpreting data (analysts) and those who must act on intelligence briefings (politicians). Whether it is highlighting the vulnerability of a signalling network, showing the likely location of an insurgent group's hideout or mapping areas where extremist propaganda flourishes online, data visualisation provides decision-makers with insights they can trust and understand immediately.

In terms of predictive analytics – an area where intelligence agencies use algorithms and models to forecast threats – data visualisation has again proved invaluable. Predictive models may suggest that particular individuals or groups are likely to pose a risk, or that certain neighbourhoods are set to become hotspots of extremist activity. While these outputs might be hidden in lines of code or statistical tables, data visualisation can bring them into the open by mapping where those threats are emerging, when risk levels spike or how different factors interact over time. As a result, decision-makers can focus resources more efficiently, deploy intervention teams more strategically and respond to threats before they materialise.

In short, data visualisation can help intelligence analysts recognise their own biases, organise information more effectively and interpret uncertain data with greater clarity. These tools encourage a more structured, critical and balanced approach to intelligence work. They help ensure that when analysts face important decisions with significant consequences, the information guiding them is not only plentiful but also accessible, easy to understand and reliable.

Yet, as discussed in Chapter 6, data visualisation can be a double-edged sword. While it can reveal hidden patterns, it can also distort reality if crafted or interpreted carelessly. The same cognitive biases that economists, analysts and politicians struggle with – confirmation bias, framing effects and groupthink – may be magnified when data is presented in visual form. A chart or network diagram can lend undue authority to a flawed conclusion – making it seem far more concrete than a paragraph of text ever could.

We have seen how theoretical models and elegant narratives can crumble when confronted with complexity. Economics teaches us that patterns may be fleeting and assumptions easily overturned. Intelligence analysis, as Heuer highlighted, is no different. The human mind craves coherence, hunts for patterns and often clings to familiar explanations even when the evidence suggests otherwise.

This is the paradox: thoughtfully applied data visualisation can help counter biases by making discrepancies and anomalies painfully visible. It can highlight not only what we see, but also what we overlook. At the same time, when handled without care, the clarity and immediacy that make a data visualisation so compelling can lull analysts into complacency. Instead of challenging preconceptions, poorly examined visuals may only strengthen them.

The lessons from economics, intelligence studies and our earlier examination of cognitive biases converge here. It is not enough to produce more charts, maps and network diagrams; we need to interpret them to see what they show. Just as economists must accept that their theories are not blueprints for an unchanging world, intelligence analysts must remember that each data visualisation is an abstraction. Every choice – what data to include, how to categorise information and which patterns to emphasise – shapes the story that unfolds on the screen.

Cultivating a habit of critical engagement is key. Analysts, politicians and their teams should consider what has been excluded from a given visual, why certain data points appear most salient and whether a different presentation might reveal a different story.

We need to remain vigilant. In intelligence work, as in economics, humility and adaptability are crucial. No matter how advanced our tools become or how skilfully we display data, the human mind remains vulnerable to error.

Handled responsibly, data visualisation can alert intelligence agencies to emerging dangers, help track the global spread of disease and uncover early indicators of food insecurity or potential mass migration. In other words, it can guide us away from the brink of our own self-destruction.

If we learn to read these visual clues without succumbing to illusion, and if we remain humble and vigilant in the face of our biases, then data visualisation can serve as a compass. It can point us towards a future where we do not merely survive but thrive. Used wisely, it may help us understand and address the existential threats we face. In that sense, data visualisation benefits not only intelligence agencies, but also anyone who relies on human ingenuity to navigate the uncertain path ahead.

KEY TAKEAWAYS

- Data visualisation techniques – such as network diagrams, heat maps and time-series plots – enable telecom operators and intelligence agencies to identify anomalies, locate threats and intervene before crises unfold.
- Ethical issues arise when governments or institutions use these vulnerabilities and visual tools for surveillance, highlighting the importance of oversight, accountability and the protection of civil liberties.
- In counterterrorism, visualising communication networks, financial transactions and geospatial patterns helps analysts spot key individuals, predict attacks and respond more effectively.
- Heuer's insights into cognitive biases emphasise that visualisations can both clarify and distort understanding. They can not only counter biases by revealing hidden patterns but also risk reinforcing preconceived notions if handled carelessly.
- Building on lessons from Chapter 6, embracing humility and critical thinking ensures that data visualisation does not become a misleading crutch, but a tool that encourages curiosity and challenges assumptions.
- Ultimately, responsible data visualisation not only aids in tackling threats such as terrorism or cybercrime but can also guide humanity towards addressing existential challenges. By making complexity visible and actionable, it can help protect human life and support our long-term survival.

Chapter 9

Visualising the Climate War

I stood motionless at the summit of Moosfluh, my heart thumping as I gazed down across the pristine ski piste. A decade ago, I would never have imagined myself here – at thirty-something transplanted into Switzerland by chance and now about to attempt my first venture down this very slope.

'Ready?' Hans Peter said grinning in his deeply Swiss-German accented English. His weathered face creasing into a knowing smile. At sixty-something, he was a mountain sage who wore his years of experience like a badge of honour. No helmet for him – just a bandana, his silver hair peeking out at the sides.

'Just ... just taking it all in,' I replied, my breath visible in the cold air.

'Stop!' he suddenly commanded, pointing his ski pole behind his head in the opposite direction. 'Come with me. We go here first. I want to show you something.'

As we walked towards a nearby viewpoint, he spoke, his voice softening with memory. 'Remember that big house earlier? That's where I grew up. My parents worked there. We were surrounded by all this beauty.'

Below revealed a huge, majestic glacier covered in winter snow, yet clearly visible.

'The Aletsch,' he continued, his tone changing. 'When I was a boy, it reached almost two kilometres further down that valley. See!' He fell silent for a moment. 'People can argue about many things, but this ...' he gestured at the retreating ice 'this I've seen with my own eyes. The world is changing, but we are not.'

The Aletsch Glacier, the largest in the Alps, is not just a breathtaking spectacle, but it's also a visual testament to global warming. This river of ice, a sculptor of the Alpine landscape over millennia, is shrinking at an alarming rate. While it has lost 3.2 km since 1870, a staggering 1.3 km of that retreat occurred since 1980. In 2006 alone, it pulled back more than 100 m. Scientists warn that this glacier could lose up to 90% of its ice mass by the end of this century.

The glacier that once snaked all the way down that valley now withers day by day. Satellite measurements reveal it sheds over one billion tonnes of ice each year. Every droplet of meltwater carries away not just ancient ice, but also millennia of climate history encoded in its frozen layers. This is not just a Swiss problem either, but it's also a global story written in the ice of that ancient glacier, one that we need to see if we want any hope of changing it.

Cutting Through Climate Data Overload

Most people today accept that climate change is real and urgent. We have moved beyond basic awareness. The challenge is now twofold: the sheer scale of what we are facing and the ease with which our attention drifts in a world overloaded with information. Why focus on climate change when wars are raging in the Middle

East and Ukraine, tensions are rising between the United States and China, while our minds are already stretched thin?

The sheer volume of data exacerbates the problem. We are bombarded with temperature trends, emissions estimates, ice loss measurements and sea level forecasts. The complexity is not just in the science, but it is also woven into politics, economics, human behaviour and the fragile balance of the systems that keep our world stable. This torrent of facts, coming from every angle, can lead to a sense of paralysis, even despair. How can we possibly grasp, let alone solve, such a multifaceted crisis?

A big part of the solution lies in how we communicate that data. Charts and statistics mean nothing if they do not connect with our senses or provoke an emotional response. This is a constant struggle I face with my own clients. It is never just about the fancy tech, sleek graphics or mood-setting music. What makes information resonate in my data visualisations is the story it tells and how that story makes people feel. That is the art to good data visualisation.

Data visualisation has the power to cut through the noise and make climate change tangible, relatable and actionable. It's about transforming raw data into compelling stories that speak to both our intellect and our emotions. Consider the now-iconic 'warming stripes' created by climate scientist Ed Hawkins. You have to see it in colour to really appreciate it. If you have a smartphone or laptop nearby, just Google it. There are many variations now, but they all tell the same story. Each stripe represents a year's average global temperature, colour-coded from blue (cooler) to red (warmer).

No words are necessary. The visual progression from cool blues to fiery reds is a powerful, intuitive representation of our planet's warming trend. It's a visceral experience that transcends language barriers and scientific jargon. Have a look at the chart shown in Figure 9.1. You get the underlying message here within seconds: our planet is heating up. Just look at 2016.

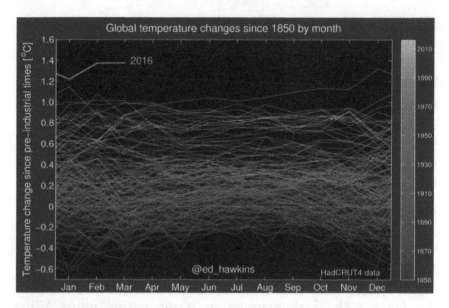

Figure 9.1 Global temperature changes since 1850 by month
Source: Ed Hawkins, climate scientists at the University of Reading/Wikimedia Commons/CC BY SA-4.0.

Interestingly, when Ed Hawkins published this chart, it was in colour. But you don't need to see it in colour to understand the message it conveys.

But it's not just about aesthetics. Effective data visualisation uses principles of cognitive psychology and visual perception to maximise impact. Warm colours such as red and orange evoke urgency and danger, while cool colours like blue can represent calmness or the past. In financial data visualisation, I reverse this colour scheme: shades of red signal negative returns, while shades of blue indicate positive performance. Nevertheless, the emotional impact and subtle signalling achieve the same effect.

The strategic use of colour gradients works so well because it can instantly convey trends and even be used to highlight anomalies. Choosing the right type of presentation is also very important and can impact how you use colour. There are actually many different types of line charts you can create: static, animated and interactive. And each will have an impact on how you use colour.

When Animation Speaks Louder than Words

Carbon Brief's data visualisations demonstrate temperature warming through a gradient effect, although you cannot see that here in black and white. Figures 9.2 and 9.3 plot calendar years of temperature records from 1940 onwards. I've created an animated version of Figure 9.3 myself. The animation allows me to reveal each year's temperature line sequentially, displaying both the year and its monthly temperatures as it unfolds. As each calendar year completes, its line remains on the chart, either dimmed or thinned,

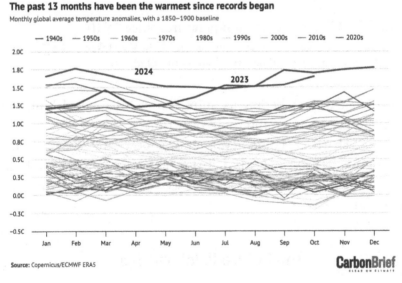

Figure 9.2 Monthly global average temperature anomalies
Source: Reproduced from State of the Climate: 2024 Now Very Likely to Be Warmest Year on Record.' Chart by Carbon Brief/Carbon Brief Ltd.

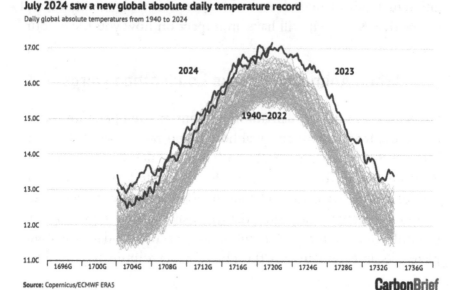

Figure 9.3 Global average temperatures since 1940
Source: Reproduced from 'State of the Climate: 2024 Now Very Likely to Be Warmest Year on Record.' Chart by Carbon Brief/Carbon Brief Ltd.

while the next year begins its animation. This gradual build-up reveals the Earth's warming trend over time.

These charts become even more powerful when made interactive – exactly as Carbon Brief has done on their website. Viewers can hover over any year to see specific temperatures for that period.

The Future Is Interactive

Figure 9.4 demonstrates a particularly effective interactive design. Its heat map features an intuitive interface that lets viewers zoom in to examine monthly temperature data points while maintaining the context of the calendar year. The colour gradient cleverly captures warming trends on a monthly basis, making complex

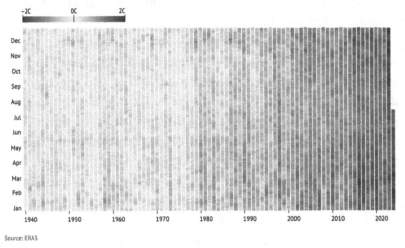

How daily average global temperatures have warmed since 1940
Compared to 1850–1900 average

Source: ERA5

Heat map of daily temperatures for each day from 1940 to present (22 Jul. 2024) from Copernicus/ECMWF ERA5. Anomalies plotted with respect to a 1850–1900 baseline. Chart by Carbon Brief.

Figure 9.4 Global average temperatures since 1940
Source: Reproduced from State of the Climate: 2024 Now Very Likely to Be Warmest Year on Record.' Chart by Carbon Brief/Carbon Brief Ltd.

temperature patterns immediately clear when you view it as a static data visualisation.

In my opinion, it is the most effective of the three. However, it may not necessarily be the most impactful. This is important to consider. I chose to animate Figure 9.3 because I knew it would instantly grab attention and communicate the point I wanted to get across – the Earth is warming. As a communication tool it was far more powerful than Figure 9.4, even though it is less precise.

I actually posted Figure 9.4 as well, but it didn't get nearly the same level of engagement as the animated version of Figure 9.3.

This is a point that I feel needs addressing. Some in the data science community shun animated data visualisation because it sacrifices precision, accuracy and scientific interpretation. But when you are trying to get a point across quickly on social media, you are in a thinking fast game, where the viewer may not have the cognitive bandwidth to fully understand the granular depth of information that you have.

In this situation, the objective is to get the point across as quickly as possible to as many people as you can. You want that data visualisation to go viral, get copied, shared and reposted to as many people in an ever-expanding network graph of connections that benefit from that message. If you want to warn people about climate change, this is what you must do. You don't have time to expect your audience to care about the same level of data precision and data exploration as you do. You want to grab your audience by the lapels and say, 'listen to me, you will lose everything if you don't act now – the climate is warming!'

The type of chart you use matters a lot. Line graphs excel at showing trends over time because they present the entire data set at once. You can see both past and present, making comparisons easily if you wish. And when it comes to animating line charts, you have multiple options.

You can create charts as shown in Figures 9.2 and 9.3, where each calendar year's line reveals the rising temperature trend through animation. Alternatively, you could design an exploding line chart that expands along the x-axis and adjusts the y-axis whenever the line reaches a new maximum. This second type that I have described is the one I use most frequently. The exploding line chart has proved so engaging because the line appears alive. The motion seems to capture attention.

Other types of charts can be equally powerful. Bar charts excel at comparing different categories with precision. Traditionally, as a static data visualisation, the bar chart has been one of the most precise and robust data visualisation formats you can produce, offering far more accuracy and elegance than alternatives like pie charts.

While a standard bar chart does not typically capture time-series data like a line chart, there is one notable exception – the animated bar chart race. Though it cannot preserve past data points in the same way a line chart does, it can still convey time-series information through animation. What makes these visualisations so compelling is their ability to show how rankings evolve over time, revealing powerful stories that hold the viewer's attention. If you don't know what I am talking about, or you are finding it hard to visualise what I am describing, just search for bar chart races on YouTube.

As a communication tool, racing bar charts have arguably been one of the most effective forms of animated data visualisation to date. At one point, bar chart races were apparently demonetised on YouTube and their popularity has led to controversy. They were even banned on some subreddits, like 'Data is Beautiful' and remain a contentious form of data visualisation among data scientists.

Criticisms generally focus on them being distracting, hard to follow or too focused on rankings rather than absolute values. Yet these shortcomings often stem from poor design rather than inherent flaws. Edward Tufte's critiques of chartjunk are particularly relevant here, reminding us that careful attention to clarity and purpose is key.

When designed well, however, bar chart races can highlight trends in a more engaging and memorable way. Concerns about tracking moving bars or emphasising rank over values become less significant if the goal is to convey an urgent message, such as the unfolding realities of climate change.

To enhance the story within a bar chart race, you can limit the number of categories, use clear labels and add annotations where needed. While bar chart races are not ideal for deep analysis of complex datasets, that is not their purpose: they are a powerful storytelling tool that can capture the imagination of an audience very quickly, which is especially useful if the message being delivered is important.

Another powerful type of data visualisation for tackling climate change is maps. This should be unsurprising as they are among the oldest forms of data visualisation known to humankind. Remember the *Imago Mundi*?

An animated or interactive map can show how wildfires spread, how global temperatures change over time or how deforestation intensifies in the Amazon Rainforest. Interactive maps are especially powerful because they let users explore different scenarios and zoom into specific areas. Just as people often browse Google Maps and Street View for enjoyment, interactive climate maps create a similar sense of discovery, inviting you to explore the data more intimately and making it both memorable and impactful.

Emphasis on data exploration is key. Data visualisation, whether a chart, an animated graphic or an interactive map, relies on more than just acquiring and cleaning data. It also involves uncovering the story hidden within. In fact, data exploration is one of the most crucial components of this process. Typically, a data visualisation project follows three phases: data acquisition, data exploration and finally data presentation. What we are focusing on here is that central step – discovering patterns, insights and stories within the data.

This exploration can happen in two ways. First, the creator of the visualisation can thoroughly investigate the dataset, identifying the story they wish to convey. Alternatively, data exploration can be handed over to the audience. By designing an interactive data visualisation, users can examine the information themselves, finding their own patterns and insights that might otherwise remain hidden. In doing so, data visualisations enable viewers to derive personal meaning from data, deepening engagement and fostering a richer understanding of the subject.

Interactive data visualisations give them the ability to find out and see for themselves what that story is about, by allowing them to move their cursor over the data visualisation. This is why I now believe that the most powerful form of data visualisation is one that you can interact with, search through and discover with very little guidance.

Although I am more widely known for my animated data visualisations, my true love lies with those that are interactive. I do build these myself. In fact, I do them all the time for my clients. I only use animation because I am limited by the technology offered by social media platforms.

You cannot embed code into a social media platform post, but you can embed video, and this is why I tend to rely on either video or static data visualisations. However, interaction is very much the future of data visualisation, and if you look at the stories produced by Carbon Brief, you will find you can interact with their charts and even see the underlying data points when you run your cursor over them. The beauty is that you instantly see and feel the information in front of you. You no longer need a detailed explanation of what the colours mean because you can discover this for yourself by searching and feeling your way through these data visualisations.

I think this is incredible because it allows people to interpret data for themselves.

When I posted my own work on Reddit or LinkedIn, the part I value most is the comments I receive. These responses are data, revealing the views and perspective from my followers that I might never otherwise have discovered myself.

This is the twenty-first century of data visualisation. We are only just scratching the surface of what we can achieve, and so I am always hesitant to confine myself to the conventional wisdom prescribed by the traditional data science community. If we are genuinely going to challenge issues like climate change, we need to open our minds to how we treat data and how we view it. More importantly, though, we need to improve how we communicate with it.

Only then can we truly tackle the problems we face. We need everyone to be able to access data, to feel it, to explore it and to know what it means. This is what we must do. We must do it now if we want to prepare ourselves mentally to make those tough decisions that will help us live more sustainably in the future.

Shining a Light on Climate Injustice

For instance, data visualisation can do more than just illustrate the effects of global warming; it can reveal the deeper injustices behind climate change that have been ignored for far too long. We speak so simply about climate change because we are not cognitively prepared for the complexity it entails. Yet data visualisation can create and present a much richer story that our minds can absorb and understand, preparing us to make the right decision now and not later.

Climate change is not a black-and-white story. It is not simply about right or wrong, or good versus evil. It cannot be reduced to the simplistic moral outrage of a social media post, nor should it ever be treated as a momentary meme like a passing remark. Climate change threatens the survival of our species. We must take it seriously and use every tool at our disposal to communicate this risk, including data visualisation.

What data visualisation does is dare us to look closer. It is not merely about numbers and charts but about shining a light on uncomfortable truths. Maps, graphs and other visual tools can lay bare the brutal disparities of climate change, showing at a glance who suffers the most, who caused the problem and who continues to benefit. Once confronted by these images, we can no longer claim ignorance. We must acknowledge that as the atmosphere warms, some will pay a far higher price than others.

Consider the wealthy nations of Western Europe and North America. Their fortunes were built during the Industrial Revolution and much of the twentieth century, a time when they freely burned through the planet's carbon reserves. A well-chosen data visualisation – a historical emissions chart or a global heat map – makes it clear how these countries soared to prosperity by relying on fossil fuels. Today, they appear shielded behind their wealth and infrastructure that they previously created by burning fossil fuel. This has left them better positioned to adapt to a lower-carbon future.

But what about those regions of the world that suffer through no fault of their own?

In the Sahel, satellite imagery and drought indices reveal fields shrivelling beneath a relentless sun. In Tuvalu, the Maldives and countless other low-lying islands, elevation maps and tide gauges show rising seas threatening to wash entire communities from their homes. These people did not spark this crisis, yet each data point and carefully plotted line show that they bear consequences they never asked for. This is climate injustice made visible: those least responsible are forced into the fiercest struggle against the damage created elsewhere.

Meanwhile, the West often points proudly to declining emissions and investments in renewables. Data visualisation, however, can also trace another telling line – the path by which we outsourced our dirtiest industries to emerging markets. By overlaying trade flows with emissions data, we see how we imported comfort and luxury while exporting environmental costs. Our age of unprecedented wealth, as the figures confirm, rested on a hidden transaction that mortgaged the planet's future.

Now, as interactive charts highlight decades of skyrocketing carbon dioxide levels and maps pinpoint the world's most vulnerable regions, we stand before a moral reckoning. The data tells a story of shared responsibility and unfulfilled promises. Emerging economies now seek what we once claimed for ourselves: prosperity and opportunity. Is it fair to deny them the path we took, simply because we have already overspent our carbon budget?

These visuals – maps of emissions and floods, and charts of deforestation and drought – refuse to let us look away. They distil complexity into patterns we can understand, reminding us that behind every pixel lies a human story. If we truly absorb what these data visualisations reveal, perhaps we can find the will to change course. Our comfort came at a cost. Only by facing that cost, laid out so vividly before us, can we begin to forge a fairer way forward?

But understanding this alone is not enough. We must also find ways to communicate such complex issues effectively. In our modern age, data visualisation can achieve what words alone cannot. It allows us to convey intricate ideas in ways that feel deeply human and innately familiar, akin to the cave paintings and ancient maps that once guided our ancestors. Why should we not use these tools now, when the stakes are so high?

The carbon in our atmosphere is not our only poison – we are also choking on data. While the climate crisis demands urgent action, we find ourselves paralysed by information overload. Our inability to cut through the noise and see what truly matters is no mere inconvenience; it is the barrier preventing us from taking meaningful action on every existential threat we face.

We do not risk becoming obsolete in an age of artificial intelligence – we risk forgetting who we truly are. Humans were never meant to be walking databases. We were made to dream, to understand and to care. Our purpose is not to know everything, but to use what we know wisely, ensuring the Earth remains a home worth inheriting.

To do this, we must embrace the tools at our disposal – our technology, ingenuity and innate resilience. We are an extraordinary species that has always risen above its limitations, from the first wheel to the first written word. But we must listen, adapt, debate, explore, discover, solve, resolve and push on because that's what human do.

Burning Embers and the Paris Agreement

When climate scientists first unveiled their colour-coded diagram showing how global climate risks escalate with rising temperatures, they couldn't have predicted its lasting impact. Created decades ago, this data visualisation still influences climate science today.

The diagram, aptly named 'The Burning Embers', was developed for the IPCC's Third Assessment Report in 2001 (McCarthy, et al. 2001). Its purpose was elegant yet ambitious – to capture in a single, intuitive image the mounting dangers our planet faces as temperatures rise.

Burning Embers divides climate risks into five distinct pillars, called Reasons For Concern: 'Unique and Threatened Systems', 'Extreme Weather Events', 'Distribution of Impacts', 'Global Aggregate Impacts' and 'Large-Scale Singular Events'.

In 2001, the IPCC thought warming of about 2°C would keep risks relatively moderate, with only gradual increases for unique and threatened systems. But as our understanding grew, this view changed dramatically. By 2009, their next version acknowledged that '2°C' was no longer safe, with more embers igniting on the diagram (Golnaraghi 2009).

The 2014 version added purple hues to show even greater danger, signalling that risks were intensifying at lower temperatures than previously thought.

Today's latest IPCC Assessment Report paints an even starker picture. Higher risks now occur at lower temperatures across all five areas. Warm-water corals, for example, entered the high-risk zone at just 1.1°C of warming. This shift shows that even the 1.5°C target, while crucial, carries significant dangers. The darker, more intense colours serve as a clear warning: we're approaching – and in some cases have already crossed – critical thresholds that seemed distant in 2001.

The evolution of Burning Embers shows how powerful data visualisation can be in communicating climate threats. Each IPCC update brought greater urgency, using visual changes to make rising temperatures feel real and immediate. Take the fifth pillar: in 2001, risks of major events like ice-sheet collapse were thought to become severe at around 5.5°C of warming. By 2018, new evidence about ice-sheet loss meant this threshold had dropped below 2 °C. The changing colours of the embers made these insights both clear and compelling (Masson-Delmotte et al. 2018).

This data visualisation has proven invaluable to climate science. It transforms complex scientific findings into images that everyone can understand and feel. The diagram's evolving colours and structured pillars help both scientists and the public grasp climate risks at a glance, highlighting where urgent action is needed to prevent crossing points of no return.

Another example is Al Gore's 2006 documentary *An Inconvenient Truth*, which used data visualisation as part of its strategy to communicate climate change to the public.

While the film's story moved audiences, its use of data visualisations was extremely powerful, especially the famous 'hockey stick' graph.

This graph, created by climate scientist Michael E. Mann and his team, showed global temperatures over the past thousand years (Figure 9.5) (Mann and Bradley 1999). For centuries, the line barely moved – then, as industry arose, it shot upwards like the blade of a hockey stick. This single image captured the film's core message: human activity since industrialisation has dramatically altered our planet's climate.

The graph's power came from its simplicity. It turned complex science into something anyone could grasp. Global warming was no longer abstract – it became a clear, undeniable trend. *An Inconvenient Truth* brought this stark message into homes worldwide, winning two Academy Awards and commercial success. But its real achievement was changing minds. Surveys showed most viewers came away with a new understanding of climate change's reality and urgency. The film sparked educational programmes, energised environmental activism and shifted how society viewed climate change.

Such a powerful message inevitably faced criticism. Some questioned certain claims, arguing that predictions like a 20-foot sea-level rise were alarmist. The hockey stick graph itself became

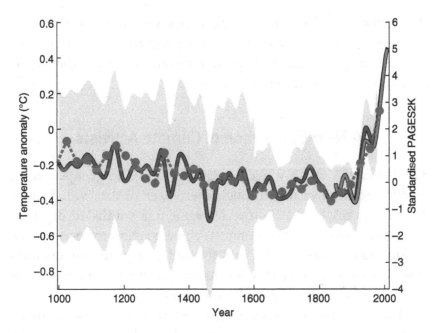

Figure 9.5 The hockey stick chart

Source: Klaus Bittermann/Wikipedia/https://en.wikipedia.org/wiki/File:T_comp_61-90.pdf/CC BY 3.0/last accessed on 27 January 2025.

controversial, with critics challenging its methods. Yet these challenges led to more research, which ultimately confirmed the graph's accuracy and strengthened its position as a reliable picture of long-term temperature trends. Scientists consistently backed the film's main message: human-caused climate change is real, urgent and demands action.

Since *An Inconvenient Truth* first shocked audiences, climate visualisation has evolved rapidly. We mentioned new tools like Ed Hawkins' 'warming stripes' earlier on in this chapter. He is also famous for the 'climate spiral' – an animated view of rising global temperatures which have made it even easier to show climate science clearly.

These data visualisations help shape public understanding, inform policy debates and help teachers explain climate change in classrooms. The film and its hockey stick graph proved that clear, compelling data visualisations can do more than communicate — they can inspire change, shape discussions and drive the urgent action we need to face climate change.

A New Generation of Climate Activists

This is exactly what we need today, and there are groups actively working to achieve this through the power of data visualisation. Take, for example, the Sunrise Movement, a youth-led organisation founded in 2017 that connects climate action to social justice. Unlike earlier movements that focused solely on conservation, Sunrise recognises that climate change intertwines with workers' rights, racial equality and economic fairness.

They use data visualisation not just to show rising temperatures but also to reveal societal inequalities. Their visuals expose how climate change hits marginalised communities hardest — showing that those least responsible often suffer the most severe impacts. This approach to presenting data helps make these injustices both visible and understandable.

When the Sunrise Movement campaigns for a Green New Deal and the end of fossil fuels, they use data to tell a story far more profound than one of greenhouse gases alone. Their data visualisations show how communities on the margins, already burdened by pollution and flooding, will suffer most as temperatures rise. For them, renewable energy does not simply address the environmental crisis, it paves the way for better jobs, healthier neighbourhoods and a more equitable society.

By combining climate science with social justice advocacy, the Sunrise Movement has built a diverse coalition pushing for comprehensive climate solutions. Their work, from organising climate strikes to advocating for the Green New Deal, relies on data-driven stories to show why we need systemic change.

Other youth movements like Fridays for Future and Extinction Rebellion Youth also use data visualisation to mobilise support. They present clear evidence of the climate crisis to draw media attention and public engagement.

Uniting Science, Society and Justice

These movements share a core belief: climate change isn't just an environmental issue, but it's also a crisis of social justice, inequality and human rights. By using data visualisation strategically, they turn complex information into accessible stories that can inspire action. Their goal is to build a global community working towards a more sustainable and equitable world.

Data visualisation helps empower this type of activism as does the technology that supports it. For instance, take the Climate Action Tracker (CAT) for example. It shows how data visualisation can make climate action clearer and more accountable. This independent scientific project tracks how government climate policies measure up against the Paris Agreement's goals – keeping warming well below 2 °C and trying to limit it to 1.5 °C.

I should mention the Paris Agreement – a pivotal moment in climate action that came years after the early warnings from scientists. This 2015 international treaty, adopted at the UN's COP21 conference, set a clear target: limit global warming to well below 2 °C above pre-industrial levels and try to keep it to 1.5 °C.

While the 2001 IPCC Third Assessment Report had raised awareness about global warming's impacts – as shown in the Burning Embers diagram – it took until the Paris Agreement in 2015 for nations to commit to specific temperature targets. This 14-year gap between understanding the problem and agreeing on action shows how challenging it can be to move from scientific evidence to global policy.

But now that we have agreed to do something, we have to track it, otherwise this is no more than a bunch of empty pledges. That is what the CAT's Data Explorer does. It lets users examine and compare how different countries are addressing climate change. Through interactive tools, anyone can explore emissions data and see how nations rate against their climate promises.

By turning complex climate data into clear charts and graphs, CAT helps everyone – from the public to policymakers – understand what's happening. This clarity matters because it shows the gap between what countries are doing and what they need to do to tackle climate change effectively. By creating this level of clarity, this holds every signature to this agreement in Paris accountable. This is why data visualisation is so important.

The power of good data visualisation lies in its ability to turn complicated science into compelling stories. Take Ed Hawkins' climate spiral – this simple animation shows global temperature changes in a way that makes warming feel real and urgent. Tools like these can shift how people think about climate change and encourage them to act.

These platforms bridge the gap between complex climate data and public understanding. By making the information clear and accessible, they help hold governments accountable and encourage better climate policies.

This approach lifts the climate debate above mere temperature targets. It transforms dry statistics into compelling evidence of layered injustices calling out for remedy. Like all powerful data storytelling, it takes numbers and weaves them into narratives that stir empathy and inspire action.

If the Aletsch Glacier's retreat helps us visualise the stark reality of climate change, the Sunrise Movement's arguments show us the breadth of what is at stake. Understanding the scale of the problem is not enough; we must also grasp that solving it means addressing social, economic and political issues simultaneously.

This intersectional framing does not dilute the climate message – it enriches it. It makes climate action relevant to everyone, especially those who might otherwise feel excluded. When presented well, these data-driven narratives bridge distant concerns and everyday struggles, reminding us that climate change will define the quality of life for current and future generations.

This is where data visualisation and narrative storytelling converge. If done thoughtfully, they can tear down mental barriers and reveal that climate change is not an isolated threat; it is woven into the fabric of our societies. The Sunrise Movement understands this, harnessing every available tool – policy proposals, vivid graphics and clear charts – to make their case.

Evidence alone will not save us, but how we present that evidence can turn confusion into clarity, apathy into resolve. By connecting the dots in ways that feel both urgent and just, we may finally find the courage to treat climate change not as a distant environmental problem but as the defining human challenge of our era.

The climate war is a battle for our future, and data visualisation is one of our most potent weapons. Let us wield it wisely.

KEY TAKEAWAYS

- Climate communicators face two main challenges: explaining an incredibly complex crisis while cutting through today's information overload – this is where data visualisation can prove invaluable.
- Simple but powerful visuals, such as Ed Hawkins' 'warming stripes' or the 'hockey stick' graph made famous by Al Gore, can change how people see climate change by showing trends clearly and immediately.
- Different charts serve different purposes. Line charts show change over time, bar chart races grab attention, and animated

maps reveal patterns and interactive dashboards let people explore deeply. Each tool has its place, from quick social media posts to detailed research presentations.
- Animated and interactive visuals work well because they tell stories quickly, reaching viewers who might find raw data or static graphs overwhelming.
- Groups such as the Sunrise Movement and youth campaigns use data visualisation to expose climate injustice, showing how communities that contributed least to climate change often suffer its worst effects.
- Important visuals – from the IPCC's 'Burning Embers' to Hawkins' 'climate spiral' – have shaped both policy discussions and public understanding, showing how data visualisation can drive awareness and action.
- Well-designed data visuals reveal climate change as more than an environmental issue. They show it as a social, economic and political challenge that demands worldwide cooperation.

Chapter 10

Poverty and Wealth

The world cannot be understood without numbers. But the world cannot be understood with numbers alone.

–Hans Rosling

The fluorescent lights droned overhead as Ethan stared at the conveyor belt, sorting packages for the eighth hour in a row. His calloused hands, once adept at crafting spears and igniting fires, now moved cardboard boxes from one endless line to another.

The irony weighed on him. These hands that had once brought down mammoths were reduced to shuffling parcels filled with things he barely understood.

How he missed the hunt.

Still, it wasn't all bad, he told himself. His body, once lean and hardened by a harsh hunter gathering life, had filled out thanks to regular meals and better nutrition. No more waking at dawn, shivering in the dark or slipping into restless sleep with an empty stomach after an unproductive hunt.

The supervisor's voice crackled over the warehouse intercom, signalling the end of his shift. Ethan gathered his belongings – the cheap plastic ID badge, the synthetic jacket he had been given on arrival and the keys to his cramped apartment.

Outside, the setting sun was perhaps the only constant. The car park was full of vehicles whose glossy surfaces reflected the orange glow. He passed them all, heading for the bus stop. He could have learnt to drive – they had offered to teach him – but a car was out of reach on his wages, so why bother.

His apartment was on the third floor of a concrete block that crammed hundreds of people together like prey animals in a trap. The keys jingled as he opened the door, a sound that still felt strange to him. Inside, the air was perfectly warm. No need for fire, no need to gather wood and no need for anything but to press a button on a wall for instant light. His son was in the living room doing his homework, which Ethan couldn't understand.

He was just another low-wage worker living pay cheque to pay cheque in a world where even those deemed poor possessed more material wealth than the mightiest tribal leaders from his time. Yet everyone kept wanting more, always more. They had light without flame, water without labour and heat without fuel but still they complained of lacking.

Was he really that poor?

To be fair, we should probably ask ourselves the same question. It is challenging to answer because it is all about perspective and what you believe to be true.

In Aravind Adiga's novel *The White Tiger* (Adiga 2008), Balram Halwai considers India's poor to be like caged animals in a rather cruel way. The poor, according to him, often choose the safety of steady work over the risks of freedom. He called this the 'Rooster Coop' where people stayed trapped by fear of losing their security and putting their families at risk even as they watch others around them struggle. This powerful metaphor of caged animals and freedom leads us to another novel – Yann Martel's *Life of Pi*.

Through the eyes of Martel's protagonist Pi, a zookeeper's son, we learn that animals don't long for freedom the way humans think they do (Martel 2018). Instead, they value routine, safety and clear boundaries more than open freedom. Pi's unique position as both observer and caretaker reveals something surprising about the nature of confinement and contentment.

In his family's zoo, Pi notices how animals thrive with reliable shelter and food, protected from the dangers of the wild. This contentment with security over freedom, he suggests, says more about what humans want than what animals need. His insights make us question our assumptions about freedom and security, particularly when we think about human society and progress.

These literary explorations of freedom, security and human nature – from both Adiga and Martel's novels – directly connect to Hans Rosling's groundbreaking work. Rosling was a Swedish physician and gifted speaker who died in 2017. He used data visualisation to challenge our misconceptions about global poverty and development. Through his engaging charts and presentations, he proved that the world isn't simply divided into rich and poor – the reality of human progress is far more complex and connected. Like Pi's observations about zoo animals and Balram's insights about the Rooster Coop, Rosling's work makes us reconsider what we think we know about freedom, security and human well-being.

Rosling's work painted a more complex picture of human progress. His most famous creation – the Gapminder bubble chart, also known as 'The Wealth and Health of Nations' – transformed dry statistics into a compelling story of global development.

In this animated data visualisation, each coloured bubble represented a country. The colour represents the continent that the country is from, and the size of the bubble represents the size of the population. I actually created this same animated data visualisation early on in my data visualisation journey and unsurprisingly it went viral.

In Figure 10.1, you can see a static snapshot, which is freely available to enjoy and distribute. It's also available in colour, so you can distinguish between the different continents that the countries belong too. If you want to see the updated animated version, just go to Gapminder and you will find it easily. It is one of the most famous animated data visualisations ever made.

When you hit play, what you see are these bubbles moving over time. What is particularly uplifting is the dramatic progress the world has actually made according to our definition of extreme poverty.

If you do visit the Gapminder project website, do take some time to explore the other data visualisations. It is one of the best data visualisation websites out there, and the data shown are truly beautiful.

This beauty and accessibility didn't happen by chance. Hans Rosling's 2006 TED Talk, 'The Best Stats You've Ever Seen' was a defining moment in data storytelling. In just 20 minutes, Rosling transformed what could have been a dry statistical presentation into riveting theatre. Using his Gapminder bubble chart animation that I mentioned, he showed 200 years of global development to that audience and in doing so shattered common misconceptions about world poverty.

Rosling was so ahead of his time. I only started my own data visualisation story in 2018 and produced my first animated project at the end of 2020, during the coronavirus disease 2019 lockdown. Just to emphasise how revolutionary his 2006 animated data visualisation was, he produced it just a year after YouTube was founded in 2005 and more than a decade before bar chart races took YouTube by storm.

His presentation in 2006 was truly revolutionary. With infectious enthusiasm, Rosling brought statistics to life, literally running across the stage to follow his animated bubbles as they traced the path of countries from poverty to prosperity. The audience watched, captivated, as decades of human progress unfolded before them.

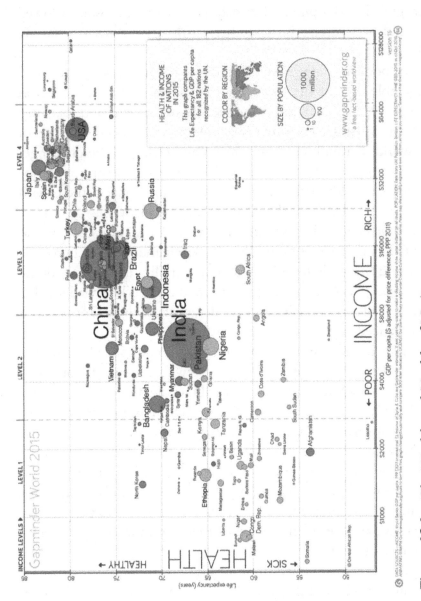

Figure 10.1 The Wealth and Health of Nations

Source: The Gapminder World Map/Gapminder/https://CC BY 4.0/www.gapminder.org/downloads/updated-gapminder-world-poster-2015, last accessed on 27 January 2025.

This talk became one of TED's most watched presentations, viewed millions of times. It changed how people thought about both global development and data presentation. Rosling showed that statistics weren't just numbers – they were stories waiting to be told.

His book *Factfulness* builds on these groundbreaking ideas and is arguably one of the best data science books I have ever read (Rosling 2019). Drawing from decades of research and teaching, Rosling explains why so many people misunderstand the state of our world. Through engaging stories and examples, he challenges common myths – like the belief that poverty is getting worse or that global health crises can't be solved – and replaces them with evidence-based analysis drawn from data visualisation.

Factfulness actually deepens the themes Rosling first showed at his TED Talk. He goes on to discuss the remarkable global progress the world has made in reducing child mortality, expanding education and fighting extreme poverty. While he acknowledges that serious challenges remain, Rosling demonstrates how far the world has advanced in the past two centuries.

These improvements, he argues, often go unnoticed because of our tendency to focus on negative news and cling to outdated views. The book reinforces his central message from that memorable TED Talk: seeing the world accurately requires us to follow data, think critically and question our assumptions.

Now just imagine if we could plot Ethan's journey on one of these Gapminder charts – from prehistoric survival to modern life – we would see a striking transformation. By today's measures, his living standards would have improved enormously. He no longer walks miles to find food or fuel. A minor injury or illness no longer threatens his survival.

We can actually trace some of his economic journey, though not quite back to Ethan's prehistoric times. Figure 10.2 shows global gross domestic product (GDP) from 1 CE onwards, which is close enough. It's presented by Our World in Data, a nonprofit

Poverty and Wealth

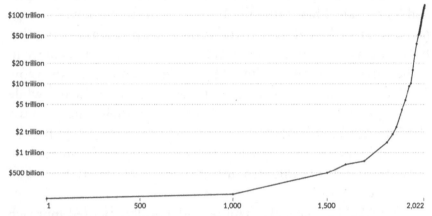

Figure 10.2 GDP over the long run

Source: Our World in Data. However, there is an important distinction that needs to be made, which becomes ever more apparent as this chapter progresses.

organisation founded by economist Max Roser at the University of Oxford in 2011. This group provides comprehensive data about global challenges that we face, covering everything from poverty to health and climate change. Their goal is to help policymakers, economists and public officials make more informed decisions about global challenges through data visualisation.

Note that we have used a log scale in Figure 10.2. The log scale is crucial for understanding this economic story. Without it, centuries of early human history would be compressed into an almost invisible line, dwarfed by modern growth. The log scale transforms exponential growth into something our eyes can better interpret — a steadily rising line rather than an impossibly steep curve.

Yet even with a log scale this simple line chart is quite a shock. For most of history, global GDP grew at a glacial pace due to the limitations of pre-industrial societies with their basic technologies and local trade. Then came the Industrial Revolution, which triggered unprecedented growth, creating a sharp upward curve that has dominated recent centuries. What took millennia to achieve in earlier periods has been eclipsed by modern economic expansion.

The logarithmic scale helps us understand this growth – while recent growth rates have remained fairly stable, their impact on the absolute size of the global economy has been staggering. It confirms and supports exactly what the Gapminder project presents – extraordinary economic progress in a relatively short period of humanity's history.

Our World in Data takes a more academically oriented approach than Gapminder, offering in-depth analysis of long-term trends rather than solely engaging data visualisation as a storytelling tool. While Gapminder focuses on dynamic charts and storytelling to challenge global misconceptions, Our World in Data, founded by economist Max Roser, acts as a comprehensive research platform that looks at historical context and delves deeply into pressing global issues such as poverty, health and climate change. Both organisations share a commitment to clear data visualisation, but Our World in Data places particular emphasis on thorough exploration of the evidence and detailed historical comparisons. In short, it goes deeper, which is what we need if we want a better bearing of where humanity is heading.

Let's return to Ethan. This GDP chart doesn't tell the whole story. It's too zoomed out and also lacks context. In doing so, it misses the key risks that the human race faces. If this chart could actually go back to prehistoric times, even with a log scale, you wouldn't be able to grasp Ethan's sense of freedom, his bond with the land and even his kinship with fellow hunters. There are these intangible riches that Ethan might have enjoyed, like communal bonds, self-reliance and a deeper connection to nature, which cannot be captured by data.

In fact, this is an observation I've even made with my own experiences. One of the reasons I moved to Switzerland was for a better quality of life, especially for my children. In my town of Wädenswil, just 20 km from Zürich, children as young as four walk to school alone because they can. It's actually a fiercely defended Swiss tradition, promoting the Swiss sense of independence, fortitude and strength at a young age. This is a country that is incredibly safe where everything works like clockwork, and that pun is fully intended.

My children enjoy an extraordinary childhood – nothing like my upbringing in Croydon which is still one of London's poorer boroughs. Here, my kids come home for lunch, have rich social lives and are surrounded by nature. We buy food directly from local farmers if we want, go for walks in the mountains and enjoy all the cultural richness this country has to offer. Here, they can immerse themselves in countless activities: music lessons, ice hockey, football, breakdancing and more. Weekends mean skiing in winter or swimming in lakes in summer and having a barbeque.

From flawless healthcare to exceptionally resourced schools and smooth roads and pavements, the infrastructure is remarkable. It is the day before Christmas Eve right now and outside it is snowing heavily. Yet everything still works. The roads are constantly ploughed and the buses and trains are working. You don't even need to shovel the pavement outside your house – they have mini pavement snow ploughs for that.

Yet sometimes my children complain that Switzerland is boring. Well, I embrace boring. I'll take boring over the excitement of my teenage years in Croydon. Having a bottle thrown at you for being brown after walking down the wrong street isn't pleasant. Nor is having to divert your journey because a whole neighbourhood has been closed off by the police because of a shooting or stabbing. Most sobering of all was when a classmate was thrown under a train just for graffitiing on the wrong wall.

I'll take boring Switzerland thank you very much. Sorry kids! Boring is fantastic. Yet, even living in Switzerland isn't perfect.

For all its efficiency and jaw-dropping landscapes, Switzerland illustrates some of the hidden costs that come with high living standards.

Like many developed nations, it depends on massive imports of skilled labour to fill roles in finance, pharmaceuticals, watchmaking and specialist engineering. Attractive salaries pull in talented newcomers, driving up wages and, inevitably, the cost of living. Housing, food, insurance and everything else become more expensive, leaving even middle-class families feeling a financial squeeze that often goes unseen because, by global standards, no one in Switzerland is truly destitute.

The economic problem hasn't been solved. My kids still find Switzerland boring because they have no frame of reference for what is worse. This then leaves them exposed to seeing only the problems they face: they don't get enough pocket money, everything is expensive and they live in a town 20 km from Zürich where all the action is happening.

However, being discontent with the way the world isn't a bad thing. It gives us a reason to fight for change and desire progress. I don't want my kids to be content with the status quo. I want them to dream and have desires that might take them beyond Switzerland.

If we ever want to progress as a species, we must never get too comfortable, otherwise we become complacent. Today, we are fragile because we can't see our weaknesses due to the technology we rely on and the damage we do to the planet that we continue to ignore.

It is true that human progress has been monumental, especially in the last few centuries. Fewer children die before their fifth birthday, more families can afford food and shelter and more nations are lifting themselves out of poverty. But at the same time, these improvements have been neither linear nor evenly distributed. If they were, I would not have moved my family to Switzerland.

Colonial history, brutal world wars, changing economic policies and generational advantages warp wealth across nations and their underlying populations.

For centuries, colonial powers extracted vast amounts of resources from colonised regions – labour, raw materials and

Poverty and Wealth

agricultural products. Once they departed, they often left local populations impoverished and infrastructure underdeveloped despite claims that those countries were better under their former governance.

This exploitation concentrated wealth and industrial capacity in the hands of the colonisers, creating economic imbalances that still persist to this day. These countries built their prosperity on the back of this inequity while former colonies often faced economic stagnation, political instability and social divisions long after achieving independence. I'm British, so I'm pretty aware of what my country did. We stole, we plundered and we flourished economically. Should I celebrate this?

Let's examine some data from Our World in Data, focusing on two charts. Figure 10.3 shows the number of European overseas colonies by continent. At its peak, Africa had an overwhelming

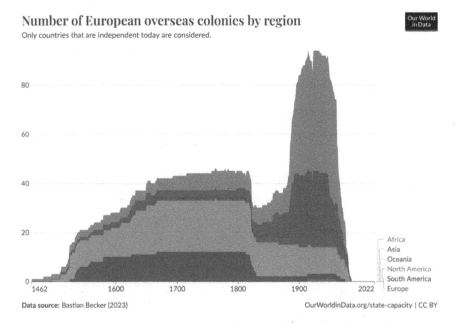

Figure 10.3 Number of European overseas colonies by region
Source: Bastian Becker (2023)/Our World in Data/CC BY 4.0/https://ourworldindata.org/grapher/number-of-european-overseas-colonies-by-region, last accessed on 27 January 2025.

number of colonies, with nearly the entire continent under European control, leading to extensive exploitation of its resources and people. Figure 10.4, in contrast, depicts GDP per capita across various regions over time. I have selected GDP per capita rather than total GDP because it captures the average economic output per individual and allows for meaningful comparisons across regions with vastly different population sizes. The disparity between these charts is striking.

However, these datasets are not directly comparable. They originate from different sources, use varying definitions for regions and cover different time scales. Despite these limitations, a broader narrative emerges: many regions that were heavily colonised have

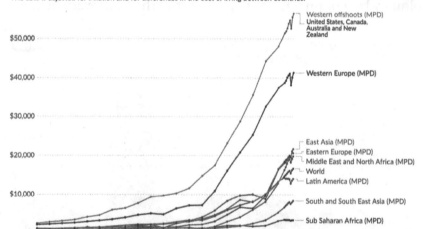

Figure 10.4 GDP per Capita 1820 to 2022

Source: Bolt and van Zanden/Our World in Data/CC BY 4.0/https://ourworldindata.org/what-is-economic-growth, last accessed on 27 January 2025.

struggled to achieve the same levels of economic prosperity as those less affected. This observation, while compelling, is nuanced and does not fully capture the complexities at play.

For instance, the United States began as a group of British colonies that fought for independence and eventually united to form one of the world's largest and most powerful economies. Similarly, Australia was established as a settler colony without a war of independence. In both cases, the colonisers settled permanently, established new political systems and focused on local development.

In contrast, many colonies in Africa and India remained under European control for extended periods, with colonial powers prioritising resource extraction over local development. These regions were often left with fragile political structures, uneven economic foundations and deeply ingrained inequalities. This underscores the complex relationship between colonialism and long-term economic outcomes, indicating that the narratives suggested by these charts require careful interpretation.

It is also important to recognise that drawing a direct causal link between colonisation and slower GDP per capita growth may overlook numerous other factors that shape economic trajectories. Variables such as geographical advantages, access to resources, technological diffusion, governance and political ideology all play significant roles. A more robust statistical model that tests multiple variables side by side could offer deeper insights. The historical legacies of colonisation undoubtedly matter, but they should be examined in conjunction with a multitude of interacting social, political and economic factors that have evolved over time.

Building on this, colonialism also shaped global trade patterns to favour the colonisers and establish lasting dependencies. Many formerly colonised nations were pushed into exporting raw materials while importing finished goods from European powers. This arrangement widened the development gap by steering these nations towards low-value exports and limiting opportunities for higher-value manufacturing. Even after independence, such economic structures often remained in place – supported by international trade and financial frameworks that tend to disadvantage developing regions – making it harder to boost GDP per capita or compete on equal footing.

As these countries strive to improve living standards, they face another pressing issue: the carbon emissions required to create the infrastructure that Western nations have enjoyed for decades. This raises difficult ethical questions. Should we expect developing countries to restrict their own industrial growth for the sake of combating climate change even though Western nations once used unrestrained industrial expansion to build their wealth? This dilemma reveals a tension between global environmental goals and the desire of postcolonial economies to catch up economically.

Yet, claiming that colonisation alone caused slower GDP per capita growth can be misleading. Geography, governance, access to resources, technology and trade policies all shape economic outcomes. Relying on a single explanation may overlook these influences and distort our understanding of why some countries advance more quickly than others. Colonial legacies do matter, but they do not operate on their own.

We must also guard against misreading data and drawing sweeping conclusions without considering other variables. Historical conditions, domestic policies and external factors often play a greater role than we assume. If we treat correlations as proof of causation, we risk overlooking how different forces interact and evolve. Recognising the limits of our data stories allows us to avoid simple narratives that ignore the real complexity behind economic development.

Sometimes there are multiple layers to a situation and the frustrations people feel often stem from factors that overlap in complicated ways.

Yes, it's true that life has improved for the vast majority of people worldwide in the past few centuries, but beneath that progress lie thousands of messy data stories that shape the advances we have achieved. These gains haven't been distributed evenly nor do they always reflect deeper issues such as historic inequalities, technological disparities and environmental impacts. Recognising this allows us to see that while the overall picture is positive, the path has been shaped by complex forces that don't always move in harmony. By looking beyond the aggregate figures, we can better understand the uneven trajectories of development and work towards more equitable progress in the future.

Let's examine another example that reveals the subtle details behind what appears to be general progress. Even in the developed world, wealth disparities exist despite generally high living standards. In recent decades, those disparities have grown to staggering levels, yet they do not always follow the typical notion of a clear divide between rich and poor.

Take the past four decades. Older generations benefited from gradually falling interest rates, which made mortgages and loans more accessible, causing property prices to surge and boosting their wealth. Meanwhile, a favourable job market offered them greater security along with pensions and benefits that enhanced long-term financial stability. This picture does not match the usual rich-poor narrative often heard in political debates.

We tend to imagine the rich as a small group with far more than everyone else, yet we rarely consider who they might be. They could be people close to you – perhaps your parents – who are not commonly seen as wealthy but may appear so if you are a young adult struggling with high living costs.

Young adults now face a very different economy to that of their parents. Housing prices have spiralled beyond reach in many urban centres, leaving young people with either steep rents or an almost impossible path to a home deposit (see Figure 10.5). At the same time, the cost of higher education has soared, trapping graduates in debt for years – sometimes decades – after graduation.

On top of that, the modern job market is often characterised by gig work, short-term contracts and limited chances to advance

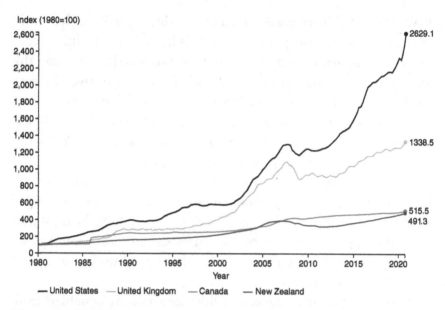

Figure 10.5 House prices since the 1980s
Source: Data from OECD.

(Figure 10.6). This makes it difficult to build both immediate financial stability and longer-term wealth. Pension systems in many places are also under strain, shifting the burden onto younger workers and raising the possibility that some may never fully retire or may risk dying poor.

In this climate, it is no wonder the younger generation may not feel any more prosperous than Ethan did when he first stood dazzled by the neon lights of a rapidly modernising world. Technological progress, digital connections and global markets have changed how we live but have not necessarily ensured greater financial security or social mobility for young workers. These realities gnaw away at the optimism once promised in an age of unending economic growth.

By highlighting this generational wealth divide, we see another instance of the 'messy data stories' that underscore how progress is not always straightforward. Although conditions have improved for

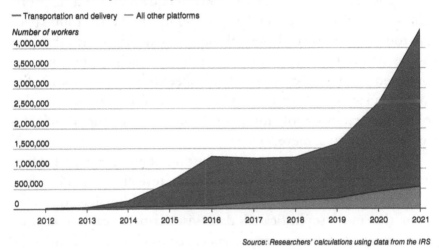

Figure 10.6 Growth in gig workers with platform payments
Source: Adapted from Andrew Garin et al. (2021).

many, the benefits are not distributed evenly even within prosperous countries. This adds yet another layer to the complexities you have been exploring. Beyond the broad metrics of global advancement, we must also examine the shifting circumstances that define people's everyday experiences.

In the investment world, we warn that past performance doesn't predict future returns. The same could be said about Rosling's economic progress maps. If you're a young worker in today's brutal, fast-paced economy, what comfort is there in knowing how life improved over 200 years? That history offers little guidance for navigating today's financially repressive world that is technologically driven and changing faster than ever before.

Furthermore, there is a darker side to all this global economic progress. Consider the carbon dioxide pumped into our atmosphere, necessary to achieve this level of economic development.

Yes, child mortality has dropped and we're living longer but how do future generations maintain these gains?

Understanding these generational inequalities – and their origins – is crucial for creating fair policies for the future. Young people today face unprecedented challenges: a housing crisis that puts home ownership out of reach, overwhelming student debt and outdated labour laws that don't reflect modern working life. Without tackling these issues head-on, the financial security that older generations took for granted may remain impossible for today's youth to achieve.

Data visualisation is more than just numbers on a page. It offers a glimpse into the deeper forces at play, revealing persistent inequalities, unexpected areas of progress and cultural patterns. Yet even the most sophisticated data visualisations cannot capture every nuance of human experience. Rosling's enduring message, carried forward by Gapminder (the organisation he co-founded), is that understanding human progress through facts can guide us towards wiser action.

Nevertheless, Rosling's focus on historical data and past victories risks creating a misleading impression that our trajectory of progress will continue unbroken. Yes, we have improved child mortality rates and extended life expectancy, but our reliance on fossil fuels has propped up these advances. That reliance is becoming unsustainable.

We can look back on centuries of rising living standards, yet we often forget that civilisations have collapsed before. From the destruction of the Library of Alexandria to the dark ages in Europe, history shows that regressions are possible and we are just as susceptible if we ignore warning signs.

We must acknowledge that today's global economy heavily depends on fossil fuels for everything from manufacturing to transport. Abruptly ceasing their use would undermine the living standards that so many now enjoy. Yet, continuing on the same path invites equally dire consequences.

The tension between preserving current gains and avoiding ecological catastrophe is palpable. If we fail to find innovative, cleaner ways to fuel economic growth, we risk social unrest, widening inequalities and even war – scenarios that could unravel the very progress Rosling's charts so vividly depict. By celebrating how far we have come without planning for an uncertain future, we may lull ourselves into a false sense of security.

Moreover, despite the upward trend in global averages, major disparities persist. Improvements captured by global data can mask the realities of those left behind or disenfranchised. True progress means not only preserving our present achievements, but also ensuring that the path ahead is sustainable and inclusive.

If we do not adapt, future generations might look back on our era with the same bewilderment we reserve for civilisations that lost their way. We can honour Rosling's legacy – and Ethan's longing for deeper meaning – by recognising both the fragility of what we have gained and the urgent need to safeguard it, lest we drift into our own modern dark age.

KEY TAKEAWAYS

- While global averages show advances like lower child mortality, many regions and social groups lag behind. Data visualisations make it clear that one country's rapid progress may not apply elsewhere, reminding us to look beyond big-picture statistics.
- Colonial histories and generational divides still shape who benefits from economic growth. A mere upward trend on a graph can mask systemic injustices and the long-tail effects of exploitation and resource extraction.
- Global trends shown in data visualisations tell us part of the story, but they can't capture everything. While charts help us see the big picture, they need to be balanced with real human experiences and historical context that numbers alone can't show.

- Progress does not guarantee stability. Past civilisations have collapsed due to ignoring hidden risks. Today's reliance on fossil fuels, social inequalities and climate pressures can threaten the very gains data shows us achieving.
- Recognising improvements should not lead to complacency. Discontent with current problems is what drives further progress, and data can show precisely where we fall short and how urgent our next steps must be.
- Good data visualisations can reveal hidden problems and highlight possible solutions. They help us understand where we stand now and guide us towards better decisions for the future.

Chapter 11

Data Deception in Politics

Christopher Wylie stood outside Cambridge Analytica's office, the weight of London's grey sky pressing down on him. The young Canadian data scientist never imagined he would find himself here in late 2013, about to step into what would become the epicentre of a global political storm five years later.

The office he entered projected corporate sophistication. Consultants moved between meeting rooms while analysts worked quietly at their desks. At the heart of it all moved Alexander Nix, who carried himself with the polished assurance of his Eton education. It was hard not to be seduced. Hailing from an earlier career at Barclays' investment bank, he was extremely convincing. His confidence made everyone believe they were part of something revolutionary.

In those early weeks, Wylie witnessed the company's ambitious pitch. The language was all about 'microtargeting', 'psychographic modelling' and 'persuadable voters' – Cambridge Analytica claimed they could predict and influence voting behaviour by analysing vast amounts of personal data, the vast majority gleaned from Facebook accounts.

When potential investors visited, the presentations were slick and confident. Data visualisations showed how personality data could supposedly sway voter behaviour. Wylie watched these demonstrations with a mix of fascination and growing unease about what the technology might mean.

Over time, that unease grew into something more troubling. Wylie discovered how Cambridge Analytica had harvested those millions of Facebook profiles without proper consent. At first, he tried to rationalise his concerns. After all, he had come to London to work at the cutting edge of data science. But his doubts became impossible to ignore when a colleague showed him a spreadsheet that labelled individuals as 'persuadable', categorised by their vulnerability to issues like immigration or gun rights. These weren't just data points in a database. They were real people, being targeted through their personal fears and anxieties.

After just a year, Wylie quit in late 2014, troubled by the ethical lines he had seen crossed. However, it would take another three years before he began working with journalists to expose the truth, with the story finally breaking in March 2018 across several news outlets: *The New York Times, The Observer* and *The Guardian* (Cadwalladr and Graham-Harrison 2018), followed days later by Channel 4 News catching Alexander Nix on camera boasting about using dirty tricks to influence elections (Channel 4 News Investigation Team 2018). Wylie's decision to become a whistle-blower had revealed to the world how personal data had been weaponised against democracy itself.

Given the intensity of the revelations, we can only imagine the daily reality inside Cambridge Analytica's offices. Yet Wylie's experience raises profound questions about ethics in data science. His decision to become a whistle-blower, knowing it could damage his career, showed remarkable courage. It's easy to say we would do the same, but standing up against unethical practices – especially when surrounded by people who treat them as normal – takes extraordinary resolve.

Cambridge Analytica's Origins and Influence

Cambridge Analytica was a British political consulting firm founded in 2013 as an offshoot of SCL Group (Strategic Communication Laboratories). SCL, established in 1990, described itself as a 'global election management agency' that specialised in 'behavioural change' programmes, working in the shadowy world of the military industry and with intelligence agencies. Cambridge Analytica emerged from this heritage but focused specifically on political campaigns, becoming notorious for its claims of using data-driven psychological profiling to influence voters.

Behind Cambridge Analytica stood powerful figures from America's political elite. Robert Mercer, a billionaire hedge-fund manager, poured at least $15 million into the company's vision of data-driven persuasion. Steve Bannon – who would later become Donald Trump's Chief Strategist – served as a vice president, holding shares worth millions. By 2016, the company had secured its place in political history, working on Trump's presidential campaign. Their method? Using personal data harvested from millions of unwitting Facebook users to craft political messages that would tap into voters' deepest fears and desires (Halpern 2018).

The Dark Side of Politics

The information had been harvested from Facebook profiles via a third-party app, where they had used their Facebook profile as a sign-in method. Users who thought they were taking harmless personality quizzes or casually clicking through social media unknowingly allowed their data, and in many cases that of their friends, to be collected and repurposed (Scott and Dickson 2018). This was then transformed into psychological profiles designed to influence voting behaviour. When Cambridge Analytica was investigated, it scrambled to defend itself, insisting all data were legally obtained, even as critics questioned the ethics and legality of the methods used.

The public saw a darker side of political campaigning, which they had not experienced before. Revelations included footage of Alexander Nix discussing entrapment methods and political dirty tricks. Journalists uncovered evidence that millions of Facebook profiles had been processed without clear permission. Lawmakers in the United States and the United Kingdom opened hearings, calling tech CEOs – including Facebook's Mark Zuckerberg – to testify.

In the wake of the uproar, Cambridge Analytica collapsed in 2018, though its techniques of large-scale data harvesting and psychographic targeting have not disappeared. The scandal served as a warning about how personal information – often collected invisibly through apps and online services – can be harnessed in ways that go far beyond its intended uses, raising serious ethical and privacy concerns.

While the firm Christopher Wylie helped expose is now gone, some valuable lessons were learnt. Cambridge Analytica showed that voter manipulation is not just about pushy door-knocking or sensational headlines, but it is also about how data can be used – the millions of data points quietly gathered from social networks and then used to craft messages that can slide into an individual's feed at precisely the right time. Such tactics blurred the line between persuasion and psychological warfare, leaving many wondering what really happens to their private information once it's out there in the digital ether.

As Wylie learned first-hand, revolutionary ideas in technology can also carry a dangerous edge. Cambridge Analytica saw data as the raw material for shaping political outcomes but left a trail of ethical and privacy concerns in its wake.

Facebook Data Turn from Asset into Liability

Before the Cambridge Analytica scandal, Facebook's vast trove of user information was regarded as its crown jewel – a colossal repository of personal data unlike anything traditional survey firms could imagine. Investors hailed it as an unparalleled asset. I too regarded it as a fascinating, game-changing phenomenon with the power to disrupt industries and provide marketers with an unprecedented view into user behaviour. Then, in an instant, that glittering promise turned into a credibility crisis – forcing us all to confront the murky trade-off between value and privacy in the digital age. Facebook's data ultimately turned out to be a liability, not an asset.

Given the rapidly changing landscape, it is useful to elaborate: Facebook seemed to know nearly everything about its users. This privileged position stemmed from the company's ability to gather an enormous volume of data, including their users' interests, political leanings, shopping habits and social connections.

In the years before the Cambridge Analytica scandal erupted in early 2018, many businesses viewed Facebook data as a marketing dream. Instead of conducting slow and expensive surveys with limited samples, advertisers could tap into a global user base of billions, slicing and dicing the population into highly specific target groups via Facebook's advertising tools. As the supply of available data exploded, its cost plummeted.

For example, if a user liked Coca-Cola on Facebook, the platform could correlate that preference with other data points: how old the user was, where they lived, whether they preferred watching sports content, which restaurants they checked into and so forth.

Facebook's sophisticated algorithms would then cluster this data with countless other user signals, allowing marketers to glean patterns like 'people in midwestern states aged 18 to 25 who like Coca-Cola also tend to be fans of these sports teams or TV shows'. Over time, advertisers could drill down further, discovering niche segments – for instance, 'college students at specific universities who engage with certain fast-food brands' and then serve them tailored ads. This went far beyond traditional demographic breakdowns, enabling targeting based on what people did, read or liked on the platform.

One of Facebook's key advertising products, Audience Insights, demonstrated the platform's ability to offer advertisers granular, anonymised data. By providing detailed breakdowns of who liked a page, clicked on an ad or responded to an event, Audience Insights allowed advertisers to see which regions and age brackets engaged most with their content, as well as the brands and interests commonly shared within a group.

While the tool itself was not implicated in scandals like the Cambridge Analytica case, it exemplified Facebook's capacity for precision targeting – a feature that later drew criticism. Broader concerns about Facebook's advertising practices began to include issues such as enabling microtargeting for political ads, partnerships with data brokers to combine online and offline consumer data and allegations of discriminatory ad targeting. Although Audience Insights operated within these dynamics, it was not directly linked to any controversies but remains part of the ecosystem that has faced scrutiny over privacy and transparency.

For marketers, however, this was a huge revelation at the time and was believed to be a disruptive game changer for the industry. In contrast to older methods – telephone polls or focus groups with just a few hundred or thousand participants – Facebook appeared to provide real-time feedback from hundreds of millions, if not billions, of users around the world. Entire marketing strategies could revolve around continuous testing of different messages, designs or calls to action, watched over by Facebook's live metrics. Everything happened at lightning speed: budgets could be reallocated overnight to the best-performing ads, and new target audiences could be found with a few clicks.

But then came the Cambridge Analytica scandal. In March 2018, investigative journalists revealed that data from tens of millions of Facebook accounts had been harvested under questionable pretences and passed on to Cambridge Analytica. The firm then developed psychological profiles for political advertising, potentially influencing elections in the United States and abroad. While Facebook had long been viewed as a marketing gem, these revelations cast a harsh spotlight on its data-handling practices, prompting serious concerns about privacy and exploitation of personal information.

In the immediate aftermath, many users felt betrayed. Hashtags like #DeleteFacebook began trending, and public trust in the social media giant plummeted. Large numbers of people either deactivated their accounts or tightened their privacy settings, worried that their data might be used for similarly murky purposes. Regulators around the world – from the US Federal Trade Commission (FTC) to the UK's Information Commissioner's Office – launched investigations into Facebook's conduct. In 2019, Facebook was fined $5 billion by the FTC in one of the largest privacy-related penalties in American history, and it was required to submit to new oversight measures (Federal Trade Commission 2019).

Re-evaluating Facebook's Transparency

From a marketing standpoint, this controversy prompted a re-evaluation of how much user data Facebook should share and how transparently it should inform both advertisers and users about data usage. Some of its targeting functionalities were scaled back, and rules for third-party data access were made stricter. Nevertheless, advertisers still sought the granularity Facebook offered – the ability to zoom into particular neighbourhoods or focus on very narrow interest groups – but they found themselves under increased scrutiny too, especially when it came to political or potentially sensitive ad targeting.

Overall, the scandal illustrated just how powerful Facebook's data had become. No longer merely a tool for marketing consumer products, it had morphed into an engine capable of influencing societal outcomes on a global scale. Indeed, the precision once hailed as a marketer's dream was revealed to be a double-edged sword, capable of being misused in ways that ordinary users never intended and governments only belatedly began to regulate. The lasting impact was a profound shift in how both the public and officials viewed the collection, storage and targeting of personal data online – and a reminder that today's digital world wields insights into our behaviour that once seemed unimaginable.

After years of legal battles and media scrutiny, the final lesson is that these tools are here to stay. Whether they are used for constructive engagement or for manipulating entire populations will depend on how vigilantly the public, lawmakers and technologists watch over the ever-growing deluge of personal data that powers modern life.

Election Misinformation and Data Manipulation

Progress in preventing data manipulation remains slow. The aftermath of the Cambridge Analytica scandal was still fresh when new concerns emerged during the 2020 US presidential election. Though different from Cambridge Analytica's tactics, these new challenges showed how data could still be misused to mislead the public.

During the 2020 United States presidential election, certain groups circulated false claims of voter fraud based on so-called 'spikes' in vote totals reported in swing states. These claims typically hinged on charts or screenshots that appeared official at first glance – some were taken from live election data feeds, while others were custom-made graphics overlaying numbers or percentage changes.

A prominent example arose in Michigan, where a popular chart claimed to show a sudden '138,000 vote spike' for Joe Biden at around 6:31 a.m. local time. The graphic displayed what looked like a near-vertical line in Biden's tally, sparking allegations of foul play. However, investigations revealed that the spike resulted from a clerical error in Shiawassee County, which was quickly corrected. Although the data feed was updated within hours, screenshots of the misleading chart continued to spread across social media (PolitiFact 2020).

Another chart gained traction in Wisconsin, purporting to prove a suspicious '4 a.m. Dump' of votes in the city of Milwaukee. Viewers saw a line graph where Biden's vote count jumped steeply in a single update. In reality, Milwaukee officials process large batches of postal votes and then post the results in one go – creating an abrupt increase on time-series graphs. Reuters noted that despite this being part of normal election procedures, screenshots of the spike were taken out of context and presented as proof of cheating (Reuters 2020).

By the time data analysts and election experts clarified that these patterns were perfectly consistent with standard vote-reporting practices, the misleading charts had already been widely shared, amplifying doubts about the legitimacy of the election. Although such events differed from the Cambridge Analytica scandal, they illustrated a similar threat: complex data can be selectively showcased, adorned with authoritative-looking data visualisations and used to undermine public confidence in democratic processes.

By 2023, artificial intelligence and other digital editing tools had begun fuelling a new wave of online disinformation. In India, a group of female wrestlers were protesting against a prominent political figure, alleging sexual harassment and other misconduct. Tensions escalated when an image began circulating on social media that seemed to show these wrestlers smiling in a police vehicle following their arrest – a scene apparently contradicting the seriousness of their cause.

In reality, the photograph was had been digitally manipulated. The wrestlers' faces were modified – likely with AI-driven or advanced editing tools – to give the impression they were amused or untroubled by their detention. Although forensic analysts eventually proved the women's expressions in the original image were sombre, the altered version had already been shared thousands of times, creating confusion among supporters and casting doubts on the gravity of the wrestlers' claims. This incident highlighted how even minor alterations can drastically change the public's interpretation of an event, illustrating the broader risk of weaponising technology to undermine legitimate protests (Menon and Khare 2023).

Deepfake videos have now become a staple concern in politics, which we covered back in Chapter 4. Here, prominent figures are made to appear as though they are saying or doing things they never actually did. If you remember from Chapter 4, one widely discussed instance arose in 2018, when film-maker and comedian Jordan Peele worked with BuzzFeed to create a video featuring former US President Barack Obama seemingly insulting a public figure (BuzzFeed 2018). This experiment was intended to demonstrate how convincing deepfakes could be, yet the clip later circulated on social media without the original disclaimer – leaving viewers uncertain about its authenticity.

A more alarming example occurred in March 2022, when a deepfake emerged depicting Ukrainian President Volodymyr Zelensky calling on Ukrainians to lay down their arms during Russia's invasion (Allyn 2022). Although Ukrainian news outlets quickly debunked it, and the video was soon flagged on multiple platforms, it underscored a growing threat: video evidence can be synthesised from scratch to influence public opinion, undermine leaders and sow confusion. These incidents highlight that the dangers of deepfake technology extend beyond entertainment or parody – they pose serious risks to democratic discourse and global security, as manipulated visuals are readily believed if disseminated by influential online actors.

Online Manipulation and the Arms Race Against Fake Accounts

Political actors have not limited themselves to mere visual deceptions. Bots and fake accounts on platforms such as Twitter and Facebook have been deployed to inflate apparent support for political movements or distort trending topics. In mid-2018, Twitter announced it had removed over 70 million suspicious accounts in just two months, noting that many were linked to spamming or possible political interference (Timberg and Dwoskin 2018). Yet the company admitted it was impossible to stop every bad actor because new bot networks emerged as quickly as old ones were shut down.

Facebook likewise undertook large-scale removals of networks originating from countries including Iran and Russia, in some cases deleting tens of thousands of accounts and pages designed to disrupt elections or sow confusion (Facebook Newsroom 2018). The sheer volume of these takedowns underscores how widespread organised misinformation campaigns have become. In one specific incident in September 2020, Facebook removed a network of accounts tied to foreign groups masquerading as American activists discussing divisive topics such as race relations and environmental crises (Meta 2020). By adopting the veneer of grassroots movements, the network aimed to exploit existing social tensions, deepening political divides and polarising debate. This episode was a striking illustration of how even a modest team of determined actors can engineer powerful illusions of public opinion – provided they know how to harness social media algorithms.

How Data Visualisation Can Help

Data visualisation has an important role in combatting disinformation campaigns in politics if used properly. We must remember, though, that these techniques can also be part of the problem when they are used to deceive or mislead. However, they do offer a real opportunity to strengthen democracy.

Well-designed data visualisations can highlight patterns of suspicious activity, making it easier for journalists and citizens to spot irregularities. One noteworthy illustration of this approach comes from the Stanford Internet Observatory, which has produced network graphs displaying clusters of Twitter accounts believed to share a common origin (Figure 11.1). By mapping out how these accounts retweet or share the same images, researchers can show how apparently diverse users might all stem from a single source. This kind of visual analysis reveals the underlying links in a large dataset – helping to uncover coordinated manipulation and protect the integrity of public discourse.

Data visualisation can also help the public parse genuine electoral data. *The New York Times* Upshot and *FiveThirtyEight* produced interactive maps during recent US elections showing how votes shift at different reporting times. Viewers could see, for instance, that urban areas with more mail-in ballots might release large chunks of votes late in the evening, which explained sudden jumps in tallies. These clear, dynamic charts served as an antidote to superficial graphs circulated by conspiracy theorists. Rather than fuelling alarm, they demonstrated the normal rhythms of vote reporting (The New York Times 2024).

Researchers at the European Digital Media Observatory created a 'misinformation tracker' that mapped false stories across various countries in real time (https://edmo.eu). Colour-coded markers indicated the frequency and topics of disinformation, letting policymakers and journalists identify hotspots of fake news. By pinpointing spikes in fabricated content, authorities could direct

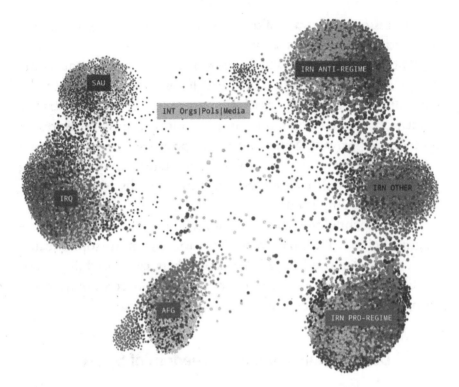

Figure 11.1 Community network map of covert Twitter assets by regional influence
Source: Evaluating five years of pro-Western covert influence operations, 2022/ Stanford University.

fact-checking resources where they were most needed. This sort of visual analysis not only exposed orchestrated campaigns but helped reduce the impact of false narratives before they escalated further.

Ultimately, data visualisation on its own cannot erase the motivations behind disinformation, nor it can convince those already committed to certain narratives. However, when used effectively – drawing on credible data sources and presented in an accessible, intuitive format – it becomes a powerful tool to counter confusion. By illustrating how a few manipulated videos or concentrated bot networks can distort entire debates, data visualisation can be used to restore a measure of transparency and encourage the public to question sensational claims.

The key question is whether governments, social media companies and citizens will take these lessons seriously. After the exposure of Cambridge Analytica, there were calls for stricter regulation of data collection and for more robust measures to protect user privacy. Some legislative proposals, including those in the United Kingdom and the United States, hinted at banning microtargeted political ads or requiring full disclosure of how voter data is being used.

Yet as technology speeds ahead, many worry regulations are lagging behind. Deepfake tools are growing more sophisticated and can be deployed faster than lawmakers can pass bills. Social media platforms are reluctant to adopt overly strict ad restrictions, citing free speech concerns and competitive pressures.

Data Visualisation and Freedom of Speech

In political discourse, freedom of speech stands as a fundamental principle. Yet, as the 2024 UK riots demonstrated, this freedom can be severely tested when the platforms that enable and amplify speech lie in private hands. X – formerly Twitter – has effectively become a modern public square, a battleground for information in which narratives are formed and contested. Elon Musk's 2022 takeover of Twitter transformed its moderation policies, prompting new questions about how to preserve open debate while containing dangerous falsehoods.

The UK riots in the summer of 2024 that followed a tragic stabbing at a children's summer dance class in Southport – which we covered in Chapter 3 – is a good example. Almost immediately, misinformation circulated that the perpetrator was a Muslim asylum seeker who had entered Britain illegally by boat. In reality, the attacker was a British citizen, born in Cardiff to Rwandan parents.

Nonetheless, the rumour spread at an alarming pace on social networks, fuelling mobs that targeted individuals they believed to be asylum seekers. Over the course of a week, far-right groups hijacked the false narrative to foster chaos and fan fears of a wider plot (Krasodomski 2024).

When Musk assumed control of Twitter, he envisioned it as a bastion of free speech, rolling back various forms of content moderation. Some hailed this as an overdue shift away from what they perceived as heavy-handed censorship. Others warned that loosening the reins would invite disinformation to flourish. Musk himself has repeatedly stirred controversy – from re-sharing edited headlines to amplifying incendiary hashtags – muddying the line between hosting open dialogue and appearing to condone dubious claims. This has led to public clashes with politicians such as Prime Minister Keir Starmer, who criticised Musk for allowing inflammatory content to remain on X during the 2024 unrest.

For many, the Southport case stands as a stark illustration of what happens when misinformation – in this instance, a baseless rumour – is left unchecked. Yet these platforms also contain tools that could counter distortions, if deployed effectively. Fact-checkers increasingly use data visualisations to lay bare fraudulent claims by clarifying timelines and identifying the real actors behind incidents. During the riots, news outlets and watchdog organisations produced digital timelines showing how quickly the 'asylum seeker' story took hold, juxtaposing this with verifiable details of the attacker's background. Network maps of retweets showed the far-right accounts that propelled the rumour from fringe corners into mainstream conversation within hours.

Such data visualisations can uncover suspicious patterns on a large scale – revealing, for example, how a few inflammatory posts can be magnified by bot networks or tightly knit user groups. They also allow journalists and the public to track how a rumour morphs over time, sometimes mutating into entirely new conspiracy theories once the original claim is refuted. Presented clearly and intuitively, these charts highlight the fact that misinformation rarely goes viral by chance. It is often driven by coordinated efforts designed to warp reality for political advantage.

Musk's interpretation of free speech, however, complicates efforts to harness these visual tools as correctives. He argues that an open environment encourages robust debate and that beneficial content will rise to the surface if left to compete freely. Critics counter that such ideals overlook the emotional triggers that make disinformation so potent as well as the rapid pace at which bad actors can manipulate trending topics. They point to the destructive impact of rumours that incite violence, witnessed in the UK riots where lives were upended by a single viral lie.

Ideally, platforms would partner with fact-checkers to present immediate, transparent data whenever suspect content appears. There could be an automated overlay that flags sudden surges in hateful messages in a specific area, or a system showing how a trending hashtag originated from a handful of identical posts. The same analytics once employed for targeted advertising could be repurposed to expose how ostensibly grassroots narratives might, in fact, be orchestrated by a small network of accounts.

Yet the choice to introduce such features lies with the platform owner. By rebranding Twitter as X and advocating a more radical free-speech doctrine, Musk has opened the door to content that may remain unchecked indefinitely. While he asserts that open dialogue is vital for democracy, the Southport riots highlight what is at stake when inflammatory falsehoods go unchallenged.

Ultimately, freedom of speech must not encapsulate inflammatory lies – a point increasingly echoed by lawmakers striving to regulate platforms like X. Some in the United Kingdom are calling for stricter rules on how quickly fake news posts must be removed or labelled. Others propose banning certain forms of targeted political advertising – a policy briefly adopted by Twitter in 2019 but reversed under Musk.

In this landscape, data visualisation emerges as a powerful means of reconciling free speech with the need for accuracy. It does not silence any viewpoint; instead, it places every claim in context, revealing which narratives stand up to scrutiny and which disintegrate upon closer examination. By mapping information flows, journalists, civil society groups and ordinary users can better grasp how disinformation spreads, who fuels it and how it impacts the real world.

The technology for such oversight already exists. Governments, academic institutions and analysts regularly develop dashboards to monitor online threats. As the Southport episode showed, the main obstacle is not a lack of data – it is a lack of incentive for platforms to implement rapid, real-time visual checks or swiftly respond to corrected information. Whether Musk's X – or any privately owned social media platform – will commit to these measures remains an open question. Yet if we value free speech alongside the integrity of public debate, data visualisation offers a clear route back to truth when lies begin to cloud the social media sphere.

A Future Balanced on Data

If data is the currency of modern politics, the Cambridge Analytica scandal served as a dire warning of how it can be spent unethically. But it also revealed that data analysis, used ethically, can promote transparency. When combined with thoughtful data visualisation, it gives citizens the means to scrutinise campaign claims, recognise voter-suppression tactics and see exactly how electoral processes work. Journalists and watchdogs can point to clear graphs that explain the real likelihood of voter fraud, show the normal distribution of votes over time or unmask networks of fake accounts.

As technology continues to evolve, it is likely we will see more sophisticated attempts at disinformation, whether through advanced AI-generated content or next-level social media manipulation.

The question is not whether these threats will arise – they will – but whether the safeguards we develop can keep pace. Data visualisation stands out as one of the most potent ways to counter mass confusion, but it relies on open data, skilled interpretation and public trust. That last element – trust – remains the hardest to secure in a climate where polarisation and suspicion run high.

Nevertheless, if society can cultivate a culture of critical engagement with data, the tide may yet turn. We have glimpsed the extent of damage that comes from using personal information as a political weapon, as happened with Cambridge Analytica. We have also seen how quickly deepfakes and AI-driven forgeries can cloud basic truths. Yet we have tools at our disposal – advanced forensic methods, interactive dashboards and network mapping – that can expose the hidden patterns behind orchestrated campaigns of deception. Whether we choose to deploy them widely and effectively could well determine the health of democracy in the face of data-driven manipulation.

KEY TAKEAWAYS

- Data visualisation helps uncover patterns of suspicious online behaviour, revealing how disinformation campaigns operate and spread.
- Interactive charts and graphs enable journalists and researchers to spot irregularities, such as sudden 'vote spikes' or coordinated posts from seemingly diverse accounts.
- Visual mappings expose how a small group of orchestrated users or bots can amplify misleading narratives, making them appear more widespread than they really are.
- Presenting complex datasets in an accessible format allows the public to understand how disinformation circulates and when it might be artificially boosted.

- Real-time visual dashboards can warn policymakers or fact-checkers about emerging threats and prompt quicker responses to harmful rumours.
- Using visual evidence helps counter conspiracy theories by clarifying legitimate vote-reporting practices and disproving deceptive charts or manipulated media.
- Demonstrating the flow of misinformation through network graphs underscores that viral rumours often stem from coordinated efforts rather than organic grassroots movements.

Chapter 12

Visualising Healthcare for a Better Tomorrow

Priya arrived to work early, just before her shift. The intensive care ward hummed in the hush before dawn, where the world felt suspended between night and day. She stepped through the double doors and past the rows of monitors either side of her. They beeped faintingly, speckling dots of colour intermittently against the walls and curtains. Pulsing lines flashed on their screens, forming an unbroken vigil over the ward's sleeping patients.

She took a moment to look and scan the main digital display by the main desk, studying each patients' vitals over the last 24 hours. All seemed well. In previous years, she would have been buried in paper charts, sifting through scribbles of ink left by the other nurses to spot any clue of a patient's decline. Now that screen synthesised everything with unnerving clarity – each time a patient shifted, or even breath, a flicker of green or yellow recorded the activity.

A single blinking icon drew her gaze. One patient's heart rate line, usually steady, had begun to climb at a worrying angle. Adrenaline flooded her system as she zeroed in on this anomaly – a sudden red glow flickering insistently on her screen. Her training kicked in at once and she crossed the ward with swift, purposeful strides, the ward lights seeming to shiver as she moved.

When Priya reached the bed, the man's breath seemed too quick and his pulse pounded beneath her fingers. She administered a rapid series of medications, only glancing back at the monitor to see whether his heart rate had begun to settle. It did, mercifully, returning to its normal cadence as dawn's first light broke through the high windows.

That small spike on the dashboard had been the difference between a stable morning on the ward and a catastrophic episode. It struck her how, not so long ago, she would have relied on the occasional manual check to catch such an early sign. Now, multiple examples of advanced data visualisation had sounded the alarm before he'd even broken a sweat.

Priya took a moment to reflect on the silent hero of the night – that subtle colour shift on the screen. Its quiet yet urgent signal had spurred her into action, helping preserve a life in the fragile predawn light.

These seemingly quiet moments capture the profound impact of data visualisation in modern healthcare. When patient data transforms from abstract numbers into visual data, it can revolutionise clinical decision-making. Healthcare professionals – from physicians to nurses – can now spot crucial patterns and respond to emerging threats with unprecedented speed and precision.

In many hospitals around the world, multi-coloured dashboards summarise health data from electronic records, wearable sensors and diagnostic machines to reveal patterns that would be invisible if those same data existed only as rows in a spreadsheet. In fact, we take them for granted because this technology has been around for decades, just like the modern PC. However, that's what it is – data visualisation. It plays a huge role in modern medicine, even if we do not realise it.

As the pace of medical innovation accelerates, hospitals, research institutions and public health agencies increasingly rely on data visualisation to reveal everything from bedside care to long-range health policy.

Data visualisation in healthcare has of course grown more sophisticated as each year passes, although this progress often goes unnoticed. A decade ago, clinicians typically saw line graphs of patient vitals or occasionally a basic chart showing disease incidence in different neighbourhoods.

Today's interactive systems – computer platforms that integrate real-time data with predictive analytics – use machine learning to forecast which patients could develop complications and to pinpoint groups at higher risk during an epidemic. Researchers exploring the potential of artificial intelligence (AI) in medical imaging produce three-dimensional (3D) scans with colour-coded zones indicating tumour probability, while epidemiologists rely on dynamic heat maps that track disease spread, often updating in real time. Visual analytics has evolved from an innovative tool to an essential part of modern healthcare. It helps doctors and nurses spot important changes in their patients' conditions that might be missed in pages of numbers and test results.

Electronic Health Records and Patient Monitoring

The evolution of hospital record-keeping marks a dramatic shift in healthcare delivery. From the paper charts that were once use – prone to errors and slow retrieval – to electronic health records, we've seen a transformation in how medical data is stored and accessed. The crucial innovation came with visual interfaces that help healthcare workers rapidly interpret this wealth of information.

Today's doctors can quickly scan a colour-coded dashboard to identify critical metrics rather than sifting through pages of test results. These modern interfaces mirror aircraft cockpits, offering real-time monitoring and subtle alerts that guide clinicians towards areas needing closer examination.

In intensive care units, these visual tools have proven particularly valuable. Staff can monitor patient vitals continuously, with subtle colour changes indicating when readings drift from normal ranges. Advanced systems now incorporate predictive algorithms, comparing current vital signs against historical patterns to warn staff about potential deterioration risks. This visual approach to patient monitoring helps prevent critical oversights in busy ward environments. Rather than replacing clinical expertise, these tools enhance it by making crucial information immediately visible and easier to interpret.

Data visualisation is starting to be used to coordinate complex patient care across departments such as cardiology, oncology, radiology, finance or admissions. Some advanced facilities now use visual journey maps to track patient appointments, results and procedures, helping coordinate care between different consultants such as cardiologists, endocrinologists and neurologists. Where fully implemented, these dashboards used in patient care can highlight connections between different aspects of care and help reduce scheduling conflicts and administrative errors. This is a problem that many patients have had in the past, including myself. You end up feeling like you are running around in loops sometimes, coordinating with various different types of doctors who don't really communicate with each other.

This can be pretty important when patients have more complicated needs. For example, cancer care requires quite rigorous planning. Being able to create a visual timeline or treatment can be incredibly useful for both patient and healthcare provider. There are many healthcare systems around the world that are working towards creating this level of integration. It's still early days yet and a lot of progress still needs to be made. But we are getting there. The benefit from getting rid of fragment healthcare systems is huge as they are both frustrating for patients and costly for healthcare providers.

Medical Imaging and Diagnostics

In the world of medical imaging, data visualisation is already transforming both diagnostic accuracy and how patients experience their care. Technologies such as CT, MRI and PET produce enormous volumes of data, often in three dimensions.

Traditionally, radiologists have examined these data in two dimensions, as black-and-white slices to spot fractures, tumours or other irregularities. If you have ever been for an X-ray, then you will know what I'm talking about.

Modern techniques, however, allow them to generate interactive 3D models on screen, complete with colour highlights that draw attention to potential problems. By rotating these models, doctors can view, for instance, a tumour from every angle, helping surgeons plan complex procedures with greater confidence.

Machine learning pushes this progress even further. In many hospitals, AI-enhanced imaging systems flag suspicious areas in bright, unmistakable colours, steering pathologists towards regions that need closer inspection. The ultimate decision remains with human experts, but algorithms reduce the likelihood of missing subtle anomalies and can accelerate the overall diagnostic process.

Real-time 3D reconstructions also help track how tumours evolve under different treatments, giving medical teams a clearer picture of whether a therapy is working. Equally important is the benefit for patients: rather than hearing a vague update that 'the tumour has shrunk by a few millimetres', they can actually see a 3D animation showing how the mass has changed, which often makes them more engaged in their own treatment decisions.

Data visualisation now extends to new frontiers as well, including advanced microscopic imaging. Researchers can don virtual reality headsets to examine molecular structures at a scale invisible to the naked eye. In these immersive simulations, they literally 'walk around' proteins to observe how potential drugs bind to target sites (O'Connor et al. 2018). While still emerging, this cutting-edge blend of biology, software engineering and medicine could revolutionise drug discovery. By seeing molecules in action, scientists may spot promising interactions more quickly than they would by analysing data in abstract charts, potentially shortening the path to breakthroughs.

Taken together, these advances are reshaping diagnostics, surgery and even the research lab, signalling a future in which visual immersion and data analysis go hand in hand to improve patient outcomes.

Disease Surveillance and Epidemiology

Data visualisation does not merely enhance clinical work within hospitals, but it also serves as a powerful medium for large-scale disease surveillance, enabling investigators to detect outbreaks early and mount effective responses. Yet the recent pandemic illustrated how, despite meticulous preparation and simulations warning of a looming crisis, the world still failed to act decisively in time.

If you remember in Chapter 2 we recounted two striking examples of this. The first was Crimson Contagion, a large-scale exercise in 2019 that engaged multiple US federal agencies, state health departments and hospitals, revealing serious flaws in pandemic coordination. Soon after came Event 201, overseen by Johns Hopkins, the World Economic Forum and the Bill & Melinda Gates Foundation, which likewise underscored the importance of data sharing and public–private collaboration in containing a hypothetical coronavirus outbreak. Let me reiterate that both simulations were carried out prior to the outbreak of coronavirus disease 2019 (COVID-19).

Despite these prescient warnings, the actual pandemic exposed how theoretical insights can be lost in the absence of compelling visual communication. When the real crisis struck, vibrant heat maps lit up social media, depicting how infections spread and intensified in alarming shades of red and orange. Government agencies worldwide erected sophisticated dashboards to display case counts, hospital capacity and fatalities in near real time.

In the United Kingdom, the official COVID-19 dashboard allowed individuals to see local infection trends and compare them with broader national data. In the United States, the *COVID Tracking Project* aggregated testing figures from state health departments, building interactive charts that showcased how positivity rates spiked or subsided by county. Rather than a static grid of numbers, these sites allowed people to track the pandemic's ebb and flow, often gauging the effect of measures such as lockdowns or masking policies.

Crucially, these dashboards made visible the pandemic's uneven impact. Many included filtering options to show how older adults and residents of low-income neighbourhoods suffered disproportionately, pointing to deep-seated healthcare inequities (Centers for Disease Control and Prevention 2010). Media outlets frequently embedded such graphs in coverage, making it plain that COVID-19 was never just about raw case numbers. Behind the scenes, epidemiologists and health officials relied on time-series data visualisations to correlate infection curves with specific interventions, such as the closure of schools or public gatherings, assessing whether policies curbed transmission (Wu et al. 2020).

Network diagrams proved equally vital in the pandemic's early phases. Their web-like connections illustrated how a single infected individual could trigger a whole chain of secondary and tertiary cases, often through social or communal gatherings.

Where these contact-tracing tools functioned effectively, health departments identified 'superspreaders' who had inadvertently exposed large numbers of people. Armed with such visual insights, local authorities could target resources and isolation measures more strategically, containing outbreaks before they grew unmanageable (Muntoni et al. 2024).

One resource rose above the rest in terms of global attention: the Johns Hopkins University COVID-19 dashboard (coronavirus.jhu.edu/map.html). It offered an interactive world map and timeline that updated confirmed cases, deaths and test numbers daily. Countless people visited the site each morning, their decisions about family visits or personal precautions guided by the evolving data. For many, this dashboard was far more than just a statistical tool – it was tangible proof of data visualisation's power to unify diverse, fast-changing streams of information into one accessible portal.

Yet these tools were not without limitations. In some corners of the Internet, partial data or selective presentations underplayed the severity of the crisis, fostering confusion. Different dashboards sometimes published conflicting numbers due to differences in reporting timetables or definitions of a 'case', causing in some cases public distrust.

Nonetheless, the broader lesson stands: data visualisation does not merely illustrate a situation, but it also actively shapes public discourse, informing policymaking and crystallising a shared awareness of the risks we face. The pandemic revealed how quickly visual platforms can transform our collective understanding, drawing millions into conversations about epidemiology and community health that would have been unthinkable just a few years earlier.

All of this arrives with a pointed irony. Crimson Contagion and Event 201 had plainly foreshadowed the enormous challenges that a virulent new pathogen would pose. Insights from these exercises remained tucked away in official reports, overshadowed until the world was already on its back foot. Had we visualised those concerns with the same clarity we brought to real-time pandemic dashboards, perhaps global leaders and the public would have grasped the danger in time to mitigate it. The fact that data visualisation took centre stage only after the outbreak was well under way underscores both its transformative potential and the cost of ignoring it. Combining the advanced analytics forecast by these simulations with compelling visual storytelling could be the difference between early intervention and a catastrophe on the scale we witnessed. Such is the power of sight: by making threats visible, we stand a better chance of addressing them before they spiral out of control.

A Shocking Murder and the High Cost of Healthcare

If anything, healthcare needs data visualisation more than ever to help tackle some of the biggest problems faced by the industry. We've already covered how data visualisation could have left us better prepared for the pandemic in 2020, but we miss that opportunity. The upshot is that we quickly realised the value data visualisation offered during the pandemic. The medical industry now faces a whole set of new challenges.

In the early hours of 4 December 2024, Midtown Manhattan bore witness to a chilling act of violence that has since reverberated through the corridors of corporate America and the public psyche alike. Brian Thompson, the 50-year-old CEO of UnitedHealthcare, was fatally shot near the New York Hilton Midtown, where he was scheduled to attend an investors' meeting. The assailant, described as a masked figure, approached Thompson from behind and fired multiple times before vanishing into New York's urban labyrinth.

The subsequent investigation led authorities to Altoona, Pennsylvania, where on 9 December they apprehended 26-year-old Luigi Mangione. At the time of his arrest, Mangione was found in possession of a 3D-printed firearm – a so-called 'ghost gun' devoid of serial numbers – along with a suppressor and multiple forms of false identification. These items bore a striking resemblance to the weaponry described in the Manhattan attack.

Mangione, an Ivy League graduate with no prior criminal record, now faces a litany of charges, including first-degree murder as an act of terrorism. If convicted, he could spend the remainder of his life behind bars. His legal counsel has entered a plea of not guilty, setting the stage for a complex and highly scrutinised trial.

Beyond the immediate horror of the assassination, Thompson's death has ignited a fervent public discourse surrounding the American healthcare system. In the digital aftermath, social media platforms became hotbeds of vitriolic commentary, with some users expressing a grim satisfaction over the demise of a figurehead in an industry often criticised for its perceived profiteering and bureaucratic inertia.

While no rationale can justify the taking of a life, the circumstances surrounding Thompson's murder have prompted a deeper examination of the systemic issues that continue to plague American healthcare.

Thompson had become a symbolic figure for critics who blamed rising insurance premiums, opaque billing practices and the frequent denial of necessary treatments for patients in financial distress. Public demonstrations outside Mangione's pre-trial hearings offered a disturbing sign of how deeply resentment had rooted itself in parts of the American populace. Many commentators suggested that this killing reflected a breaking point, although the real impetus ran deeper than any single individual or incident. The cost of American healthcare, combined with uneven outcomes, has been a long-running national crisis.

Figure 12.1 shows a snapshot of an animated data visualisation that I published a week after this incident. Unsurprisingly, it went viral. The United States has one of the most expensive healthcare systems in the world and what you see here is very telling and visually shocking.

Americans pay far more for healthcare than people in other developed nations, yet they often have worse health outcomes. The United States appears as a lonely outlier in Figure 12.1, far to the right on cost, but shows no better results for life expectancy or managing chronic diseases.

The reasons for these high costs are numerous: complex administration, expensive drugs, defensive medical practices and profit-driven insurance and healthcare systems. Each aspect of this problem can be seen through data visualisation. Administrative costs appear as oversized slices in pie charts. Drug prices shoot upward in graphs, climbing far faster than inflation. Color-coded maps reveal how

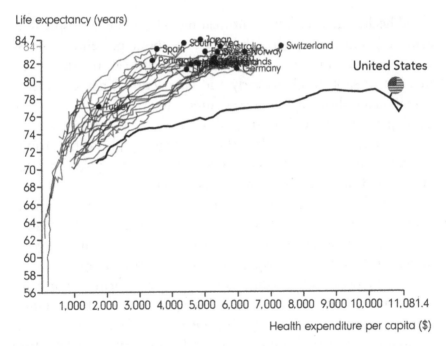

Figure 12.1 Life expectancy vs health expenditure per capita (1970–2023)

Source: UN, World Population Prospects (2023); OECD Health Expenditure and Financing Database (2023). Health expenditure data is expressed in US dollars, PPP converted at 2015 prices.

healthcare quality varies across states, often worse in areas dominated by large hospital groups that face little competition.

While Thompson's murder cannot be justified, it has highlighted a healthcare system in urgent need of reform. Rather than letting public frustration boil over into violence, we need reasoned debate leading to real change. Data visualisation can help by showing exactly where problems lie and providing solid evidence for reform discussions. When complex healthcare challenges are made visible and clear, meaningful solutions become possible.

Public Health and Population-Level Interventions

Good healthcare isn't just about treating sick people in hospitals or managing insurance claims, but it's also about preventing illness across entire communities. Public health teams can use data visualisation to spot problems early and take action. They can create digital maps showing where children aren't getting vaccinated, helping them target those neighbourhoods with mobile clinics. They can design clear graphics showing how people's eating habits affect health, making it easier to run effective campaigns against obesity and diabetes. When residents worry about pollution, heat maps can be used to show exactly where dangerous chemicals concentrate in their neighbourhoods, giving them solid evidence to demand change. In every case, these visual tools help everyone understand what's really happening in their communities.

Figure 12.2 vividly demonstrates the transformative impact of the measles vaccine in the United States. Before the vaccine's introduction in the early 1960s, the United States saw tens of thousands of cases annually – with some years exceeding 400,000 reported cases. This data visualisation illustrates the dramatic decline in cases across all states following the vaccine rollout. By the 1980s, measles cases had dwindled to fewer than 5,000 per year, and in 2000 the disease was declared eliminated in the United States.

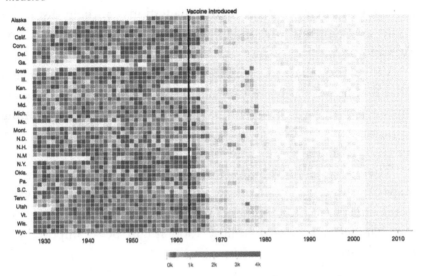

Figure 12.2 Measles incidence in the United States (1930–2010)
Source: This chart is adapted from 'Battling Infectious Diseases in the 20th Century: The Impact of Vaccines', by Tynan DeBold and Dov Friedman, originally published by *The Wall Street Journal* on 11 February 2015. Data are drawn from the US Centers for Disease Control and Prevention (CDC), measuring the number of reported measles cases per 100,000 people across all 50 states and the District of Columbia. Reproduced with permission from *The Wall Street Journal*.

Yet this hard-fought victory remains under threat. Isolated outbreaks continue to occur – particularly in communities with low vaccination rates. For example, in 2019 the United States reported over 1200 measles cases according to the National Foundation of Infectious Diseases, primarily among unvaccinated populations. This resurgence highlights the dangers posed by vaccine hesitancy, often fuelled by misinformation.

The power of this particular data visualisation lies in its ability to counter such hesitancy. By clearly showing the near eradication of measles after vaccination campaigns began, this evidence serves as a compelling argument for vaccination. It provides a stark visual contrast between the pre- and post-vaccine eras, underscoring the critical role of immunisation in public health. For parents reluctant to vaccinate their children, such visualisations can help dismantle myths and illustrate the undeniable success of vaccines in saving lives and preventing disease.

Visual tools help us see how populations are changing and what that means for healthcare needs. When charts show that certain areas will have many more elderly residents in the coming years, hospitals can plan ahead – adding more heart specialists, cancer treatment centres and end-of-life care services.

These tools also reveal how social factors affect health. Interactive maps can show, for instance, how neighbourhoods without grocery stores often have more residents with high blood pressure, suggesting that better access to healthy food might be as important as medical care.

Clinical Research and Drug Development

Developing new medicines is a massive puzzle, and data visualisation helps researchers see the picture more quickly. Picture a multi-hospital study tracking thousands of patients – there are so many numbers flying around that even the best statisticians need a clear way to spot critical trends. That is why forest plots are so popular.

During the RECOVERY trial (Randomised Evaluation of COVID-19 Therapy) – a large clinical study in the UK testing potential treatments for hospitalised COVID-19 patients – data visualisation immediately showed which patient subgroups benefited most from dexamethasone, a commonly used corticosteroid that reduces inflammation. This allowed scientists to see at a glance whether younger or older adults gained the biggest advantage.

Survival curves introduce another layer of insight. In cancer research, they let clinicians compare how well patients fare on new treatments like pembrolizumab (Keytruda) – an immunotherapy drug that helps the immune system attack cancer cells – versus older therapies. Being able to see, at a glance, that one line stays higher on the graph is incredibly powerful: it tells you that more people are living longer on the new drug.

Data visualisation goes beyond the clinical stage too. Drug discovery often starts in the lab, where teams use advanced 3D modelling tools like Schrödinger's software – a suite of computational chemistry and molecular modelling programs – to predict how a potential drug compound might bind to its target protein.

In the early days of the pandemic, these models helped researchers grasp how remdesivir interrupts a crucial protein in the severe acute respiratory syndrome coronavirus 2, speeding its path to clinical trials. Such visuals, with colour-coded chemical bonds and interactions, help scientists predict both efficacy and side effects, cutting down on time spent chasing false leads.

Once a drug heads into human trials, data dashboards become vital for tracking enrolment numbers and spotting potential safety concerns right away. Pfizer and Moderna made extensive use of visual monitoring to ensure their COVID-19 vaccine trials included a diverse mix of participants in terms of age, ethnicity and pre-existing conditions. It is not just about numbers – seeing how different groups are filling up the enrolment slots helps researchers keep the trials on the right track.

When trials end, regulators, doctors and patients want clarity above all else. That is where bar charts, risk plots and simplified graphics shine. AstraZeneca's COVID-19 vaccine results were often shown in neat visual formats that spelled out both effectiveness and rare side effects. According to research in the *BMJ*, doctors absorb this sort of data faster and with more confidence than when it is buried in reams of text or raw tables. In other words, a carefully presented Kaplan-Meier curve can make the difference between a drug languishing in bureaucracy and hitting pharmacy shelves with public trust already on board.

Healthcare Resource Management

Hospitals might be where we go for treatment, but behind the scenes they resemble logistical juggling acts. Administrators must coordinate everything from staffing and operating theatre schedules to bed availability in multiple wards. Data visualisation transforms these complexities into something that can be managed at a glance. Think of Gantt-like charts that show which departments are nearing capacity or colour-coded maps that highlight hotspots in the emergency room. The moment a particular ward is about to overflow, a red flash can prompt managers to shift staff or open extra beds.

This kind of real-time insight becomes especially crucial in emergencies – whether it is a natural disaster or a pandemic. If a surge of respiratory infections is on the horizon, for instance, interactive dashboards can integrate local infection numbers with hospital occupancy figures, predicting when each ward will be swamped. Hospital leaders can then test what-if scenarios to see how adding triage tents or extra ventilators might smooth out patient flow. Instead of relying on guesswork and anecdotal evidence, they get a semi-quantitative roadmap for crisis management.

Resource visualisation also plays a growing role in healthcare supply chains. Pharmaceutical distributors track shipments through live dashboards, making it harder for counterfeit drugs or price gouging to fly under the radar. Meanwhile, some hospitals in medical tourism hotspots give patients upfront procedure cost estimates with slick interactive calculators – a nod to improving transparency, even if critics point out that it does not always solve deeper cost issues. At minimum, it sheds light on how money and equipment move within the healthcare ecosystem, setting the stage for more informed discussions about fairness and efficiency.

Cognitive Biases in Medicine and the Role of Visualisation

Imagine a busy emergency ward late on a Saturday night. A junior doctor rushes from one patient to the next, relying on a swirl of test results, quick evaluations and gut instinct. In that hectic environment, it is easy to see how cognitive shortcuts – or biases – might creep in.

A memorable case from the previous week, for instance, can linger in the mind, prompting the doctor to suspect the same ailment in someone with entirely different symptoms. Psychologists refer to this tendency as availability bias (Kahneman 2011). Or perhaps the physician gets fixated on a lab result from earlier in the night and fails to register new information that contradicts that initial impression. This is known as confirmation bias.

Data visualisation alone cannot erase these human quirks, but it can help counteract them. Well-designed dashboards encourage clinicians to review every piece of information, not just the eye-catching or familiar details. That might mean presenting multiple indicators side by side so no single data point dominates the narrative (Saposnik et al. 2016). Or it could involve colour-coded alerts that draw attention to an outlier the doctor might otherwise dismiss. When used thoughtfully, data visuals guide clinicians towards patterns rather than random exceptions.

The flipside, of course, is that a poorly planned data visual can amplify bias. Overemphasised short-term fluctuations might tempt a doctor to chase false alarms, while design choices that highlight old data can trigger hindsight bias: everything looks obvious once you already know the outcome (Saposnik et al. 2016). This points to why data visualisation requires far more than adding a glossy chart to a screen. Designers must collaborate with healthcare teams, making sure that the final layout actually supports real-world workflows.

Medical education is starting to catch on. Today's trainees often receive lessons in data literacy, learning not just how to navigate digital dashboards but how to question them. Is the data set complete. Could there be hidden filters or flawed assumptions. Have we validated these results. By encouraging critical habits early, the next generation of doctors, nurses and allied professionals will be more adept at spotting both the insights and the blind spots that arise when human intuition meets digital information.

Reshaping the Narrative of Healthcare

Some might wonder how a line graph or an interactive map can shift an industry as massive and complex as healthcare. But consider how we change our minds: often it takes a moment of clarity, a stark realisation that the status quo is neither inevitable nor acceptable. A carefully crafted chart can deliver that moment. It might show an alarming uptick in drug prices or a dramatic gap in infant survival rates between rich and poor areas. Suddenly, a problem that once felt abstract becomes immediate. Policymakers, hospital administrators and even the broader public can rally around evidence that speaks volumes in just a few seconds' look.

Visuals also connect everyday human stories to bigger policy debates. A single mother describing her struggles with medical bills resonates more profoundly when accompanied by a graph showing that thousands of families in her region face the same issue. Facts gain emotional weight through visual context. That is why journalists and advocates alike rely on data visualisation: it communicates complexity swiftly, without drowning readers in dense text.

Of course, data can be manipulated. A narrow data set or hidden assumptions can skew the results. If a dashboard's methodology is opaque, or if crucial details are missing, it can be weaponised to push a false narrative (Saposnik et al. 2016). This is where ethical design and transparent sourcing matter most. At its best, data visualisation clarifies reality. At its worst, it masks it. Understanding which is happening requires ongoing vigilance.

Towards a Healthier, Data-Driven Future

We all end up navigating healthcare's labyrinth at some point in our lives, whether for ourselves or our loved ones. Recognising how data underpins everything – from diagnosing a tricky disease to deciding national health budgets – can help us imagine a fairer, more effective system. Already, we see glimpses of what is coming. Picture an operating theatre where surgeons use augmented reality to see a patient's arteries in real time, or epidemiologists layering climate projections onto infection maps to predict outbreaks in vulnerable regions.

The common thread is that data visualisation can bring clarity to chaos. In medicine, time and attention are precious. A few seconds saved by a well-placed colour-coded indicator could mean a faster diagnosis and maybe a saved life. That is not hyperbole; it is the reality of high-stakes decision-making. Beyond the ward, data visuals can show lawmakers and voters how a proposed policy might shift resources or reduce wait times. They can highlight pockets of success, encouraging replication in other areas, or reveal glaring gaps that need urgent fixes.

No chart alone can fix every broken part of the healthcare machine. But an honest visual – grounded in solid data and designed with people's real needs in mind – can illuminate a path forward. Rather than forcing doctors or patients to wade through mountains of spreadsheets, it draws attention to what truly matters. In the end, that is the promise of data visualisation in healthcare: not to override human expertise or empathy but to amplify both so we can deliver care that is smarter, kinder and, more crucially, available to all who need it.

In many ways, healthcare offers a microcosm of the challenges that threaten our collective future: complex systems, competing interests and the ever-present risk of disaster if we fail to grasp the warning signs in time. Data visualisation cuts through the fog of bureaucracy and endless spreadsheets, transforming opaque figures into insights that spark action.

By revealing hidden patterns in patient outcomes, highlighting health disparities across entire populations or shedding light on the ballooning costs of care, effective visual design can rally disparate groups around a common understanding. The same tools that help Priya catch an emergency at dawn can guide world leaders to confront a looming pandemic or expose the glaring inequities that drive people to desperation.

This is how data visualisation holds the potential to safeguard humanity from extinction. By highlighting what is too big, too subtle or too urgent to perceive through raw data alone, it calls us to respond before crises spiral beyond control. It does not replace expertise, compassion or political will, but it amplifies each one, forging a clearer path towards prevention and reform. If we can harness its power not just in hospitals but across every domain where life, technology and society intersect, we stand a better chance of resolving our most daunting threats. This clarity is the bedrock on which we can build strategies to protect ourselves and generations to come – a vivid reminder that, given the right tools, we need not stumble blindly into the next catastrophe.

KEY TAKEAWAYS

- Data visualisation in healthcare does more than present information: it can trigger life-saving actions by making subtle patient changes immediately obvious.

- Electronic dashboards, predictive algorithms and interactive maps enable doctors and nurses to detect deterioration early and allocate resources more efficiently.
- Machine-learning-enhanced imaging tools help radiologists, surgeons and pathologists identify tumours, track treatment progress and improve patient communication.
- Large-scale disease surveillance dashboards transform community-wide issues such as COVID-19 into plans of action, influencing policy and public understanding.
- Visualisations can highlight the uneven costs and outcomes of healthcare systems, propelling reforms that target hidden inefficiencies and inequities.
- Clinical research relies on compelling charts and graphs to reveal which treatments work best, speeding regulatory approval and building trust among both doctors and patients.
- Real-time hospital resource tracking (like Gantt charts or colour-coded occupancy maps) cuts through bureaucratic complexity, turning crisis management into a transparent, data-driven process.
- Cognitive biases, from availability to confirmation bias, can be offset by data visualisations that guide medical professionals to patterns rather than anecdotal outliers.
- By offering clarity in an otherwise confusing system, data visualisation stands as a powerful force: one that not only improves healthcare outcomes but may help avert larger crises threatening humanity.

Chapter 13

Educating Through Data Visualisation

Gita stared at the glowing dots and lines projected on the interactive wall of her classroom in Mumbai. She was a newly qualified secondary-school teacher, yet she felt more like a detective that morning. Her Class 10 pupils had just begun investigating the global spread of infectious diseases. Their textbook offered blocks of text and statistics, but these did little to bring the topic to life, especially with board exams looming. Instead, Gita turned to an online interactive chart – recommended by the World Health Organisation – that showed the historical trajectories of cholera, smallpox and other diseases across different continents. Using touch-sensitive controls, her students zoomed in on country-by-country data, turning raw numbers into vivid patterns that they could see on screen.

Within minutes, the class was alive with curiosity, captivated by the whirling display of information appearing simultaneously on the big screen and on their tablets. In an instant, they were interacting with an immersive data visualisation that let them explore how each disease spread.

One group debated why certain diseases dipped in the 1980s, while another examined a sudden spike in the twenty-first century that aligned with conflicts or the breakdown of healthcare systems in particular regions. All around, students hypothesised, tested ideas and refined their understanding.

That morning, Gita glimpsed the power of data visualisation in education: her pupils were grappling with real-world questions, guided by visual evidence rather than abstract figures in a static table. Later, as she reflected on the lesson, she realised that this new educational tool had opened a window onto the complexities of the world, bridging the distance between her classroom and a rapidly changing global landscape.

It might seem like a modest moment, yet in a world saturated with data, such experiences can be transformative. Perhaps nowhere is the need for data visualisation more urgent – or more full of potential – than in education. If you have children, you will recognise the challenge: getting them off their devices can feel impossible and capturing their interest in anything that requires thinking – such as reading, learning or exploring the world outside – is often an uphill battle.

Distractions are everywhere, especially when it comes from smartphones and tablets. Yet, it doesn't have to be that way. We can compete for their attention by making education more captivating. Data visualisation and storytelling are powerful tools to achieve this. I once had an English teacher who claimed he had served in the SAS before becoming a teacher, or so the story goes. Of course he had not, but the story captured the attention of his students instantly. It was his form of click-bait before social media even existed.

Once he had their attention, he could direct that energy towards teaching because the whole class was listening to them.

Educators today are up against fantastically addictive social media content. It's addictive because of the dopamine-driven rewards delivered through personalised content and endless scrolling designed to keep kids hooked. It taps into their deep needs for validation, connection and novelty, creating a cycle that's hard to break. Kids have therefore become used to being constantly stimulated by addictively clickable headlines and bite-sized videos that demand little from them. If education cannot keep pace, curiosity can fade and that precious little attention that they have goes online.

Improving the learning experience through a more dynamic and interactive approach to teaching – including creative uses of data visualisation – could help change the outcome of this battle for attention. By tapping into their innate curiosity, we could deliver something genuinely exciting, motivating children to discover rather than tune out.

It's not just children who need our attention, but adults too. In a fast-paced, tech-driven world where changes happen at breakneck speed, we are constantly being challenged to learn new skills and stay curious. Although we have artificial intelligence (AI) and the Internet ready to supply instant answers, this same convenience can make us complacent.

To remain competitive and to keep our minds agile, we must embrace lifelong learning, continuously reskilling and upskilling as our fields and interests evolve. We might have access to endless information, but it still takes effort and motivation to apply that knowledge in a way that is meaningful. If your role is replaced by AI, then you need to be prepared. Lifelong learning will help you switch jobs and careers more easily. Moreover, it makes you still relevant in a world dominated by AI. If we fail to do this, then what is our purpose in life? What is the point of our existence?

If our education system fails, then this makes us fragile as a species. It's not AI that will wipe us out, but our own ignorance.

Data visualisation could help us tackle the immense challenges we face in learning and understanding our world. When we visualise data, we can help different fields of study work together, make complex issues easier to understand, and spot, question and respond to important trends in society. Whether we are examining climate change, inequality, biodiversity loss, global health issues or conflicts over resources, our ability to interpret and act on information may well determine whether we endure or disappear.

Our rapidly evolving, technology-driven world presents us with risks that could lead to our extinction if we fail to adapt. Throughout this book, I have tried to show how data visualisation could be a powerful weapon against those threats. Ultimately, however, the choice to harness it responsibly lies with us.

Education Is Crucial in a Data-Saturated World

We live in an age saturated with data from social media, satellites, smartphones, medical sensors and online transactions to research labs and much more. For many people, this flood of numbers, graphs and charts feels overwhelming rather than enlightening. Instead of offering clarity, excessive amounts of data create confusion.

Hans Rosling showed how powerful data visualisation can be when it is harnessed as a tool for learning. Through his Gapminder project, he transformed raw statistics on poverty, fertility, literacy and health into animated data visualisations that sparked curiosity and wonder. Learners of all ages could suddenly see the complexity of our world and marvel at how data itself can be beautiful.

I would really recommend reading his book *Factfullness*, which he miraculously managed to finish even during his dying days fighting pancreatic cancer. You can see throughout his entire career he spent a great deal of time using data to try and challenge biased world views using data.

Another challenge with promoting continuous learning and encouraging people to be more curious to pursue knowledge is how our economy has evolved. We now inhabit a hyper-specialised society, which has created barriers to an intra-disciplinary exchange of ideas. Medical researchers might never cross paths with marine biologists, engineers may not delve into population studies and social scientists could remain unaware of the intricacies of supply chain logistics.

This compartmentalisation drives progress in specific fields but often weakens our collective ability to innovate and tackle broader challenges that might impact the world. Addressing climate change, for instance, requires not just climatologists but also economists, sociologists, political scientists, data modellers and educators working hand in hand.

For instance, DNA's unique properties could be used to tackle engineering challenges. For example, engineers could use DNA's ability to self-assemble and store information to design nanoscale materials, novel computing systems (DNA computing) and even data storage devices. Bridging biology with traditional engineering principles could open up new ways to solve problems in medicine, energy and environmental sustainability. The best ways to achieve this is to break down those barriers in education.

I live in the German-speaking part of Switzerland where I leant about this concept called *Bildung*. If you literally translate this German word, it means 'education' in English. But this translation doesn't give justice to its deeper meaning. *Bildung* goes far beyond formal education and vocational training. It embodies a lifelong devotion to personal growth, intellectual curiosity and cultural enrichment.

It is a lifelong process of personal and cultural maturation, drawing on the Ancient Greek concept of 'Paideia', the seventeenth-century Protestant Pietists' emphasis on spiritual and moral growth, and the ideas of late eighteenth- and early nineteenth-century thinkers such as Herder, Schiller and von Humboldt.

It goes beyond formal education or job training to encompass self-cultivation, intellectual curiosity and cultural enrichment. It is about harmonising your heart and mind to fostering both individual autonomy and social responsibility. It's the ultimate freedom of expression.

Bildung encourages people to explore a wide range of fields. For example, a medical doctor might become interested in physics, or a scientist might study economics. This holistic approach embraces technical competence, while also cultivating a deeper understanding of the world through the search for knowledge.

One of the greatest cultural hubs for *Bildung* came from Europe's past, in the form of pre-1938 Vienna. It was a city that once thrived as a nexus of art, music, science and philosophy. Vienna was famed for producing polymaths during what was a golden cultural renaissance. These individuals refused to confine themselves to a single field, weaving together music, art, philosophy and science to generate groundbreaking discoveries. Many of those great minds were Jewish as well as Catholic. There were no religious barriers in the pursuit of knowledge.

Its legendary coffee houses and salons became arenas for intellectual exchange during *Privat Seminars*, while royal patronage funded creative and scholarly pursuits. In that environment, experts who might normally stay in their silos – from architects to composers – engaged with each other's fields. This spirit of boundary-crossing collaboration shaped Europe's evolution in art, music, science and philosophy. And natural aspects are still felt next door in Switzerland to this day.

Switzerland has had, therefore, a huge impact on my life. It was here that I discovered my own *Bildung* – my personal drive for continuous learning. I would never have had the opportunity to do what I do today if I had stayed elsewhere. Living in this country gave me the space to explore my interests beyond my career in asset management. Although I studied economics at university and spent over

20 years working in this industry, my curiosity spans physics, mathematics, history and psychology. I also love art, colour and music.

I am now known for my data visualisations these days, even though I never formally trained in that field. Most of my time is spent on coding despite having done little more than dabble in it as a teenager. I am neither a data scientist nor a software engineer by training, yet in Switzerland I found the freedom and resources to learn these skills.

It proved that sometimes all we need is a supportive environment to unlock our hidden passions. Switzerland is one of the most innovative countries in the world, but that innovation didn't just pop out of nowhere. It's the system over here that allows innovation to thrive and I experienced this myself.

When I visited my daughter's secondary school recently, one of her teachers showed me how she might become an engineer, which is her current dream. He explained the multiple routes available within the Swiss education system to help her reach that goal, recognising that every student has a unique personality and preferred way of learning. Believe it or not, what he showed by was a network diagram.

They also encourage children to explore interests that might not immediately seem obvious to them. Why not have a go at art, cooking or sport. It's not all academic. If you want to be an engineer, you do not necessarily need to follow an academic path. While some students do thrive on more traditional exam-focused learning, others are more suited to a more hands-on approach. In Switzerland, these academically inclined learners often attend what is known as the *Gymnasium* (similar to a grammar school in the United Kingdom).

Personally, I would never have fitted well into that sort of school. I spent much of my teenage years dealing with ADHD and dyslexia, and I received no real support except from one dedicated English teacher, Mr Hargreaves. He was the only person who noted my struggles and fought hard to get me extra help. In truth, I did not find substantial support until I started university, where the resources were more extensive for someone like me. Even then, I only truly flourished when I moved to Switzerland in my 30s and discovered the immense pleasure of lifelong learning and thinking slowly.

That is something we must not forget: learning has to be enjoyable and accessible. If it is not then it is society that will suffer from the loss of what we might have accomplished.

Specialisation Can Actually Make Us Fragile

Returning to the issue of over-specialisation we discussed earlier, students with narrowly focused academic paths often miss how different fields intersect. Data visualisation, however, can connect seemingly unrelated information sets, revealing hidden relationships that might otherwise remain invisible.

Picture, for instance, an interactive map that links deforestation in the Amazon to consumer demand in Europe and shifting rainfall patterns in Africa (Bourgoin et al. 2024). Viewed this way, global cause and effect becomes far clearer, showing how local actions can reverberate worldwide.

However, this mindset and this way of learning has to start at a young age, otherwise knowledge is acquired in isolation and it's not applied holistically. I believe that education today stands at a turning point. Our education systems often lag behind the rapid pace of technological and social change, leaving many teachers untrained in data literacy or the use of visualisation tools (OECD 2019).

Meanwhile, misinformation spreads easily on social media and conspiracy theories thrive when audiences cannot interpret or question their sources (European Commission 2018). If we wish to push back against these trends and harness data for the greater good, data visualisation in education is not just a 'nice to have' – it could be pivotal to our collective survival.

Education is key to preventing people from being misled by misinformation and fake news. By starting at a young age, encouraging students to challenge the status quo, analyse evidence and search for truth rather than simply accepting statements as fact, we can reduce these risks. When students develop critical thinking skills early, they become better equipped to navigate the complexities of information in the digital age. Rather than passively consuming content, they learn to question, verify and evaluate the credibility of sources – essential skills for identifying and resisting misinformation.

These are skills that are not being practiced enough, but I believe data visualisation offers the chance to help bridge this gap by making data and the truth that it holds much more accessible.

Data Visualisation Taps into the Power of Visual Thinking

One reason data visualisation is so powerful is that it speaks to our deep-rooted capacity for visual thinking. Early in this book, we noted how one of humanity's earliest data visualisations was the *Imago Mundi* – the oldest known world map, used by ancient Mesopotamians to make sense of their surroundings. Even today, our brains excel at processing visual information. In the book *Brain Rules* (2014), developmental molecular biologist John Medina argues that we retain significantly more information when it is presented visually than when it is conveyed purely in text. Some studies suggest we may recall around 65% of what we see, compared with only about 10% of what we read after three days (Medina 2009). While the exact figures vary, the main point remains clear: tapping into our natural preference for images can greatly improve our understanding and memory.

Visualising data also reduces cognitive load, relieving us of the need to juggle numerous figures and relationships in working memory (Mayer and Moreno 2023). Instead of painstakingly parsing rows of numbers, you can focus on interpreting the patterns directly in front of you. This benefit becomes vital when dealing with large or complex datasets – from genomics to real-time satellite imagery.

Raw data, typically presented as tables or lengthy blocks of text, demands high-level interpretation skills. Even in well-educated groups, only a small fraction of people can fully explore extensive datasets and uncover their underlying messages. In the book *Show Me the Numbers* (2004), Stephen Few shows how effective data visualisations can transform daunting collections of figures into more approachable representations. By visually highlighting key patterns, we can swiftly and clearly glean what might otherwise remain hidden in dense numbers (Few 2004).

Picture two ways of looking at the same information: scrolling through endless rows of numbers in a spreadsheet or looking at a simple scatter plot. The plot immediately shows you something important – how closely greenhouse gas emissions and ocean temperatures rise together. One glance tells you the story that might be hidden in those thousands of spreadsheet rows.

A clear data visualisation does more than compress complexity – it also encourages deeper inquiry. Instead of feeling overwhelmed by a sea of numbers, students can ask, 'What causes this spike?' or 'Why do these anomalies appear here?' A good data visualisation, therefore, becomes an invitation to investigate further rather than a daunting wall of data.

From an educational perspective, combining data with visuals can be especially powerful. Interactive graphs, timelines and heat maps help students notice patterns quickly, prompting them to pose questions and form hypotheses. Rather than passively absorbing information, they actively engage with the data and, by extension, the real-world phenomena behind it.

Bring the World into the Classroom

Imagine a typical science classroom. Students often memorise chemical formulas or read about historical experiments, without connecting these lessons to major global challenges. At least that was generally my experience when I studied science at school.

Data visualisation can bridge that gap by linking classroom concepts to live information. For example, NASA's Earth Observing System shares real-time dashboards on carbon dioxide levels and temperature anomalies around the world. Interacting with these visuals can spark questions like 'Why is it so hot in this region right now?' or 'What causes that sudden jump in CO_2?'

You don't need to be a scientist to find this interesting. I do, even though it was not my academic discipline. That's why data visualisation is so powerful. It makes knowledge much more accessible and enjoyable to obtain, especially when you can interact and explore data that holds those learning experiences.

A similar idea works in social studies or economics. Public data on trade balances, inequality or unemployment can be turned into interactive charts. Platforms such as the World Bank's DataBank or the UN's SDG Tracker offer a wealth of information. Students might compare how gross domestic product aligns with literacy rates or track trade imbalances over time. Seeing these trends on a graph invites deeper thinking about root causes and potential solutions.

Today's classrooms are perfectly positioned to embrace multi-disciplinary learning through data visualisation. For example, biology and geography classes could work together, using interactive maps to explore the relationship between habitat loss and human development. At university level, this collaborative approach could extend even further – economics and natural science students might partner to visualise how carbon market fluctuations influence forest conservation efforts. These cross-disciplinary projects bring abstract concepts to life, helping students understand complex relationships between different fields of study.

By seeing how everything is linked, students develop a mindset that is ready to address large-scale problems, which is what we need to do today. That broader perspective is essential if they are to help tackle and possibly prevent crises that threaten humanity both now and in the future.

We can start tracking these problems at a local level. For instance, students living in an urban environment might track their neighbourhood's air quality and compare it with national pollution patterns, while rural students could examine local farmland use and its relationship to worldwide drought risks. This approach grounds abstract global issues in students' daily lives, showing them that these challenges are neither remote nor insurmountable.

These local-to-global connections are already making an impact through various educational programmes. The GLOBE Program, supported by NASA and the National Science Foundation, exemplifies this approach. Students collect environmental data in their own communities, which then appears on global maps. This visual representation helps them see how their local observations contribute to our understanding of worldwide environmental patterns.

Overcoming Misinformation Through Visual Literacy

We have seen how immersive data visualisations can light up a classroom, but data can also be dangerously misleading if used without integrity. As discussed in the previous chapter, misinformation has become a significant threat to rational discourse. Social media platforms, with their rapid-fire sharing features, can provide a fertile ground for conspiracy theories and half-truths to go viral.

Data is not immune to such distortions – a single misplaced axis, selective sampling or manipulated colours can turn valid statistics into false narratives. Misinformation can then be dressed up in charts that look credible on the surface but are riddled with errors or bias. We have briefly touched on this already, but now let's delve a bit deeper.

As mentioned before, younger generations face a serious risk if they lack the tools to interpret and critique visual information. Without these critical skills, they may accept misleading visual claims without question. Educators must play a central role here. Data literacy is not just about reading a bar chart, but it also requires a basic grasp of statistics, an appreciation of how sampling works and a healthy scepticism towards any visual that does not cite its sources.

Personally, this is a massive bugbear for me. If you follow me on social media, you will note that I hate unsourced content. There is too much copying and pasting, which adds to the confusion and misinformation that spreads across social media platforms. If you use content that is not yours on a social media platform, then say so and say where you got it from. We do it in academics for a reason. If you can't find the source of that information or verify whether it's true, it is bad data.

This is why we need to teach students at a young age to challenge these types of issues.

By teaching pupils to ask, 'Who created this chart?' and 'What assumptions might be hidden in the dataset?' we inoculate them against manipulation.

Teaching critical data visualisation literacy also goes beyond formal lessons in mathematics or IT. Pupils should learn how easily scales, axes and colours can be altered to amplify certain findings or mask uncomfortable truths. Classroom activities might invite students to 'fix' a misleading infographic, challenging them to spot how truncated axes or missing legends warp the facts. This approach demystifies data visualisation, empowering them to distinguish between evidence-based arguments and deceptive design.

When coronavirus disease 2019 struck, countless flawed charts began circulating online. Some featured distorted timelines to suggest sudden spikes in cases; others compared disparate metrics, sowing confusion. In schools, if data interpretation skills were routinely taught, students would be able to spot these inconsistencies without much effort.

How Technology Can Be Used for Data-Driven Learning

Recent advances in technology have also broadened the possibilities for data-based education in schools and university. Tools such as Tableau, Power BI, Google Data Studio or open-source platforms such as RAWGraphs and Datawrapper can now allow teachers and students to produce interactive data visualisation with relative ease. They don't need to code in JavaScript and Python like I do. There are so many different ways you can create data visualisations.

When it comes to technology, I admit that there is still a long way to go. Data visualisation is not accessible enough. But the emergence of these tools is nonetheless a good sign of progress. Used properly and they can help foster a culture of lifelong learning among students. We should never underestimate the power of what is learnt in the classroom. I remember learning how to write an excel formula at school almost 30 years ago. Those same excel skills that I learnt back then, I remember and still use today.

Rather than poring over pages of raw numbers, interactive data visualisations can allow students to manipulate filters, zoom in on specific years or compare multiple data sets to see real-time trends. This taps into the spirit of exploration, transforming static lessons into hands-on investigations. It is important to teach these lessons now as they can have huge impact on the future. One of things I was never taught at school was how to explore data. This is arguably one of the most important skills you need to learn if you ever want to create your own data visualisations. A huge part of creating a data visualisation is being able to not just acquire data but also to explore the data set for the hidden meanings within.

This is actually a skill that can take years, if not decades, to master. You learn from experience. And being able to do this well makes the difference between your data visualisation having an impact on the world and influencing people or just being a misaligned social media post. These are lessons that really ought to be taught in schools. As far as I know, at the time of writing, there are no school systems anywhere in the world that teach these skills.

We need to show kids in school that data visualisation can be really cool. For example, showing them how to create dashboards might not be the best way to inspire a student. I know many CFOs that struggle to take in the dashboards that their finance departments have created for them and they are adults.

There are more interesting ways to visualise data. For instance, virtual reality (VR) and augmented reality (AR) can push data immersion even further and encourage students to take a greater interest. Can you imagine, for instance, walking through a three-dimensional climate model or visualising temperature changes across decades. Similarly, an AR app could overlay historical flood levels or pollution data onto the physical space around them. Neuroscientific studies suggest that such immersive experiences can enhance both emotional engagement and long-term memory (Christou 2010).

Gamification offers another route to make data interactive and meaningful. The classic city-building game SimCity was never intended as a formal teaching tool, yet it demonstrated how data – from population density to pollution metrics – can be visualised and managed. Modern educational simulations build on this principle, letting students experiment with different policies or resource allocations while instantly seeing the consequences. In this way, data becomes a living thing rather than a static entity, encouraging systems thinking.

Barriers and Ethical Dilemmas

Despite these exciting developments, we must acknowledge the barriers. Not all schools around the world have reliable Internet connections or budgets for advanced digital tools. In many regions, even a simple computer lab is a luxury, meaning that interactive dashboards or VR headsets might be out of reach. Inevitably, a 'digital divide' emerges, risking further educational inequality. Open-source software and community-led initiatives can help reduce costs, but addressing infrastructure gaps often requires governmental support.

Data privacy raises further concerns. When students collect or analyse local data – for example, on health or income – there is a risk of re-identifying individuals, even when names and addresses are removed. Protecting personal information is not just a legal obligation, but it is also an ethical one. Young people need to understand why privacy matters, learning how to anonymise and aggregate data responsibly.

Data Visualisation as a Catalyst for Global Awareness

One of the points we have not yet addressed in this chapter is the role data visualisation plays when it comes to empathy. Strongly linked, which is why human beings have such a love for data visualisation evidence the dawn of human history. We mustn't forget this.

Data visualisation can spark profound empathy on certain topics. Many of us won't remember the iconic 'Earthrise' photograph captured by the crew of Apollo 8 back in 1968, but it was probably one of the most iconic images from that decade.

It revealed Earth, a beautiful glistening blue and green marble glowing the darkness of empty space. That single image helps shift public perception on many environmental issues. It transformed humanity's sense of unity and collective responsibility.

Robert Poole later wrote an influential book titled *Earthwise*, taking its name from this watershed moment. The book delves deep into the moral dimensions of environmental stewardship. In it, Poole explores how this unprecedented view of our planet catalysed the modern environmental movement (Poole 2008). The photograph's impact helped lay the groundwork for initiatives like Earth Day and embedded ecological concerns deeply within public consciousness.

Similarly, contemporary data visualisations can provoke an equally visceral response. These visualisations – whether depicting retreating ice sheets, shifting refugee movements or patterns of deforestation – serve a powerful purpose. They illustrate that climate change and humanitarian crises are not mere abstract concepts that you hear about on the new, but stark realities affecting millions of lives.

In the classroom, such images can spark important discussions about global responsibility and our moral duty to protect our shared home, planet Earth. Students who witness, in real time, how tropical storms devastate vulnerable regions or how rising seas threaten coastal communities can better comprehend the pressing need for action. As *Earthwise* argues, once we acknowledge our fundamental interdependence and recognise that the planet's well-being is inextricably linked to our survival, we can no longer ignore our moral obligation to safeguard our collective future.

Well-designed data visuals can galvanise collective action. A group of students might build a dashboard tracking local air pollution levels and then use it to push local authorities for greener transport policies. By harnessing accessible, transparent data, communities can hold decision-makers accountable and students discover the power of evidence-driven advocacy. In that sense, data visualisation can become a tool for social engagement, not merely an academic exercise or a sensationalised social media post.

If we wish to navigate the storms of a data-saturated age and safeguard our collective future, we must empower ourselves, and especially the next generation, with the critical skills to visualise, interpret and share data responsibly. By embracing data visualisation across our educational systems, we inject excitement into the learning process and provide students with the tools to see beyond their narrow specialisations. In doing so, we enhance our collective intelligence, accelerate the discovery of cross-cutting solutions and encourage a global mindset capable of tackling existential risks.

Such an approach equips us not merely to withstand the onslaught of misinformation and growing technological complexity but also to remain curious, inventive and resilient. These are the very qualities that have historically propelled our species forward and may help us avert extinction or slip into irrelevance in this data-saturated world.

KEY TAKEAWAYS

- Data visualisation is a powerful educational tool that can transform abstract numbers into engaging, interactive learning experiences.
- Visual learning is more effective than text-based learning – studies suggest we may recall 65% of what we see versus only 10% of what we read.
- Data visualisation helps bridge different fields of knowledge, breaking down silos between disciplines and encouraging interdisciplinary thinking.
- Interactive data visualisations allow students to explore complex issues such as climate change, public health and global economics in intuitive ways.
- Over-specialisation in education makes societies more fragile and less able to tackle complex global challenges.
- Visual literacy is essential for combating misinformation – students need to learn how data can be manipulated through misleading visualisations.

- Technology tools (Tableau, Power BI, etc.) have made data visualisation more accessible, though accessibility remains a challenge.
- Immersive technologies like VR/AR offer new possibilities for data-driven learning experiences.
- Data visualisation can foster empathy and global awareness, similar to how the Earthrise photograph changed our perspective of Earth.
- Teaching data exploration skills is crucial but currently missing from most educational systems worldwide.

Chapter 14

Seeing Our Way to Survival

Ethan stepped off a sleek bullet train in the outskirts of Tokyo, clutching a freshly printed visitor pass. He had arrived at the Global Forum on Data Futures – one of the largest gatherings of data scientists, policymakers and activists in the world. Standing in the atrium, surrounded by towering screens pulsating with streaming data visuals, he found himself momentarily overwhelmed. Yet this time, unlike his early days of stumbling through modern civilisation, he felt a hint of excitement course through him. Over the past few months, he had been introduced to a world where data could be transformed from an avalanche of meaningless numbers into something that could actually change lives.

His mind still wandered back to the day he was a bewildered newcomer. He had wondered if modern life was a gilded cage – all comfort, no purpose. But now he sensed something else. He inhaled, looking up at a banner reading, 'Data Visualisation: From Chaos to Clarity'. It was time to see how far he, and how far *we*, could go.

The Epoch of Data

We are living in an era full of data. Satellites orbiting Earth capture high-resolution images of melting glaciers. Smartwatch and smartphones accumulate our daily movements and vital health signs. Social media algorithms ingest oceans of personal ideas and opinions. In principle, these information streams can solve problems big and small. But as the previous chapters have illustrated, data alone can also mislead, overwhelm and paralyse us into a sense of inaction.

This tension – between data as a force for progress and data as a source of confusion – has run through this book as a unifying theme. It is no exaggeration to say that our collective future may hinge on whether we learn to harness data productively rather than drown in it. Used well, data can help us track pandemics in real time, anticipate the next financial collapse, measure the true cost of our carbon footprint and reshape educational systems so that fewer students fall behind. Used poorly, data can fuel misinformation, empower authoritarian regimes to monitor and oppress or trap us in an echo chamber of lies.

Time and again, we have seen how data becomes truly valuable only when it is made intelligible. This is where data visualisation proves indispensable. Through well-crafted visuals – charts, maps, interactive interfaces, three-dimensional reconstructions and virtual reality (VR) simulations – we can reduce complexity to a form the human mind can more readily grasp. We can see patterns that would otherwise be invisible, clarifying what truly matters amid the noise.

Yet data visualisation is not a magic wand. It does not guarantee comprehension, nor does it immunise us against bias or deception. Indeed, it can be exploited to distort the truth. The challenge, then, is to use data visualisation ethically, precisely and passionately, giving us a fighting chance to avert humanity's potential downfall.

Revisiting the Warning Signs

Throughout this book, we encountered myriad threats that could – if we remain blind to them – push civilisation to the brink of collapse:

1. *Tech fragility:* Our global economy heavily leans on advanced technology whose complexity few genuinely understand. During the summer of 2024, we observed how the worst ever IT blackout saw planes grounded, surgeries cancelled and some online bank crashed, thanks to a single Microsoft Windows software patch. If we could visualise and understand network dependencies better, we might spot vulnerabilities in our technology infrastructure more easily and build a system that is more resistant to cyberattacks and accidents.
2. *Pandemic blind spots:* Despite prior simulations such as Crimson Contagion and Event 201 in the United States, the coronavirus disease 2019 still caught the world off guard. Only once dashboards emerged did policymakers and the public see the infection's spread in near real time, prompting belated but crucial interventions. Data visualisation cannot prevent pandemics, but it can help guide swift decisions needed to limit the spread, which can save lives and prevent further economic damage.
3. *Climate chaos:* For decades, raw numbers have documented sea levels rising, glaciers retreating, and storms intensifying – yet the global response has been tepid. When these changes are shown through interactive maps or animated timelines, however, public consciousness finally stirs. These data visualisations help people experience the creeping threats in their own communities and beyond. Without such compelling visuals, climate data remains merely an academic footnote, easily ignored.

4. *Misinformation and political manipulation:* As Cambridge Analytica's scandal underscored, personal data can be weaponised to manipulate voter behaviour. Deepfakes and artificial intelligence (AI)-driven image manipulation further amplify the risk. But the same data visualisation approaches – network graphs, correlation plots and real-time dashboards – can expose and debunk misinformation and political manipulation.
5. *Healthcare crises:* Hospitals often operate near capacity, juggling staff schedules, patient admissions and finite resources. Up-to-date tracking tools can prevent crises by visually showing where and when action is needed, helping medical teams respond swiftly to sudden increases in patients. Meanwhile, modern imaging presents information in greater detail, enabling faster diagnoses and clearer treatment decisions. Without these data visualisation methods, vital warning signs may be overlooked until it is too late.
6. *Economic inequalities and bias:* Our belief in endless economic growth – seen in the contrast between growing wealth and persistent health gaps or in ever-rising gross domestic product – can hide serious inequalities. Younger people worry they may never own a home, while entire nations remain stuck in poverty despite centuries of progress. By presenting data in accessible ways, we can spotlight the specific policies and historical forces that widen these divisions.

Each scenario shows how data visualisation can rescue us from ignorance, change public opinion and lead to policy change. Yet each scenario also reminds us that these tools are insufficient if we ignore the underlying signals, cling to oversimplified stories or become numb in a saturated media environment.

Data Visualisation as Human Storytelling

As we explored the journey from ancient maps like the *Imago Mundi* to AI-driven dashboards in modern hospitals, one lesson stands out: humans process stories more readily than abstract facts.

Data visualisation done right does not just present a 'picture', but it presents a story that appeals to both intellect and emotion. Hans Rosling knew this intimately. His Gapminder bubble charts soared to popularity not merely because they displayed economic and health stats, but because they told a multi-decade story of human flourishing and resilience. They made us *feel* the progress.

An effective data story, therefore, has three key elements:

1. *Simplicity of delivery:* Memorable visuals often employ colour, shapes and motion (and even music) to highlight the essence of data. Whether it is a bar chart race emphasising how country rankings shift over time or an interactive world map that glows hot red where deforestation spikes, the human brain must see the pattern quickly without deciphering endless legends or disclaimers.
2. *Integrity of source:* Audiences should trust the underlying data. Without transparency about where the numbers come from or how they were derived, even the most beautiful charts cannot be trusted. Fact-checking, reproducibility and ethical sourcing of data are vital to preserve credibility.
3. *Narrative connection:* Data alone rarely changes minds. We need real or representative characters, settings or events for the message to resonate. A climate map is more compelling when we learn about a farmer in Bangladesh losing their home to rising waters or a child in Mumbai using a data-driven app to understand cholera outbreaks in their neighbourhood.

Critically, our appetite for pictures and storytelling can also be twisted for manipulative ends. In an age of deepfakes and AI chatbots, illusions can be spun to sow discord, promote conspiracies or justify oppression. This underscores that data visualisation is a double-edged sword – we must champion visual literacy, equipping everyone to question and probe the images they see.

Ethical Frameworks and Education

Following the adage 'with great power comes great responsibility', we must establish ethics for data visualisation. We cannot simply rely on companies such as Meta or X, owned by Musk, to regulate themselves. We cannot expect AI-generative tools to spontaneously correct for biases and deception. Instead, we need:

Educational reforms: Data literacy should be part of standard curricula in school and universities. A generation that can scrutinise a suspect bar chart or detect manipulated images is a generation better prepared to resist misinformation.

Industry standards: Professional bodies in data science, journalism and design can develop codes of conduct that outline best practices from mandatory sourcing and date stamps to disclaimers about uncertainty and error margins.

Regulatory oversight: Governments must craft balanced legislation that addresses false advertising, manipulative political ads and privacy violations. This should be done in concert with researchers and ethicists, minimising censorship while maximising protection for civil society.

Global collaboration: Threats such as climate change, pandemics and disinformation campaigns affect multiple countries. We need countries to work together on common rules, or some regions might have no restrictions on how data can be misrepresented. The tools to create convincing fakes such as AI-generated videos or misleading charts are available worldwide. This means our standards for honest data presentation should also be coordinated globally.

Even with good rules and guidelines, we cannot eliminate every risk. Humans remain prone to cognitive shortcuts, tribal biases and the allure of sensational claims. But just as seat belts and traffic laws haven't ended car crashes but have significantly reduced fatalities, a strong ethical foundation in data visualisation can mitigate some of the worst outcomes.

The Imperative of Continuous Learning

If data visualisation is integral for diagnosing problems early and galvanising solutions, then ongoing education is critical. We need a holistic approach to learning that can nurture open-mindedness and encouraging professionals to cross traditional boundaries. A nurse could collaborate with an economist to reduce health inequalities, or a climatologist could partner with a supply-chain manager to design greener logistics. Such an approach can encourage out-of-box thinking and spur innovation.

The explosion in data demands that we bring academic domains together, potentially using data visualisation to show the big picture. Education systems should mirror that bridging, teaching students not just how to code or analyse spreadsheets but also how to recognise the broader patterns that emerge when separate datasets are connected.

We cannot simply rely on the next generation. Adults, too, must adapt. Rapid technological shifts can make skills obsolete overnight. Governments and companies should invest in retraining programmes that incorporate visual data tools – ensuring workers remain capable and flexible, reducing the risk of economic shocks. Data visualisation, by offering an intuitive window into new knowledge, can accelerate retraining across industries. The more accessible we make learning, the more resilient our societies become.

A Call to Arms for Change

So how do we begin? How do we truly make data visualisation a linchpin in our efforts to avert extinction-level threats?

1. *Champion open data:* Walled gardens restrict our capacity to see the full landscape. We must push governments, academic institutions and corporations to share anonymised data sets responsibly. Only then can independent analysts and civic groups build unbiased, or at least critically assessed, data visualisations that hold power to account.
2. *Invest in grassroots education:* Provide free or affordable digital tools in schools. Encourage extracurricular clubs where students tackle real data sets – on local air quality, historical election trends or epidemiological patterns – and transform them into visual stories. Let them explore interactive dashboards or VR-based simulations that connect with their daily experiences.
3. *Incentivise collaboration:* Overcome silos within academia and industry by funding cross-disciplinary data labs. Bring coders, artists, ethicists and domain experts together to produce data visualisations that tackle pressing global issues – from antibiotic resistance to energy transitions. We must treat data visualisation not merely as a final presentation step, but also as a fundamental research method that shapes how we question the world.
4. *Hold platforms accountable:* Social media networks can do more than chase short-term profits through outrage algorithms. Their sophisticated data pipelines could highlight suspicious content, label manipulated visuals and detect orchestrated campaigns – all visually summarised to the public. Regulators should require these features, balancing transparency with user privacy.
5. *Demand ethical tech development:* Deepfake generation, AI-driven chart creation and automated editing tools should embed detection systems from the start. Visual forensics can run beneath the surface, flagging content that appears artificially manipulated. This is a tall order, but ignoring these concerns invites chaos in the near future.
6. *Celebrate and reward excellence:* Events such as the Information is Beautiful Awards or the Data Journalism Awards matter, but we could do more. We can create public-facing platforms that highlight best-in-class data visualisations on health, climate, justice or governance data. Recognise professionals who push ethical, creative

and effective boundaries, inspiring others to do the same. For instance, Voronoi by Visual Capitalist is a data visualisation social media platform that encourages people to share and discuss visual data, allowing them to uncover connections that might otherwise remain hidden.
7. *Stay alert to the next frontier:* Technology evolves at breakneck speed. Just as virtual or augmented reality can help teach, they can also conjure illusions that appear terrifyingly real. As quantum computing emerges, encryption and data verification methods may need rethinking. We must remain vigilant, ready to adapt new forms of data visualisation that keep pace with reality's shifting edge.

At the core, this is a call to arms: data visualisation is not a niche or a novelty. It is a potent, necessary discipline that can guide us through the swirling data storms of the twenty-first century.

A Return to Ethan

Ethan paced the halls of the conference centre, mesmerised by interactive exhibits showing the real-time carbon footprint of every city on Earth. With a tap, the display zoomed in on hotspots, lighting up the screens with red for heavily polluted regions and blue for cleaner areas. Another exhibit displayed an animated model of antibiotic resistance genes transferring between hospital settings worldwide. For a moment, Ethan imagined each gene as a predator, slithering across continents, ready to pounce where vigilance was lacking.

He felt that old sense of purpose stirring within him – the same instinct that once drove him to read footprints on muddy ground. Perhaps he had not lost his primal instincts, after all. The hunt remained, but instead of chasing game, he was pursuing knowledge, solutions and new ideas.

A voice sounded behind him, calling him to the main auditorium. The keynote speaker, a scientist from the Pacific Islands, was about to reveal a new immersive data visualisation on sea-level rise.

Ethan found a seat near the back. The lights dimmed. A giant display flickered to life, whisking the audience into an interactive oceanic panorama. They could watch coral reefs bleach under warming waters, track storms forming in the tropics and see projected flooding along coastal cities.

As the speaker navigated the virtual space, arcs of data told stories of rising tides and shifting weather patterns. Each coloured swirl was a caution, each cluster of statistics an alarm. Yet running through it all was a sense of possibility. 'We can still act,' the speaker said calmly, 'if we can learn to see.'

Ethan could almost feel a whisper crossing centuries: the ancient hunts, the threats faced by modern man and the data swirling around them. All demanded the same skill – reading signs to survive. We have become unmoored from the environment, from each other and from our essential truths. Could data visualisation reconnect us, allowing us to see the invisible threads that shape everything from climate to pandemics to misinformation?

The keynote concluded. Applause thundered through the auditorium. People began to disperse, returning to booths and breakouts. Ethan stood, letting the echo of the speaker's words settle within him. He pictured a future where the illusions of misinformation dissolve under the bright scrutiny of well-crafted data visuals, where policy decisions revolve around clear metrics and where no child is left behind because we missed the data telling us they were failing.

He stepped into the corridor, noticing conference banners that read, '*Save the World: One Chart at a Time*'. Perhaps it was just an ambitious marketing slogan. But in his heart, Ethan realised something quite real: data visualisation could serve as our modern-day beacon fire, shining across the frontiers of possibility. If we harness it collectively, with vigilance and curiosity, maybe – just maybe – our species would endure.

Final Reflections

Data visualisation stands at the frontier of human expression, bridging the gap between knowledge and meaningful action. Where once we told stories around campfires, painting hunts on cave walls, we now encode the world in lines, bars, bubbles, nodes, shapes and arcs of colour. Throughout this book, we have seen how these representations can be weaponised, used to distort elections or overhype precarious investment trends. But we have also seen them rally communities, spark innovations in health and education and reveal solutions hidden beneath layers of numerical noise.

Why is data visualisation so crucial? Because our world has never been more complex nor so close to various tipping points that could unravel centuries of progress. In an age of nuclear arsenals and warming oceans, we must not drift into crises half-blinded by ignorance or confusion. Data visualisation, done ethically and with skill, can remove that confusion, helping us see what truly matter.

Yet none of this will happen by accident. We must commit ourselves to better data practices:

1. *Learn to read*: Not just text but also images. Hone our collective visual data literacy so that we spot illusions and lies.
2. *Learn to write*: Not just sentences but also charts, networks and dashboards. Give people powerful data visuals that guide them rather than marketing illusions that manipulate them.
3. *Confront our biases*: Understanding that every chart, map or animation emerges from choices about data selection, scale and design. Ask who made these choices and why.
4. *Foster collaboration*: Bridging different disciplines and societies. Just as data crosses boundaries, so must our solutions.

In doing so, we embed data visualisation into the fabric of education, policymaking, journalism, healthcare, environmental stewardship and all the other domains that shape human destiny. We ensure that the next wave of technological wonders – from AI to quantum computing – remains tethered to human values and insights rather than running away from them.

Yes, data visualisation can be the difference between speculation and clarity, panic and informed response, hate-driven manipulation and reasoned debate. It can also be the difference between complacent acceptance of our world's fractures and urgent, collective progress. By making the invisible visible, it can galvanise us to act, no matter how daunting the crisis. It allows us to find clarity in chaos.

From the vantage point of time, let future generations say that when we stood at the crossroads – facing pandemics, misinformation, climate hazards and societal unrest – we chose to see. We chose to interpret the signs, to reflect them back to society in patterns and colours that dispelled illusions and sparked bravery. We poured our energies into ensuring data served truth and empathy, not profit or narrow ambition. Let them say that we turned knowledge into vision and vision into survival.

This is the final call: we must embrace data visualisation as an integral tool for shaping our collective destiny. Let our charts and graphs become modern icons that rally people, strip away ignorance and guide humanity's steps away from the brink. Though no single image alone can save the world, each brilliant spark of insight can set off a chain reaction of clarity, forging the solutions our species so desperately needs.

Beyond these discussions, the story is still being written. The data streams keep coming, accompanied by new crises and wondrous opportunities. May you, the reader, carry forward the energy of each chapter – from the cautionary tales of deepfakes and hacked elections to the triumphs of advanced medical imaging and the zeal of a teacher's first interactive lessons. Envision a future where we do not just talk about data but see it, feel it, question it and use it to safeguard the most precious inheritance we have – life itself.

That is how data visualisation might help save the human race from extinction. By reminding us that knowledge alone is not enough – we must perceive it in forms our hearts and minds can grasp, weaving urgent truths into images and experiences so powerful we cannot ignore them. Let us see more clearly, act more wisely and preserve the infinite possibilities that define us as human beings.

References

Adiga, Aravind. 2008. *The White Tiger*. Atlantic Books.

Allyn, Bobby. 2022. *Deepfake video of Zelenskyy could be 'tip of the iceberg' in info war, experts warn*. 16 March. https://www.npr.org/2022/03/16/1087062648/deepfake-video-zelenskyy-experts-war-manipulation-ukraine-russia.

Anderson, Scott. 2024. *Piecing Together the Secrets of the Stasi*. 3 June. https://www.newyorker.com/magazine/2024/06/03/piecing-together-the-secrets-of-the-stasi?utm_source=chatgpt.com.

Batalla, Juan José. 2009. "The Oxford Handbook of the Aztecs." *The Historical Sources: Codices and Chronicles* (Oxford University Press) 326 (5960): 1680–1683.

Bellis, Mary. 2024. *The Invention of the Wheel*. 14 July. https://www.thoughtco.com/the-invention-of-the-wheel-1992669.

Bellizzi, Keith M. 2022. *Cognitive Biases and Brain Biology Help Explain Why Facts Don't Change Minds*. 16 August. https://today.uconn.edu/2022/08/cognitive-biases-and-brain-biology-help-explain-why-facts-dont-change-minds-2/#.

Bernstein, Peter. 1996. *Against the Gods: The Remarkable Story of Risk*. New York: John Wiley & Sons.

Born, Brooksley, Douglas Holtz-Eakin, Byron Georgiou, Heather H. Murren, Bob Graham, John W. Thompson, Keith Hennessey, and Peter J. Wallison. 2011. *The Financial Crisis Inquiry Report*. The Financial Crisis Inquiry Commission.

Bostrom, N. (2014). *Superintelligence: Paths, Dangers, Strategies*. Oxford University Press.

Bourgoin, Clement, Iban Ameztoy, Astrid Verhegghen, Baudouin Desclée, Silvia Carboni, Jean-Francois Bastin, Rene Beuchle, Andreas Brink, Pierre Defourny, Baptiste Delhez, Steffen Fritz, Valery Gond, Martin Herold, Celine Lamarche, Nicolas Mansuy, Danilo Mollicone, Duarte Oom, Stephen Peedell, Jesus San-Miguel, Rene Colditz. 2024. *Mapping Global Forest Cover of the Year 2020 to Support the EU Regulation on Deforestation-free Supply Chains*. Ispra: European Commision.

Bromberg, M. 2023. *Illusory truth effect: What it is, why it happens, how to avoid it*. Investopedia. 31 May. https://www.investopedia.com/illusory-truth-effect-7488637

BuzzFeed. 2018. *You Won't Believe What Obama Says In This Video!* https://www.youtube.com/watch?v=cQ54GDm1eL0.

Cadwalladr, Carole, and Emma Graham-Harrison. 2018. *Revealed: 50 million Facebook profiles harvested for Cambridge Analytica in major data breach*. 17 Mar. https://www.theguardian.com/news/2018/mar/17/cambridge-analytica-facebook-influence-us-election.

Cairns, Hugh, and Yidumduma Bill Harney. 2004. *Dark Sparklers: Yidumduma's Wardaman Aboriginal Astronomy: Night Skies Northern Australia*. H.C. Cairns.

Carlyle, Thomas. 1841. *On Heroes, Hero-Worship, and The Heroic in History*. London: James Fraser.

Cartwright, Mark. 2016. *Quipu*. World History Foundation. 15 February. https://www.worldhistory.org/Quipu/.

Centers for Disease Control and Prevention. 2010. *COVID-19 Racial and Ethnic Health Disparities*. Division of Viral Diseases, National Center for Immunization and Respiratory Diseases (NCIRD), Centers for Disease Control and Prevention.

Channel 4 News Investigation Team. 2018. *Exposed: Undercover secrets of Trump's data firm*. 20 March. https://www.channel4.com/news/exposed-undercover-secrets-of-donald-trump-data-firm-cambridge-analytica?utm_source=chatgpt.com.

Christou, Chris. 2010. "Virtual reality in education." *Themes in Science and Technology Education*: 59–79.

Chuang, Yaoli, and Mara R. D'Orsogna. 2019. *Mathematical Models of Radicalization and Terrorism*. Los Angeles: California State University at Northridge.

References

Costello, Thomas H., Gordon Pennycook, and David G. Rand. 2024. "Durably reducing conspiracy beliefs through dialogues with AI." *Science* 385 (6714): eadq1814.

Davis, John. 2023. *10 Areas Manufacturers Might See an Impact from AI.* 14 November. https://www.manufacturingtomorrow.com/article/2023/10/10-areas-manufacturers-might-see-an-impact-from-ai/21604?utm_source=chatgpt.com.

European Commission. 2018. *Tackling online disinformation.* https://digital-strategy.ec.europa.eu/en/policies/online-disinformation.

Facebook Newsroom. 2018. *Taking Down More Coordinated Inauthentic Behavior.* 18 August. https://about.fb.com/news/2018/08/more-coordinated-inauthentic-behavior/.

Federal Trade Commision. 2019. *FTC Imposes $5 Billion Penalty and Sweeping New Privacy Restrictions on Facebook.* 24 July. https://www.ftc.gov/news-events/news/press-releases/2019/07/ftc-imposes-5-billion-penalty-sweeping-new-privacy-restrictions-facebook.

Few, Stephen. 2004. *Show Me the Numbers: Designing Tables and Graphs to Enlighten.* Analytics Press.

Financial Times. n.d. *Data visualisation at the FT: what makes it unique.* https://professional.ft.com/en-gb/blog/data-visualisation-ft-what-makes-it-unique/.

Firth, Joseph, John Torous, Brendon Stubbs, Josh A. Firth, Genevieve Steiner, Lee Smith, Mario Alvarez-Jimenez, et al. 2019. "The "online brain": how the Internet may be changing our cognition." *World Psychiatry*, June: 18 (2): 119–129.

Friedman, Milton. 1968. "The role of monetary policy." *The American Economic Review* 58 (1): 1–17.

Galton, Francis. 1889. *Natural Inheritance.* Macmillan.

Golnaraghi, Maryam. 2009. *2009 Global Assessment Report On Disaster Reduction.* Geneva: World Meteorological Organization.

Grossman, Lisa. 2010. *Nov. 10, 1999: Metric Math Mistake Muffed Mars Meteorology Mission.* 10, 11. https://www.wired.com/2010/11/1110mars-climate-observer-report/?utm_source=chatgpt.com.

Halpern, Sue. 2018. *Cambridge Analytica, Facebook, and the revelations of open secrets.* 21 March. https://www.newyorker.com/news/news-desk/cambridge-analytica-facebook-and-the-revelations-of-open-secrets?utm_source=chatgpt.com.

Harari, Y. N. 2024. *Nexus: A Brief History of Information Networks from the Stone Age to AI*. Random House.

Heuer, Richard J. 2018. *Psychology of Intelligence Analysis*. Martino Fine Books.

Kahneman, Daniel. 2011. *Thinking, Fast and Slow*. Farrar, Straus and Giroux.

Kahneman, Daniel, and Amos Tversky. 1979. "Prospect theory: an analysis of decision under risk." *Econometrica* 47 (2): 263–291.

Krasodomski, Alex. 2024. *The UK riots force Western democracies to confront their reliance on technology giants*. 9 August. https://www.chathamhouse.org/2024/08/uk-riots-force-western-democracies-confront-their-reliance-technology-giants.

Lapsley, Phil. 2014. *Exploding the Phone: The Untold Story of the Teenagers and Outlaws Who Hacked Ma Bell*. Grove Press.

Leimdorfer, Andrew. n.d. *Data Journalism at the BBC*. https://datajournalism.com/read/handbook/one/in-the-newsroom/data-journalism-at-the-bbc.

Lewis, M. 2018. *Has anyone seen the president?* Bloomberg, 9 February. Available at: https://www.bloomberg.com/opinion/articles/2018-02-09/has-anyone-seen-the-president

Lewis, W. Arthur. 1954. *Economic Development with Unlimited Supplies of Labour*. Manchester: The Manchester School.

Leyden, John, and Simon Rockman. 2014. *White hats do an NSA, figure out LIVE PHONE TRACKING via protocol vuln*. 2014 December. https://www.theregister.com/2014/12/26/ss7_attacks/?utm_source=chatgpt.com.

Malthus, Thomas. 1798. *An Essay on the Principle of Population*. London: J. Johnson.

Mann, Michael E., and Raymond S. Bradley. 1999. "Nothern hemsiphere temperatures during the past millennium: inferences, uncertainties, and limitations." *Geophysical Research Letters* 26 (6): 759–762.

Markowitz, Harry. 1952. "Portfolio selection." *The Journal of Finance* 7 (1): 77–91.

Martel, Yann. 2018. *Life of Pi*. Canongate Canons.

Masson-Delmotte, Valérie, Zhai, Panmao, Pörtner, Hans-Otto, Roberts, Debra, Skea, Jim, Shukla, Priyadarshi R., Pirani, Anna, et al. 2018. *IPCC, 2018: Summary for Policymakers*. Cambridge: Cambridge University Press.

Mayer, Richard E. and Roxana Moreno 2023. "Nine ways to reduce cognitive load in multimedia learning." *Asian Journal of Media Studies* 56–68.

McCarthy, James J., Osvaldo F. Canziani, Neil A. Leary, David J. Dokken, and Kasey S. White. 2001. *Climate Change 2001: Impacts, Adaptations and Vulnerability*. Cambridge: Cambridge University Press.

References

McDaid, Cathal. 2016. *60 Minutes & SS7 Signalling Security: Putting the Pieces Together.* 17 April. https://www.enea.com/insights/ss7-security-putting-pieces-together/?utm_source=chatgpt.com.

Medina, John. 2009. *Brian Rules.* Pear Press.

Menon, Shruti, and Vineet Khare. 2023. *Wrestlers' protest: The fake smiles of India's detained sporting stars.* 31 May. https://www.bbc.co.uk/news/world-asia-india-65757400?utm_source=chatgpt.com.

Mercader, Julio. 2009. "Mozambican grass seed consumption during the Middle Stone Age." *Science (American Association for the Advancement of Science (AAAS))* 326 (5960): 1680-1683.

Meta. 2020. *September 2020 Coordinated Inauthentic Behavior Report.* Meta.

Muntoni, Anna P., Fabio Mazza, Alfredo Braunstein, Giovanni Catania, and Luca Dall'Asta. 2024. "Effectiveness of probabilistic contact tracing in epidemic containment: the role of superspreaders and transmission path reconstruction." *PNAS Nexus* 3 (9): 377.

Nagata, Jason M., Abubakr A. A. Al-Shoaibi, Alicia W. Leong et al. 2024. "Screen time and mental health: a prospective analysis of the Adolescent Brain Cognitive Development (ABCD) study." *BMC Public Health* 24 (1): 2686.

Naithani, Sushma. 2021. "The Origins of Agriculture." *Oregon State University.* https://open.oregonstate.education/cultivatedplants/chapter/agriculture/#:~:text=About%2012%2C000%20years%20ago%2C%20one,%2C%20Turkmenistan%2C%20and%20Asia%20Minor.

National Geographic Society. n.d. *The Development of Agriculture.* National Geographic Society. https://education.nationalgeographic.org/resource/development-agriculture/.

O'Connor, Michael, Helen M. Deeks, Edward Dawn, Oussama Metatla, Anne Roudaut, Matthew Sutton, Lisa May Thomas, Becca Rose Glowacki, Rebecca Sage, Philip Tew, Mark Wonnacott, Phil Bates, Adrian J. Mulholland, and David R. Glowacki. 2018. "Sampling molecular conformations and dynamics in a multiuser virtual reality framework." *Science Advances* 4 (6): eaat2731.

OECD. 2019. *OECD Skills Outlook 2019.* Paris: OECD, 13–19.

Pearce, Katie. 2019. *Pandemic simulation exercise spotlights massive preparedness gap.* 6 11. https://hub.jhu.edu/2019/11/06/event-201-health-security/.

Persia and Babylonia. 2019. *Archives in context: a Persia and Babylonia project.* 9 May. http://persiababylonia.org/archives/background/finding-sepharvaim-and-its-tablets-hormuzd-rassams-crowning-achievement/.

Phelps, Edmund. 1967. "Phillips Curves, Expectations of inflation, and optimal unemployment over time." *Economica* 34 (135): 254–281.

Phillips, Alban W. 1958. "The relation between unemployment and the rate of change of money wage rates in the United Kingdom, 1861–1957." *Economica* 25: 283-299.

Playfair, William. 1786. *The Commercial and Political Atlas: Representing, by Means of Stained Copper-Plate Charts, the Progress of the Commerce, Revenues, Expenditure, and Debts of England during the Whole of the Eighteenth Century.* London: T. Burton, Little Queen Street, Lincoln's-Inn Fields, for J. Wallis, Carpenter and Co., Egerton, Vernor and Hood, and Black and Parry.

PolitiFact. 2020. *No, Biden did not receive thousands of mysteriously surfaced votes in Michigan.* 4 November. https://www.politifact.com/factchecks/2020/nov/04/tweets/no-biden-did-not-receive-thousands-mysteriously-su/.

Poole, Robert. 2008. *Earthrise: How Man First Saw the Earth.* Yale University Press.

Prevelakis, Vassilis, and Diomidis Spinellis. 2007. *The Athens Affair.* 29 June. https://spectrum.ieee.org/the-athens-affair?utm_source=chatgpt.com.

Quetelet, Adolphe. 1835. *Sur l'homme et le développement de ses facultés, ou Essai de physique sociale.* Bachelier.

Reed, Stephen B., and Darren A. Rippy. 2012. "Consumer Price Index data quality: how accurate is the U.S. CPI?" *Beyong the Numbers* (U.S. Bureau Of Labor Statistics) 1 (12).

Reuters. 2020. *Fact check: Vote spikes in Wisconsin, Michigan and Pennsylvania do not prove election fraud.* 10 November. https://www.reuters.com/article/world/fact-check-vote-spikes-in-wisconsin-michigan-and-pennsylvania-do-not-prove-ele-idUSKBN27Q304/.

Ricardo, David. 1817. *The Theory of Comparative Advantage.* Vol. 1. Cambridge: Cambridge University Press.

Rosling, Hans, Rönnlund, Anna R. and Rosling, Ola. 2018. *Factfulness: Ten Reasons We're Wrong About the World – And Why Things Are Better Than You Think.* Flatiron Books.

Saadatmandi, Babak. 2015. *Is the SS7 Network open to attacks and if so what can we do about it?* 2015 September. https://www.cellusys.com/2015/09/01/is-the-ss7-network-open-to-attacks-and-if-so-what-can-we-do-about-it/?utm_source=chatgpt.com.

Salyer, Kirsten. 2019. *Live Simulation Exercise to Prepare Public and Private Leaders for Pandemic Response.* 18 October. https://www.weforum.org/press/2019/10/live-simulation-exercise-to-prepare-public-and-private-leaders-for-pandemic-response/.

Saposnik, Gustavo, Donald Redelmeier, Christian C. Ruff, and Philippe N. Tobler. 2016. "Cognitive biases associated with medical decisions: a systematic review." *BMC Medical Informatics and Decision Making* 16 (138): 1–4.

Science Atlas. 2022. *How Many Grains of Sand on the Earth?* 29 January. https://science-atlas.com/faq/how-many-grains-of-sand-on-the-earth/.

Scott, Mark, and Annabelle Dickson. 2018. *Cambridge Analytica created own quizzes to harvest Facebook data.* 17 April. https://www.politico.eu/article/cambridge-analytica-facebook-data-brittney-kaiser-privacy/?utm_source=chatgpt.com.

Shafir, Eldar, and Sendhil Mullainathan. 2013. *Scarcity: Why Having Too Little Means So Much.* Times Books.

Skinner, Burrhus Frederic. 1948. "'Superstition' in the pigeon." *Journal of Experimental Psychology* 38 (2): 168–172.

Slovic, Paul. 2007. ""If I look at the mass I will never act": psychic numbing and genocide." *Judgment and Decision Making* 2 (2), April 2007: 79–95.

Smithsonian National Museum of Natural History. 2024. *What does it mean to be human?* 3 January. https://humanorigins.si.edu/evidence/human-fossils/species/homo-sapiens.

Spencer, Amanda. 2024. *Artificial Intelligence In Retail: 6 Use Cases And Examples.* 24 October. https://www.forbes.com/sites/sap/2024/04/19/artificial-intelligence-in-retail-6-use-cases-and-examples/?utm_source=chatgpt.com.

Stangor, C., & Walinga, J. 2014. *9.3 Accuracy and inaccuracy in memory and cognition.* 17 October. https://opentextbc.ca/introductiontopsychology/chapter/8-3-accuracy-and-inaccuracy-in-memory-and-cognition/.

Sunstein, Cass R. 2017. *#Republic: Divided Democracy in the Age of Social Media.* Princeton University Press.

Taleb, Nassim. 2001. *Fooled by Randomness.* Random House.

The New York Times. 2024. *Project 538.* 5 November. https://projects.fivethirtyeight.com/2024-election-forecast/.

Thomson, Iain. 2017. *After years of warnings, mobile network hackers exploit SS7 flaws to drain bank accounts.* 3 May. https://www.theregister.com/2017/05/03/hackers_fire_up_ss7_flaw/?utm_source=chatgpt.com.

Timberg, Craig, and Elizabeth Dwoskin. 2018. *Washington Post.* 6 July. https://www.washingtonpost.com/technology/2018/07/06/twitter-is-sweeping-out-fake-accounts-like-never-before-putting-user-growth-risk/.

Toffler, Alvin. 1970. *Future Shock.* Random House.

Tufte, Edward R. 1983. *The Visual Display of Quantitative Information.* Graphics Press.

Varoquaux, Gaël, Bertrand Thirion, and Jean-Baptiste Poline. 2018. "Atlases of cognition with large-scale human brain mapping." *PLOS Computational Biology* 14 (11): e1006565.

Wald, Abraham. 1943. *A Method of Estimating Plane Vulnerability Based on Damage of Survivors.* Alexandria, Virginia: Center for Naval Analyses.

World Economic Forum. 2019. *How much data is generated each day?* https://www.weforum.org/agenda/2019/04/how-much-data-is-generated-each-day-cf4bddf29f/.

Worldometer. 2024. *Coronavirus Tracker.* 13 April. https://www.worldometers.info/coronavirus/.

Wu, Joseph T., Kathy Leung and Gabriel M. Leung. 2020. "Nowcasting and forecasting the potential domestic and international spread of the 2019-nCoV outbreak originating in Wuhan, China: a modelling study." *Lancet* 395 (10225): 689–97.

About the Author

James Eagle is an internationally recognised data visualisation specialist with a robust grounding in economics and a lifelong dedication to making complex information accessible. He began his career in the asset management industry, taking on multiple roles in major financial institutions where he discovered a keen talent for interpreting market data and translating it into compelling stories.

A decade ago, James moved to Switzerland where the breathtaking environment sparked his creativity and deepened his focus on visual storytelling. He believes our world – now brimming with more data than ever before – demands a fresh, human-centred approach to how we communicate with data. In his view, data can pose a grave threat when poorly understood yet it can also bring clarity from chaos when visualised.

James works with some of the largest financial institutions in the world across Europe and North America, guiding them to use data visualisation for sharper decision-making and a more powerful way to communicate with their investors. His keynote speeches around the globe reflect his conviction that visual methods are critical for tackling our most urgent challenges, from financial volatility to global sustainability.

Throughout his work, James promotes a measured perspective on data, celebrating its potential to drive progress while recognising its ability to mislead and overwhelm the human mind. By championing transparency, empathy and design excellence, he encourages professionals and the public alike to see beyond numbers and embrace the human stories behind data. Through his work, talks and day-to-day social media activities, James shows how thoughtful data visualisation can light up a world increasingly shaped by digital information, ultimately strengthening our shared capacity to adapt, innovate and thrive.

Index

3D modelling tools, usage, 241
3D reconstructions, usage, 270

A
Abstract thought, arrival, 9–11
Active learning (encouragement), data
    visualisation (usage), 67–68
Adaptive expectations, role (emphasis), 113
Adiga, Aravind, 188
*Against the Gods: The Remarkable Story of
    Risk* (Bernstein), 125–126
Agriculture, economic systems
    (emergence), 10
Animation, usage, 169–172
Artificial intelligence (AI)
  AI-driven chart creation, 276
  AI-driven image manipulation, 272
  chatbots, impact, 273
  collaborator, role, 75–76
  data visualisation, alliance, 63
  deskilling potential, 66–67
  feedback, usage, 75
  impact, 2

Audience Insights, Facebook usage, 212
Augmented reality (AR), usage, 263
Availability heuristic, 53, 55

B
Banks, bailouts, 85
Bannon, Steve, 209
  lies, 44–45
Bar charts
  communication tool, 173
  distortion (3D effect), 74f
Barclay, Ralph, 149
Beautiful data, 127
Bell curve, 129–130, 142
  Monte Carlo simulation, usage, 134f
  seduction, 132
  symmetry, problem, 127, 143
Bernstein, Peter, 125
Bias, 272
  confrontation, 279
Biased data, problem, 91–96
Big Data Revolution, 5
Bildung (education), 253–255

INDEX

Binomial distribution
　approximation, 126f
　visualisation (bell curve), 130f
Black Monday, 20-sigma event, 139
Blue box
　Barclay creation, 149
　Wozniak/Jobs usage, 147–150
Bostock, Mike (visual narratives), 52–53
Bostrom, Nick, 66
Box-Muller transform, usage, 134
Brain Rules (Medina), 257
Burning Embers, The (impact),
　178–182, 183

C

Cambridge Analytica
　election interference, 207–209
　exposure, impact, 220, 223–224
　origins/influence, 209
　scandal, revelation, 212–213, 272
　voter manipulation, 210
Carbon Brief stories, examination, 175
Carbon footprint, cost measurement, 270
Carlyle, Thomas, 104, 109
Causation, elasticity (relationship), 117
Ceteris paribus, term (usage), 116
Chartjunk, 72–73, 72f
　revision, 73f
Charts, birth, 19–20
ChatGPT
　attention heads, 66
　innovation, 65
Children, interests (exploration), 255
Chuang, Yao-Li, 156–158
Classrooms
　data platforms, usage, 259–260
　global responsibility discussions, 265
Clay tablets, importance, 6–7
Climate activism, 182–183
Climate change
　bar charts, usage, 173
　maps, usage, 173–174
　tangibility, data visualisation
　　(usage), 167–168
Climate chaos, 271
Climate data overload, 166–169

Climate injustice, highlighting, 176–178
Climate spiral (Hawkins), 181
Climate war, visualisation, 165
Clinical research, data visualisation
　(usage), 240–241
Cognitive biases, impact, 114
Cognitive load (reduction), data
　visualisation (usage), 258
Cognitive pitfalls, 53–55
Collaboration, fostering, 279
Collective action, galvanisation, 265
Collective knowledge, destruction, 34
Colonialism, impact, 199–200
Colonial powers, resource extraction,
　196–198
Colonisation/GDP per capita growth,
　causal link (limitations), 199
Colour-coded maps, usage, 242
Colour gradients, strategic use,
　168–169
Commercial and Political Atlas, The
　(Playfair), 19
Communication (improvement), data
　visualisation (usage), 67–68
Community-led initiatives, usage, 264
Comparative advantage, theory, 119
Complexity
　compression, data visualisation
　　(usage), 258
　issues, 39–40
Conditional Value at Risk (CVaR), 140
Confirmation bias, 53, 160
Confusion (amplification), data
　(impact), 47–49
Consciousness, map, 17
Conspiracy theories
　average belief, 70f
　debunking, AI (usage), 70–71
Conspiracy theories/falsehoods, impact, 45
Consumer Price Index, usage, 96–98
Consumption/exploitation cycle,
　continuation, 29
Continuous learning
　imperative, 275
　promotion, challenge, 253
Cost-push inflation, occurrence, 97

Index

Covert Twitter assets, community network map, 219f
COVID-19 pandemic
  clarity, importance, 39
  contact-tracing tools, effectiveness, 234
  dashboard (UK), usage, 233
  data visualisations, creation, 60
  death toll, 38
  social media claims, falsity, 57–58
COVID Tracking Project (US), usage, 233
Crimson Contagion (exercise), 36–37, 232–235, 271
Critical data visualisation literacy, teaching, 261
Critical engagement habit, cultivation (importance), 163
Critical thinking, usage, 12
CrowdStrike update, problem, 29–30
Cultural enrichment, 254

D

Data
  beautiful data, 127
  bias, 83, 95
    acceptance, issue, 99–102
  cherry-picking, problem, 96
  communication, importance, 167
  confusion, amplification, 47–49
  creation, 2, 21
  deception, 207
  democratising, 76–77, 80–81
  distortion, 260–261
  embedding, 31
  exploration, emphasis, 174
  explosions, 4–5, 20
  floods, 30–33
  forms, 18
  immersion, VR/AR (usage), 263
  liberating, 76–77
  literacy, importance, 261
  manipulation, 214–217, 244–245
  open data, misuse/violations, 79–81
  overload, hidden cost, 56
  points (extraction), AI (usage), 76
  poisoning, half-truths (impact), 54
  sharing/interpretation, questions/challenges, 22
  story, elements, 273
  threat, 1
  trick question, 47–48, 47f
  ubiquity, 270–271
  value, 270
  visual presentation, 15
  weaponisation, 2
    risks, 77–79
DataBank (World Bank), information (wealth), 259
Data-driven learning, technology (usage), 262–263
Data Explorer, usage, 184
Data-ink ratio, 72
Data pollution
  desensitisation/invisibility, 49–51
  fighting, 43
  impact, 47–49
  lies, 44–46
Datasets
  AI reconstruction ability, 77
  comparison, issues, 198–199
Data visualisation, 7, 10–11, 21–22
  adoption, delay (cost), 130
  AI, alliance, 63
  animation, importance, 169–172
  barriers, 264
  change, importance, 275–277
  combat tool, 51–53
  communication medium, power, 38–39
  creative uses, 251
  critical data visualisation literacy, teaching, 261–262
  deepfaking, possibility, 79
  depth, 204
  embracing, 280
  ethical dilemmas, 264
  failure, 86–87
  honesty, importance, 102
  human expression, 279
  human storytelling, 272–273
  immersiveness, 277–278
  importance, reasons, 279
  misuse (guarding), AI (usage), 71

Data visualisation (*continued*)
  moral responsibility, 60–61
  necessity, 40
  problems, 77–79
  quality, improvement, 75
  reconnections, possibility, 278
  reliance, 140
  role, 123
  scientists, dismissal, 129
  theory, 135
  transformative power, 35–41
Deepfakes, 220, 224, 272, 273
  generation, 276
  Obama, 78–79
  Zelensky, 216–217
Delivery, simplicity (data story element), 273
Demand-pull inflation, occurrence, 97
Detection systems, embedding, 276
Disease surveillance, data visualisation (usage), 232–235
Disinformation campaigns (combatting), data visualisation (usage), 218–220
Diversification, benefits, (enhancement), 117
D'Orsogna, Maria R., 156–158
Drug development, data visualisation (usage), 240–241

E

Earth Day initiative, 265
Earth Observing System (NASA), real-time dashboards (usage), 259
Earthwise (Poole), 265
Economic forces, impact, 96–98
Economic inequalities, 272
Economic Problem, 104–105
Economics
  Carlyle criticism, 110
  flaw, 122
  study, dismal science, 103, 109, 132
Economic theories (collapse), data visualisation (role), 111
Economic transformation, realities (capture failure), 107

Education
  barriers, 264
  classrooms, data platforms (usage), 259–260
  competitiveness, 251–252
  data-driven learning, technology (usage), 262–263
  data visualisation, usage, 249–252
  distractions, impact, 250–251
  ethical dilemmas, 264
  ethical frameworks, relationship, 274–275
  grassroots education, investment, 276
  importance, 252–257
  reforms, 274
Efficient frontier
  calculation, Markowitz methodology (usage), 136–137
  derivation, 135
  Monte Carlo simulation, usage, 136f
  problem, 137
  representation, 135–136
Elasticity/inelasticity, 117117
Elections
  charts, misinformation, 214–215
  deepfakes, problems, 216
  disinformation campaigns (combatting), data visualisation (usage), 218–220
  influence, dirty tricks (usage), 208
  misinformation, 214–217
  online disinformation, AI/digital editing (impact), 215–216
Electoral data (parsing), data visualisation (usage), 218
Electronic health records (EHRs), patient monitoring (relationship), 229–231
Empathy, 15
Engel, Tobias, 153
Enlightenment, progress, 33
Epidemiology, data visualisation (usage), 232–235
Essay on the Principle of Population, An (Malthus), 109
Ethical frameworks, education (relationship), 274–275
Ethical technology development, demands, 276

European Digital Media Observatory, misinformation tracker, 218–219
European overseas colonies, number, 197–198, 197f
Event 201 (exercise), 37, 234–235, 271
Excellence, celebration/reward, 276–277
Exploding the Phone (Lapsley), 150
Exploitation, global scale, 28–30
Extremism (defense), AI (usage), 71–75

F

Facebook
    algorithms, 211–212
    Audience Insights, usage, 212
    data, liability, 211–213
    profiles, harvesting, 208–210
    transparency, re-evaluation, 213–214
Factulness (Rosling, et al.), 59, 192, 252
Fair use policies, misuse/breaches, 77
Fake accounts, arms race, 217
False stories (falsehoods)
    data weaponisation, 110
    power, 109–123
Farming, discovery, 3–4
Feedback loops (creation), herding behaviour (impact), 141
Few, Stephen, 258
Financial sector pay, overinflation, 87f
'Firehouse of falsehoods' strategy, 45–46
Fooled by Randomness (Taleb), 50
Freedom
    defence, 155
    exploration, 189
    preservation, 159–160
Freedom of speech, data visualisation (relationship), 220–223
Free speech
    Musk interpretation, complications, 222
    reconciliation, data visualisation (usage), 223
Friedman, Milton, 113–114

Permanent Income Hypothesis, 120–121
Future Shock (Toffler), 55

G

Galton, Francis (bell curve), 129–130
Gamification, usage, 263
Gantt-like charts, usage, 242
Gapminder bubble chart ('The Wealth and Health of Nations'), 189–192, 273
Gauss, Carl Friedrich, 127–128
Generational inequalities, understanding, 204
Generational wealth divide, 202–204
Generative Adversarial Networks, lifelike representations, 79
Generative artificial intelligence
    disruption, 64–65
    output, authoritativeness (presentation), 67
Geospatial data visualisations, usage, 158–159
Gig workers, growth (platform payments), 203f
Global average temperatures, 170f, 171f
Global awareness. data visualisation catalyst, 264–266
Global collaboration, importance, 274
Global economic progress, problems, 203–204
Global Financial Crisis, 84–85
    biased data, impact, 91–96
    fragility (presence), detection (failure), 92
    pre-Financial Crisis pitchbook, examples, 93f, 94f
Global heat map, usage, 176–177
Global responsibility, discussions, 265
Global temperature changes, 168f
Global warming, trend (visualisation), 180–181, 181f
GLOBE Program, 260
Gore, Al, 180
GPT-4 Turbo, self-declared conspiracy theorists (conversations), 69–70
Graphical distortion, 73
Grassroots education, investment, 276

Great Depression, 141
Gross domestic product (GDP), 193f
  data, impact, 98–99
  GDP per Capita, 198f
    increase/decrease, issues, 200
Gymnasium (grammar school), children (attendance), 255

H
Half-truths, spread, 53–55
Hands-on investigations, 262–263
Harari, Yuval Noah, 45
Hawkins, Ed, 167–168, 181
Healthcare
  AI, impact, 229
  cost, 235–238
  crises, 272
  data-driven future, improvement, 245–246
  narrative, reshaping, 244–245
  resource management, 242
  visualisation, 227–229
Heat maps, usage, 258
Herding behaviour, impact, 141
Heuer, Jr., Richards J., 160–161
Hidden fragility, 27–28
Hockey stick chart, 180–182, 181f
Homo Sapiens, emergence, 3
House of Wisdom, destruction, 32, 33
House prices, 202f
HSBC Global Asset Management, losses, 85
Human behavior
  impact, 137, 142–143
  mathematics, 121
Humanity
  crossroads, 143–144
  data visualisation failure, 86–87
Human minds, pattern-seeking machines, 12–19
Human race extinction (prevention), data visualisation (usage), 280–281
Hydrocarbons, usage, 4

I
Ice Age, existence, 9
Ideological misinformation, data pollution (impact), 57

Imago Mundi ('Image of the World'), 8–9, 15–16, 174, 257, 272
Inaction, cost, 34
Incomplete/unclear information, challenges, 161
Inconvenient Truth, An (Gore), 180, 181
Industrialisation, promise, 106–109
Industry standards, importance, 274
Inequality (deepening), data overload (impact), 56
Inflation
  impact, 96–98
  treatment, bias, 98
Information
  accuracy, data-driven visualisations (usage), 58
  interpretation/application, civilisational strength, 40–41
  overload, 38
    navigation, 20–21
    social inequality, relationship, 55–56
  recording methods, diversity, 10–11
  understanding, data visualisation (usage), 51–52
Information technology (IT) blackout, 29–30, 35–36, 271
Innovations
  pattern-seeking, impact, 13
  requirement, 20
Intellectual curiosity, 254
Intellectual property, misuse/violations, 79–81
Interactive charts, usage, 177
Interactive graphs, usage, 258
Interactivity, importance, 170–178
Internet
  activity, increase, 5
  arrival, 4–5
Invisible hand, 109
IPCC Assessment Report, 179
Islamic Golden Age, 33

K
Knowledge, preservation, 13–14

Index

L

Lapsley, Phil, 150
Learning
  active learning (encouragement), data visualisation (usage), 67–68
  continuous learning
    importance, 275
    promotion, challenge, 253
  data-driven learning, technology (usage), 262–263
  lifelong learning, benefits, 251–252
Lewis, Michael, 44
Lewis, W. Arthur (Lewis model proposal), 106–109
  contradiction, 108
Library of Alexandria, destruction, 32, 204
Lie Factor (Tufte), 73–75
Lies (data pollution symptom), 44–45
Life expectancy, health expenditure per capita (contrast), 237f
Lifelong learning, benefits, 251–252
Life of Pi (Martel), 189
Line chart, usage, 193–194, 193f
Log scale, usage, 193–194
Loss aversion, 139
Losses, psychological impact, 138

M

Maciejewska, Joanna, 65
Malthus, Thomas, 103, 109
  mistake, legacy, 104–106
Mangione, Luigi (arrest), 235–236
Manipulated visualisations (defense), AI (usage), 71–75
Mann, Michael E., 180
Maps
  colour-coded maps, usage, 242
  creation, 9–11
  heat maps, usage, 258
  self-expression, 16–17
  usage, 173–174
Markets
  behaviour, unpredictability, 139–140
  pattern, smoothness (absence), 142
Markowitz, Harry, 136
Martel, Yann, 189

Meaning, obscuring, 31
Measles incidence (US), 238, 239f
Measurement biases, appearance, 99
Medical imaging/diagnostics, data visualisation (usage), 231–232
Medicine (cognitive biases), visualisation (role), 243–244
Medina, John, 257
Memories, multi-dimensional data, 18
Mental paralysis, 44
Mental shortcuts/cognitive biases, human cognition reliance, 53
Mercer, Robert, 209
Microsoft Windows, global disruption, 30, 271
Mining, 4
Misinformation
  credibility, problem, 260–261
  data visualisation, countermeasure, 58
  fighting
    AI, usage, 68–71
    data visualisation, usage, 51–53
  ideological misinformation, data pollution (impact), 57
  overcoming, visual literacy (usage), 260–262
  problems, 272
  spread, problem, 56, 256–257
  tracker (European Digital Media Observatory), 218–219
Modeling techniques, usage, 118
Modern Portfolio Theory, 136–137
Moivre, Abraham de, 128
  normal distribution curve, 126–128
  uncertainty, understanding, 125–126
Money, nonphysical entity, 26–27
Monte Carlo simulation, 133–144
  usage, example, 134f
Monthly global average temperature anomalies, 169f
Mosaic theory, 77–79

N

Narrative connection (data story element), 273
Nash, John (Nash equilibrium), 121–122

National security, AI (impact/implications), 77–79
Natural Inheritance (Galton), 129–130
Negative correlation, 117
Negative utility, 138
Network graphs, usage, 158–159
Networks, impact, 27–28
Nexus (Harari), 45
Nix, Alexander, 207–208
  entrapment methods/political dirty tricks, 210
Nodes/connectors, representation, 156–157, 157f
Nohl, Karsten, 153
Non-normal distributions, 140
Normal distribution
  curve, 126–128
  human behaviour, impact, 142–143
  visualisations (Galton), 131f
Numbers (meaning, loss), comparisons (necessity), 49

O

Obama, Barack (deepfake), 78–79
Online disinformation, AI/digital editing (impact), 215–216
Online manipulation, 217
Open data
  championing, 276
  misuse/violations, 79–81
Open-source intelligence (OSINT), data visualisation benefits, 159
Open-source software, usage, 264
Oral communication, fragility, 13
Our World in Data, 192–194, 197–198
  examples, 193f, 197f, 198f
Outrage algorithms, 276
Overconfidence bias, 54
Over-specialisation, problems, 256–257

P

Paideia (Greek concept), 253
Pandemics
  blind spots, 271
  impact, 34
  survival, 36

Paris Agreement, 178–182
  goals, 183
Patient
  monitoring, electronic health records (relationship), 229–231
  outcomes, hidden patterns (revealing), 246
Pattern
  persistence/collapse, 115
  recognition, usage, 118
Permanent Income Hypothesis (Friedman), 120–121
Phelps, Edmund, 113
Phillips, Alban William
  long-run Phillips curve, 114f
  Phillips Curve
    collapse, 111–115, 112f, 118
    problem, 123, 138
Phreaking, 149–151
Plane vulnerability, estimation method, 115, 116f
Platforms, accountability, 276
Playfair, William, 19–20
  graphs/charts, usage, 128–129, 133
Politics
  data deception, 207
  manipulation, 272
  problems, 209–210
Poole, Robert, 265
Population growth, agricultural production (contrast), 105f
Populist movements, data (usage), 2–3
Portfolio construction, data visualisation reliance, 140
Portfolio Selection (Markowitz), 136
Positive utility, 138
Poverty, wealth (relationship), 187
Power, global balance (distortion), 106
Predictive analytics, 161–162
Prisoner's Dilemma (game theory), 121–122
Privacy, misuse/violations, 79–81
Privat Seminars, 254
Probability distributions, 131
Productivity, complexity (correlation), 29
Progress, compartmentalisation (impact), 253

Index

Propaganda
  spread, 159
  system, amplification, 46
Prospect Theory, 139
Psychology of Intelligence Analysis (Heuer, Jr.), 160
Public health, population-level interventions, 238–240
Python, usage, 76, 137

Q
Quetelet, Adolphe, 129

R
Randomised Evaluation of COVID-19 Therapy (RECOVERY) trial, 240
Random noise, patterns (discovery), 12
Rassam, Hormuzd (excavations), 6–7
Reading, learning, 279
Real-time 3D reconstructions, healthcare usage, 231
Regulatory oversight, impact, 274
#Republic (Sunstein), 58
Ricardo, David
  advice, ignoring (result), 120
  theory of comparative advantage, 119
Risk, 125
  hiding, data visualisation (usage), 92
  underestimation, tendency, 140–141
Role of Monetary Policy, The (Friedman), 113
Roser, Max, 193–194
  historical data/past victories, focus (problems), 204
Rosling, Hans, 59–60, 190, 192, 205, 252, 273
  economic progress maps, limitations, 203
R (language), usage, 137
Russia, 'firehouse of falsehoods' strategy, 45–46

S
Scarcity: Why Having Too Little Means So Much (Shafir/Mullainathan), 56
Schrödinger's software, usage, 241
Schultz, Theodore, 107
Science/society/justice, uniting, 183–185

SDG Tracker (UN) information (wealth), 259
Self-cultivation, 254
Self-reinforcing imbalance, 142
Short message service (SMS), usage, 152
Show Me the Numbers (Few), 258
Signalling System No. 7 (SS7)
  anomalies/systemic weaknesses, revealing, 153
  usage/problems, 151–154
  vulnerabilities, data visualisation (usage), 154
Silver box, creation, 150
Simulations, impact, 34
Skinner, B.F., 141
Sleeper effect, 54
Smartphones, arrival, 5
Smith, Adam, 109
Social inequality, information overload (relationship), 55–56
Social media
  addictiveness, 251
  arrival, 5
  misinformation, spread (problem), 56, 256–257
Society
  hyper-specialisation, benefits/problems, 253
  polarization, 3
Sorensa, Lena, viral social media post attack, 1, 3
Source, integrity (data story element), 273
Southport riots, misinformation (impact), 220–221
Specialisation, problems, 256–257
Speculation, clarity (contrast), 280
Speech (freedom), data visualisation (relationship), 220–223
Stanford Internet Observatory, network graphs, 218
Statistics, Monte Carlo simulations, 133
Stories
  information, sharing, 16–17
  visualised data, 17–18
Storytelling
  data visualisation tool, 161, 272–273
  power, danger, 110

Structured thinking/systematic methods, importance, 160
Subprime mortgage-backed securities
  assumptions, flaw, 87–91
  diversification, 88
  industry, function, 90f
  origination, 88f
Subprime mortgages, failure/hubris, 85–86
Subprime retail-backed securities (RMBS), assumptions (optimism), 92
Sunrise Movement campaigns, data (usage), 182, 185
Sunstein, Cass, 58
Superintelligence (Bostrom), 66
Survival
  data visualisation, usage, 269
  warning signs, 271–272
Systems
  data, embedding, 31
  impact, 27–28

T

Taleb, Nassim, 50–51
Technological reliance, cognitive cost, 66–68
Technology
  ethical technology development, demands, 276
  failure, impact, 35
  fragility, 271
  impact, 25, 27–30
Telenor disruption, SS7 (impact), 153–154
Terrorist network
  study, 156–1581
  visualisation, 157f
Theory of comparative advantage, 119
Thinking, AI (impact), 2
Thompson, Brian (murder), 235–238
Timelines, usage, 258
Tipping points (revealing), network graph (usage), 158–159
Toffler, Alvin, 55
Trump, Donald
  communication style, psychological trick, 45
  tariff imposition, problems, 120

Trust-based architecture, structural weakness, 152
Trust-based system, vulnerabilities, 151–163
Trust (erosion), data (usage), 2–3
Tufte, Edward, 5, 52, 71–75

U

Uncertainty, understanding, 126–129
Unemployment, natural rate, 113
ur l'homme et le développement de ses facultés (Quetelet), 129

V

Value at Risk (VaR), 140
Vienna, polymaths (presence), 254
Viral social media post attack, impact, 1
Virtual reality (VR)
  simulations, 270
  usage, 263
Virtual space, navigation, 278
Visual communication, 11–12
Visual Display of Quantitative Information, The (Tufte), 5, 52, 71
Visualisation. *See* Data visualisation
  role, 243–244
Visual literacy, survival skill, 21–23
Visual narratives (Bostock), 52–53
Visuals, scientists (ignoring), 128–132
Visual thinking (power), data visualisation (connection), 257–258
Voter
  fraud, false claims, 214–215
  manipulation, 210
Vulnerability, technology (impact), 27–30

W

Wald, Abraham, 115
Warming stripes (Hawkins), 167, 181
Wealth
  concentration, exploitation (impact), 196–198
  distribution (pattern), smoothness (absence), 142
  generational wealth divide, 202–204
  poverty, relationship, 187
  progress/disparities, 201

'Wealth and Health of Nations, The.' *See* Gapminder bubble chart
Wheel, discovery, 4
White Tiger, The (Adiga), 188–189
Wisdom
 deficits, 30–33
 formation, 17
Writing
 development/benefits, 13–14
 learning, 279
 power, 14–15
Wylie, Christopher, 207–208, 210

X
X (Twitter)
 content, checking (absence), 222
 inflammatory content, Starmer criticism, 221
 information battleground, 220
 misinformation, checking (absence), 57
 Musk, control/controversy, 221

Y
Y2K, 29, 36
Young adults, economy, 201–203

Z
Zelensky, Volodymyr (deepfake), 216–217
Zuckerberg, Mark, 210